Explorations in Applied Linguistics

Explorations in Applied Linguistics

H. G. Widdowson

We shall not cease from exploration
And the end of all our exploring
Will be to arrive where we started
And know the place for the first time.

T. S. Eliot *Little Gidding*

Oxford University Press
1979

Oxford University Press
Walton Street, Oxford OX2 6DP

Oxford London Glasgow
New York Toronto Melbourne
Wellington Cape Town
Nairobi Dar es Salaam
Kuala Lumpur Singapore Jakarta
Hong Kong Tokyo Delhi Bombay
Calcutta Madras Karachi

ISBN 0 19 437080 1

© H. G. Widdowson 1979

Set in Monotype Imprint

Printed and bound in Great Britain
by Morrison & Gibb Ltd
London and Edinburgh

To S. Pit Corder

Acknowledgements

Acknowledgements are made to the following publishers from whose texts the extracts and papers below have been taken:

Centre for Information on Language Teaching and Research, for 'The teaching of rhetoric to students of science and technology', published in *Science and Technology in a Second Language*, Reports and Papers 7, 1971.
Regional English Language Centre, for 'An approach to the teaching of scientific English discourse', published in the *RELC Journal*, volume V No. 1, June 1974.
The British Council English Teaching Information Centre, for 'EST in theory and practice', published in *English for Academic Study*, an ETIC occasional paper, April 1975.
Le Français dans le Monde and Librairies Hachette et Larousse, for 'Description du langage scientifique', published in Le Français dans le Monde, No. 129, May/June 1977.
AIMAV, for 'Directions in the teaching of discourse', published in *Theoretical Linguistic Models in Applied Linguistics*, 1973; for 'The deep structure of discourse and the use of translation', published in *Linguistic Insights for Applied Linguistics*, 1974; and for 'Interpretative procedures and the importance of poetry', published in *Some Implications of Linguistic Theory for Applied Linguistics*, 1975.
Hoffmann und Campe Verlag, for 'Approaches to discourse', published in *Grundbegriffe und Hauptströmungen der Linguistik*, 1977.
Teachers of English to Speakers of Other Languages, for 'The authenticity of language data', published in *ON TESOL 76*, and for 'Notional syllabuses', published in *ON TESOL 78*.
Indiana University Linguistics Club, for 'The significance of simplification', published in *Studies in Second Language Acquisition*, Volume I No. 1, and for 'The partiality and relevance of

linguistic descriptions', published in *Studies in Second Language Acquisition*, Volume I No. 2.

Université de Neuchâtel and Librairie Droz, for 'Pidgin and babu', published in *The Notions of Simplification, Interlanguage, and Pidgins and their Relation to Second Language Pedagogy*, 1977.

Verlag Peter Lang, for 'Linguistic insights and language teaching principles', published in *Forum Linguisticum 3*, Contributions to Applied Linguistics I/II.

Indian Journal of Applied Linguistics, for 'The communicative approach and its application', published in the Indian Journal of Applied Linguistics, Volume III No. 1, September 1978.

Faber and Faber Ltd. and Harper and Row, Publishers, Inc., for 'September' by Ted Hughes, from *The Hawk in the Rain*, 1957, second edition 1968.

Heinemann Educational Books Ltd., and Harvard University Press, for an extract from *The Common Sense of Science* by J. Bronowski, 1960.

Penguin Books Ltd., for an extract (here adapted) from *Metals in the Service of Man*, by W. A. Alexander and A. Street, 1969.

Harper and Row Publishers Inc., for an extract from *Sociology* by L. Broom and P. Felsnick, 1955.

Hutchinson Publishing Group Ltd., for an extract from *Farm Animals: a basic guide to their husbandry* by F. A. W. Peregrine, A. Fox, A. P. Ingram, and A. B. Humphries, 1968.

Edinburgh University Press, for 'Rules and procedures in discourse analysis', published in *The Development of Conversation and Discourse*, 1979

The author would like to acknowledge the very considerable help of Elaine Samuels in producing fair copies of these papers from an unintelligible mass of scribble.

Contents

Introduction

This book is a selection of papers that I have written over the past eight years for presentation at courses and seminars in various parts of the world. I am prompted to bring them together in one volume because the reactions they have provoked suggest that they touch on issues of interest to many people concerned with applied linguistics and language teaching pedagogy and although most of the papers have appeared in print before they have done so in publications which are not always very easily accessible. So they are presented here in the hope that they will stimulate wider interest and debate.

Obviously I must believe that the papers have some merit and make some contribution to applied linguistic studies: otherwise I would not have had them put into print in the first place: I do not want to try to disarm the reader with the customary coy apology for publishing them.

What I do want to do in this introduction is to give some idea about the scope and purpose of these papers so the reader will know in advance what to expect and what attitude I would like him to adopt. Actually the title of the book is intended to reflect both scope and purpose, 'applied linguistics' referring to the first and 'explorations' to the second; but a gloss is needed to make this clear.

Applied linguistics, as I conceive of it, is a spectrum of inquiry which extends from theoretical studies of language to classroom practice. The papers appearing here explore issues that can be located at different points on this spectrum: some with a focus on matters of a predominantly theoretical kind, others with a primary focus on matters of practical pedagogy. But in all cases the whole spectrum is presupposed as the context of discussion: thus considerations of theory are linked to pedagogic relevance and demonstrations of practical teaching procedures are linked to theoretical principles. Often these links are made explicit. Where they are not they should be traceable.

These papers, then, are related in conforming to common principles of inquiry. They are also related in that they are all concerned with the same general theme: communicative language teaching. Here some apology is perhaps in order. Communicative language teaching is a banner which everybody nowadays wants to march behind. That is why I think it is important that I should make it clear what the purpose of these papers is. We come now to the term 'explorations' in my title.

The term is used with the quotation from T. S. Eliot (cited on the title page) very much in mind. I found constantly that intellectual excursions into theory led me back to starting points in pedagogy where old scenes now took on a different appearance. This is the familiar experience of homecoming and I do not know what importance to attach to such apparent novelty. Looking afresh at problems, placing them in different conceptual contexts, does not necessarily bring them any closer to solution. Solutions are hard to come by in any human situation and in the one with which we are concerned, which crucially involves the interaction of individuals, it is unlikely that we shall find any which are definitive enough to be universally applied. The likelihood is that any such solution would not be a solution at all as far as learners are concerned, although it may be convenient for the teacher to suppose that it is.

So no claim is made that anything has been solved in these papers. They are not meant to be read as prescriptions or conclusive arguments but as attempts to explore ideas, to work out the implications of certain insights in theory for a communicative approach to the teaching of language. What value these papers have lies in the examples they present of the process of exploration itself and in their capacity to incite other people concerned with language teaching to examine the principles of their craft and to submit their practices to critical thought. I am particularly anxious to stress the exploratory and illustrative character of these papers because there is a danger at the present time that the approach which they deal with is being accepted without sufficient examination.

Language teaching is necessarily a theoretical as well as a

practical occupation. If this were not so, discussion on the matter would reduce to an exchange of anecdotes and pedagogy would be mere pretence. Yet people concerned with teaching languages too often use the excuse of being practical to supinely accept the directives of others rather than actively think things out for themselves; to be too ready to follow the dictates of fashion without submitting them to careful scrutiny. So it was with the 'structural' approach. So it is now with the 'communicative'. If we are really serious about the teaching of communication, we cannot just exchange notions for structures, functions for forms, and suppose that we have thereby concluded the business. A communicative orientation involves a consideration of a whole host of issues:—how discourse is processed, how interaction is conducted, learning styles and strategies, developmental patterns of language acquisition, the role of learner and teacher—all these and more. There is a great deal of exploration to be done and it is time to put the banner away and start out.

So much for the scope and purpose of this book. Now, briefly, a word or two about the presentation. The papers have for convenience been arranged in eight sections each provided with a brief introduction which indicates the main lines of argument. The title of each section indicates the focal topic of the papers within it. But of course since all the topics interrelate they naturally recur in the context of other discussions as well. The sections can best be thought of, therefore, as variations on a common general theme, with the first as a prelude and the last as a reprise. This means that the papers do not fit neatly each into each in a sequence of self-contained stretches of argument. No doubt I could have refashioned them so that they did, but this would not have been consistent with the aim of the book, which is, as I have already indicated, to represent the actual process of discovery rather than to put its findings on show disposed to the best possible advantage.

The ideas expressed in these papers owe a great deal to discussion with other people—students and colleagues too numerous to mention by name. I hope that they will accept this general recognition of my debt to them. What I owe to Pit Corder, however, calls for particular acknowledgement. If he had not given me the opportunity and encouragement to pursue applied linguistic studies at the University of Edinburgh, these papers would never have been written. It is only fitting, therefore, that they should now be dedicated to him.

H. G. Widdowson
London   December 1977

Prelude

This paper represents early efforts to work out certain basic ideas and to establish broad lines of approach to communicative language teaching. To this end I draw a distinction between usage and use and between signification and value. As with other conceptual distinctions (langue/parole, competence/performance, denotation/connotation, and so on), they are a convenience whose validity can be called into question by reference to different ways of thinking. But I have found them serviceable for my purposes and they will reappear in subsequent sections.

The paper relates these notions to developments in linguistic theory. In particular there is a good deal of argument in favour of extending the concept of competence to cover the ability to use language to communicative effect. This case is no longer in court but in 1970 (when this paper was written) people were still busy preparing their briefs. I would be less ready these days to talk about revolutionary changes in linguistics: time, as usual, has altered the proportions of things. But whether or not communicative competence should be accounted for in formal models of description, I would still argue that it needs to be of central concern to the language teacher. What such competence consists of and how the teacher's concern can most effectively be converted into pedagogic procedures are questions which (as will emerge in later sections) turn out on closer inspection to be more complex than they appear to be in this paper. Here communicative competence is more or less glossed as the ability to cope with what I call rhetorical acts in isolation. There is a good deal more to it than that. In my own defence I should point out that I do make reference in this paper to how such acts 'combine to form composite communicative units'. This is an indication of the move that subsequent exploration will take in the direction of discourse.

One last point might be made on this section. There is an

assumption here that communicative competence in the form of rules of use has to be expressly and explicitly taught. This assumption is questioned in later papers, and I am now inclined to think that learning and teaching should not be regarded as converse activities at all, that the logic of a communicative approach calls for an emphasis on the learner's development of abilities through his own learning processes which the teacher should stimulate rather than determine.

1 The teaching of rhetoric to students of science and technology

In this paper I want to bring into focus a number of problems associated with the teaching of English as a second language, and by implication any other second language, in scientific and technical education. I make no pretence at being able to supply solutions. I do not myself believe that it is the business of applied linguistics to supply solutions to pedagogic problems, but only to provide some of the means by which they may be solved. It seems to me that the aim of applied linguistics is to clarify the principles by which the language teacher operates, or by which he might consider operating, if he is not alienated by arrogance.

The clarification which applied linguistics provides comes about as a result of relating the language teacher's beliefs about and attitudes to language and language learning, as they are revealed by his pedagogic practices, to the linguist's and psycholinguist's discoveries about language and language learning by means of theoretical and experimental investigation. It is particularly appropriate that applied linguistics should be concerned with English for science and technology because it happens to bring into prominence, as 'general' English teaching does not, a question which is one of the principal issues in linguistics at the present time: that is to say, the nature of language as communication. It is fairly rare that a shift in orientation in language teaching and a shift in orientation in linguistics should involve a coincidence of interest, but this, I believe, is now happening.

Let us begin with some obvious and general observations. First: what do we imagine we are doing when we are 'teaching a language'? We speak of developing skills, of making habitual the ability to compose correct sentences. We stress that the primary need is to inculcate in our learners a knowledge of the language system, and we devise drills and exercises to bring this about. At the same time, we do not wish to make our learners into automatons, mechanically repeating sentence patterns and so we insist that pattern practice and the manipulation of the language structures which are taught must be meaningful. We take pains to ensure that language is presented initially in situations which give meaning and point to the language which is being acquired. The general pattern is: situational presentation to make the language meaningful followed by exercises in repetition to make it habitual. What precisely are we teaching? We are, of course, teaching something quite abstract: we are teaching the language system: *langue*. This is not to say that we neglect *parole*. You cannot teach *langue* directly since it has to be realized in some way or another, so we use *parole* in our initial presentation and we use it in our exercises. But it is an odd kind of *parole* when you think about it: it is pressed into service to exemplify *langue*. This, of course, never happens outside a language teaching classroom. Normally *parole* only occurs as a result of some kind of social interaction: it does not just exemplify the operation of linguistic rules.

There is an important distinction to be made, then, between the *usage* of language to exemplify linguistic categories and the *use* of language in the business of social communication. When we make use of expressions like 'This is a red pencil' or 'This is a leg' or 'He is running to the door' this is language *usage* not language *use*: it exemplifies but does not communicate.

I think it is true to say that the manipulation of language in the classroom for what is known as situational demonstration or con-textualization is meant to indicate what I will call the *signification* of linguistic elements. Thus expressions like 'This is my hand', 'That is his foot', and so on, are meaningful as sentences because they indicate the signification of grammatical items like the possessive pronoun, and lexical items like 'hand', 'foot', and so on. Sentences like these are exemplificatory expressions and are meaningful as projections, as it were, of the language system or code. They are, of course, quite meaningless as utterances. It is difficult to see how they could possibly represent any message in any normal communication situation. They are meaningful as 'text-sentences' (to use a term of John Lyons') but meaningless as utterances because they have no *value* as communication.

It seems to me that it is important to stress this distinction. Language can be manipulated in the classroom in the form of text-sentences which exemplify the language system and thus indicate the *signification* of linguistic items. This is not the same as language *use*—the use of sentences in the performance of utterances which give these linguistic elements communicative *value*. In the classroom, expressions like 'This is a red pencil' are sentences; expressions like 'Come here', 'Sit down' are utterances because they have a communicative import in the classroom situation, which provides a natural social context for their occurrence.

Attempts are very often made to bestow communicative value on the language items which are introduced into the classroom, by the use of dialogue, for example. But it is done in a somewhat *ad hoc* and inci-dental way, and what I have in mind is something more systematic.

Even where there is an attempt to give communicative point to the language being learnt, it is generally left for the learner himself to work out the value. His attention is drawn to the grammatical rather than the communicative properties of the language being presented to him, and the focus is on signification rather than value. I shall return to this point later. For the moment I want to stress that the primary aim of the language teacher is at present directed at developing in his learners a knowledge of the language system, *langue*, using as much *parole* as is necessary to exemplify and establish it in the learner's mind.

I have been using the terms *langue* and *parole*. I think this distinction of de Saussure has provided theoretical sanction for the language teacher's notion as to what is involved in teaching a language. I want to question the validity of the distinction and its relevance to language teaching, and to suggest that the distinction, as de Saussure draws it, is misleading; and that in consequence the language teacher has been misled.

To begin with, though the distinction seems clear enough, when one traces it back to its source in the *Cours de Linguistique Générale* one finds it difficult to pin it down in any very precise way. Lyons says that it is intended to remove an ambiguity in the word 'language' which can refer both to potential capacity and to the realization of this potential in actual speech (Lyons 1968), and, of course, we can see what, in general, de Saussure is getting at. But although he succeeds in removing this particular ambiguity, a necessary consequence is that he introduces other ambiguities. These have recently attracted the attention of linguists; largely, I believe, because their critical faculties have been stimulated by the similar but less equivocal distinction between competence and performance introduced by Chomsky. The precision of Chomsky's formulations have the happy effect of forcing his critics to be precise as well. The ambiguities of the *langue/parole* distinction are pointed out by Hockett:

> Wittingly or unwittingly, Saussure had packed two intersecting contrasts into his single pair of terms: some of the time *langue* means 'habit' while *parole* means 'behaviour', but at other times *langue* means 'social norm' while *parole* means 'individual custom'.
> *Hockett 1968: 15.*

Householder provides his own gloss on these remarks:

> Hockett remarks quite correctly, as others have too, on the Saussurean confusion of two possible contrasts in the *langue/parole* distinction. He puts it a little differently than I would: contrast (a) makes *langue* mean 'habit' and *parole* 'behaviour', (b) makes *langue* equivalent to 'social norm' and *parole* to 'individual custom'. I would

tend to say rather that (a) equates *langue* with 'grammar' (i.e. 'competence grammar') or 'system' or 'structure' while *parole* is 'utterance' or 'performance', while (b) says *langue* is the 'common grammatical core' of a social group, while *parole* is the 'idiolect' or 'individual grammar'. Thus what is *langue* under (a) may be *parole* under (b). Of course there may be social groups of many sizes, so that in the (b) sense *parole* is the *langue* of a social group of one (if the limiting case is allowed).
Householder 1970.

The confusion which is revealed by Householder's remarks hardly needs commenting upon. From the social point of view, the distinction between *langue* and *parole*, which on the face of it seems so clear, disappears altogether. Both Hockett and Householder invoke the idea of social norms and such an invocation is fatal to the neat distinction which de Saussure is making. Once one places language in its social context, it becomes apparent that the notion of a common homogeneous system is a figment of the imagination. The paradox in the *Cours de Linguistique Générale* is that *langue* is represented as a social fact which is in some way independent of social use. As Labov points out:

. . . the social aspect of language is studied by observing any one individual, but the individual aspect only by observing language in its social context.
Labov 1970.

Once one becomes aware of the manner in which language functions in society as a means of interaction and communication, it becomes apparent that a description of language in terms of some homogeneous common system is a misrepresentation. One must accept that the linguist idealizes his data in order to do any linguistics at all, and there is nothing objectionable about this as a heuristic procedure. It could be argued that at the historical moment at which de Saussure was presenting his views the essential problem was to establish some methodological principles upon which linguistics could proceed as an autonomous discipline. This problem he succeeded in solving and linguistics has been able to develop as a result. But the linguist's area of concern as defined by de Saussure does not necessarily coincide with the areas of concern of other people involved in the study of language. The idealization represented by the *langue/parole* distinction happens to leave out of account those very aspects of language with which the language teacher must primarily be concerned.

Householder, as we have seen, glosses the *langue/parole* distinction by reference to the notions of competence and performance. I want now to have a closer look at these notions because it seems to me that they are responsible for the change in the orientation of linguistics which is now taking place.

First of all, it is clear that the competence/performance distinction is not just *langue/parole* writ large: if it were, there would presumably be no point in coining the new terms. *Langue* is represented as a concrete social fact whereas competence is represented as an abstract idealization: the perfect knowledge of the ideal speaker-listener in a homogeneous speech community. A linguistic description as an account of competence is therefore represented as a well-defined system of rules. The difficulty with an idealization upon which such a description depends is that it cuts the description off from empirical validation. Chomsky and his associates postulate the grammatical rules which constitute the system of the language by reference to their own intuitions. As for doubtful cases, they are prepared, they say, to let the grammar itself decide. As Labov has pointed out, however, it turns out that there are more doubtful cases than Chomsky imagined. This is because there is no such thing as a representative set of intuitions.

Once again, then, we run into difficulties as soon as we look at language from the social point of view. The concept of competence is meant to remove all the complications which are associated with social considerations but the result is that it also removes the possibility of what Firth called 'renewal of connection' with language in actual use. The system of the language as formalized in a generative grammar is thus cut off from the facts of use, and anomalies arise as a result: the ill-defined phenomena of human language, for instance, are represented as a well-defined system of generative rules.

The more explicit definition of competence, compared to the ambiguous definition of *langue* makes apparent the limitations of a linguistic description which depends on the abstraction of some elemental system isolated from, and unaffected by, language in use as a social phenomenon. This is not at all to belittle the achievements of generative grammar over the past two decades, but only to suggest that the depth of insight into linguistic form has been achieved by a narrowing of focus which has excluded many features of language which must somehow be accounted for in a total description. The problem is that many of these features are those with which the language teacher is principally concerned, and this is why generative grammar, as Chomsky himself points out, has such small relevance to language teaching. What exactly is excluded is indicated by Katz and Postal:

We exclude aspects of sentence use and comprehension that are not explicable through the postulation of a generative mechanism as the reconstruction of the speaker's ability to produce and understand sentences. In other words, we exclude conceptual features such as the

physical and sociological setting of utterances, attitudes, and beliefs of the speaker and hearer, perceptual and memory limitations, noise level of the settings, *etc.* (my emphasis).
Katz and Postal 1964: 4

All of these features are bundled together under *performance*. The very heterogeneity of such a collection suggests that in fact this is a covering term for everything which cannot be conveniently accounted for in the proposed model of description. Performance is, in effect, a residual category containing everything which is not accounted for under competence. The suggestion is that it subsumes everything about language which is imperfect or irregular, all systematic features being accounted for within competence, which is the repository, as it were, of the speaker's knowledge of his language. But it is clear that some of the features listed under performance are also systematic and form a part of the speaker's knowledge of his language (in any normal sense of knowledge), and should also therefore be considered as part of his competence. It is part of the speaker's competence to be able to use sentences to form continuous discourse, as Halliday points out; it is part of his competence that he should know how to use sentences to perform what Searle calls speech acts, Lyons calls semiotic acts, and I call rhetorical acts. In brief, knowledge of a language does not mean only a knowledge of the rules which will generate an infinite number of sentences, but a knowledge of the rules which regulate the use of sentences for making appropriate utterances. An utterance is not just the physical manifestation of an abstract rule of grammar: it is also an act of communication. To know a language means to know how to compose correct sentences *and* how to use sentences to make appropriate utterances.

It seems to me that a revolution is taking place in linguistics against a conceptual order which derives from de Saussure, and which, indeed, served as the very foundation of modern linguistics. There is an increasing recognition of the need to pay as much attention to rules of use, the speaker's communicative competence, as to rules of grammar, his grammatical competence, and that an adequate linguistic description must account for both. Here is where the interests of linguistics and language teaching converge. So long as our concern is with the teaching of 'general' English without any immediate purpose, without knowing in any very definite way what kind of communicative requirements are to be made of it, then the need to teach language as communication is not particularly evident. Once we are confronted with the problem of teaching English for a specific purpose then we are immediately up against the problem of communication. Teaching English as a medium for science and technology must involve us in the teaching of how

scientists and technologists use the system of the language to communicate, and not just what linguistic elements are most commonly
used. A common assumption seems to be that if you teach the system,
use will take care of itself: that once you teach, say, how to compose a
declarative sentence then the learner will automatically be able to
understand and make statements of different kinds, will be able to
define, illustrate, classify, qualify, describe, report—will, in short be
able to perform rhetorical acts and recognize the rhetorical acts of
others without much difficulty. In my view, the communicative
competence which this presupposes does not come of itself, especially
not to those learners outside the European cultural tradition. Rules of
use have to be taught with as much care as rules of grammar.

I am suggesting, then, that what I see as a revolution in linguistic
thinking should be matched by a revolution in language teaching
methodology in order to cope with the kind of challenge which English
for science and technology represents. In both cases there is a need to
shift our attention away from an almost exclusive concentration on
grammatical competence and to give equal attention to communicative
competence. Knowledge of a language involves both, and whether we
are concerned with the description or the teaching of language, we must
concern ourselves with both.

How do we set about teaching the rules of use? Rules of use are
rhetorical rules: communicative competence is the language user's
knowledge of rhetoric. Traditionally, rhetoric has been represented as a
set of prescriptive rules related to impressionistic norms, in much the
same way as traditional grammar was represented. Rhetoric is concerned
with appropriacy and grammar with correctness, and the reason why
the latter has achieved academic respectability whereas the former has
not is probably only a matter of historical accident, and probably has
something to do with the relatively recent development of the social
sciences. There seems to be no reason why rhetoric as the description
of communicative competence should not achieve similar standards of
precision as grammar has in the description of grammatical competence.
Whether the two can be incorporated into the same model of linguistic
description is a matter for speculation, but it seems clear that developments in linguistics at the present time are moving towards a rhetorical
revival. I should now like to review one of these developments and to
indicate in a rather programmatic way what relevance it might have for
the preparation and presentation of teaching materials.

The impetus behind the movement towards rhetoric has come from
two main sources: social anthropology on the one hand and linguistic
philosophy on the other. From social anthropology has come the notion
of the speech function; and from linguistic philosophy has come the
notion of the speech act.

We owe the notion of the speech act to the Oxford philosopher J. L. Austin, though I suppose it can be regarded as a development of the whole 'meaning is use' movement in philosophy. Briefly, Austin pointed out (Austin 1962) that when we issue an utterance we perform some kind of act over and above the composing of a linguistic form. Thus when I utter the expression 'I'll come tomorrow' I am committing myself to a promise or an undertaking of some kind, and if I utter the expression 'Come here' I am performing the act of command. Promises, orders, and so on are what Austin called 'illocutionary acts'. One can discover what kind of illocutionary act is being performed by making the act explicit by what he called a performative verb. Thus 'I'll come tomorrow' can be established as a promise or undertaking because one can use the performative verb *promise* and make the utterance explicit: 'I promise I will come tomorrow' or 'I undertake to come tomorrow'. Similarly one can provide a performative verb to make an order explicit: 'I order you to come here'. And so with other performative verbs.

Certain linguists, among them Thorne, Ross, and Lakoff, have made use of this insight and have postulated a deep structure in which the performative verb figures in a superordinate sentence which dominates the rest of the deep structure configuration. Thus we get deep structures roughly paraphrasable as 'I promise you I come tomorrow', 'I order you you come here', and so on. There are two difficulties about this procedure. Firstly, one has to accept that a sentence like 'I order you to come here' and 'Come here' have the same illocutionary potential, that is to say are used to perform the same act of ordering. But it seems obvious that the circumstances in which one would utter one of these are different from those in which one would utter the other. The second difficulty is related to this. In many, perhaps most cases, one cannot tell what act is being performed in the uttering of a certain sentence unless one is provided with a context. To take a simple example: 'I'll come tomorrow' may be a promise or a threat or a confirmation. 'You sound just like your mother' may be an insult or a compliment or neither.

This kind of difficulty points to the principal problem we are faced with in the study of speech acts. What other ways are there of indicating what act a sentence counts as apart from the use of the explicit performative verb? Certain linguistic features serve as signals, but they are not to be trusted: the context of utterance and the conventions of use associated with particular types of discourse very often override the linguistic indicators. One might imagine, for example, that the imperative mood is an unequivocal indicator of the act of commanding. But consider these instances of the imperative: 'Bake the pie in a slow oven', 'Come for dinner tomorrow', 'Forgive us our trespasses', 'Take up his offer'. An instruction, an invitation, advice, and prayer are all different acts, yet the imperative serves them all; and need serve none of them: 'You must bake the pie in a slow oven', 'I should take up his offer', 'Why don't you come to dinner tomorrow?', 'We pray for forgiveness of our trespasses'. But one might suppose, nevertheless, that though there are several different kinds of act that can be performed by the imperative, when an order is to be given it is always the imperative which is used. But this, of course, is not the case either. Just as one linguistic form may fulfil a variety of rhetorical functions, so one rhetorical function may be fulfilled by a variety of linguistic forms. But the forms which can serve this function are dictated by the conditions which must be met if an order or a command is adequately performed. Here we can turn to the work of Labov for illustration (Labov 1969a).

Labov points out that the conditions which must be met in making a command are as follows: when A commands B, B believes that A believes that at a time T:

1 X should be done.
2 B has an obligation to do X.
3 B has the ability to do X.
4 A has the right to ask B to do X.

Labov takes the situation of a teacher asking a pupil to do a piece of work again because it is unsatisfactory. The teacher—A—may frame his order in any of the following ways corresponding to each of the conditions:

1 This should be done again.
2 You'll have to do this again.
3 You can do better than this.
4 It's my job to get you to do better than this.

Or, making use of what Labov calls 'modes of mitigation and politeness', the command can be couched in interrogative terms:

1 Shouldn't this be done again?
2 Don't you have to do neater work?
3 Don't you think you can do better?
4 Can I ask you to do this again?

Labov also shows how the response to the command can fix upon one of the conditions, and can also be mitigated by the interrogative form.

From a different point of view, Searle (1969) also has established conditions on the performing of speech acts like promising, thanking, congratulating, requesting, warning, and so on. There is, then, a good deal of progress being made in the description of rules of use and the characterization of different rhetorical acts.

Let me now indicate what bearing I think this has on the teaching of English, and in particular on English for science and technology. What people like Austin, Searle, Labov, and others are now trying to pin down in terms of rules and conditions is precisely what language learners need to know if they are to cope with English as communication. I see no reason why the limitation stage of the language teaching process should not be a selection of rhetorical acts rather than of linguistic elements and vocabulary items. There seems no reason at all why we should not, for example, say 'For this course we will select undertakings, promises, warnings, definitions, classifications', and so on rather than 'For this course we will teach the simple present tense, present continuous, count and mass nouns', and so on. In fact, on the face of it, there would seem to be a very good reason for focusing on the former. Teaching rhetorical acts like promises and orders necessarily involves the teaching of different linguistic elements and vocabulary items, which are taught meaningfully because they are given a definite communicative import. You do not necessarily teach rhetorical acts when teaching linguistic elements and vocabulary items, as we all know, and what communicative competence the learners do acquire tends to be picked up incidentally. Once we accept the teaching of communicative competence as our prime objective, and once we can see—as I believe we now can see—how communicative competence can be described, then the logic of basing the preparation of teaching materials —limitation *and* grading—on the rhetorical units of communication rather than the linguistic units of the language system seems inescapable.

This approach seems to me to be of especial relevance in the preparation of English for science and technology teaching materials. I mentioned earlier that the conventions of use associated with particular types of discourse very often override linguistic indicators of rhetorical acts. Scientific discourse can be seen as a set of rhetorical acts like giving instructions, defining, classifying, exemplifying, and so on, but the manner in which these acts are related one with the other and the manner in which they are linguistically realized may be restricted by accepted convention. There are many ways of linking different acts to compose larger communicative units like, for example, a report or an exposition or a legal brief, and there are, as we have seen, several ways of performing the same basic act. My guess is that the best way— perhaps the only way—of characterizing different language registers is to discover what rhetorical acts are commonly performed in them, how they combine to form composite communication units, and what linguistic devices are used to indicate them.

Labov has said:

It is difficult to avoid the common-sense conclusion that the object of linguistics must ultimately be the instrument of communication used by the speech community; and if we are not talking about *that* language, there is something trivial in our proceeding.
Labov 1970: 33

I think it is possible that in language teaching we have not given language as an instrument of communication sufficient systematic attention. We have perhaps been too concerned with language system, taking our cue from the linguists, and in consequence there has often been something trivial in *our* proceedings. Now that we are turning our attention to the teaching of English for special purposes, and in particular to English for science and technology, we must take some principled approach to the teaching of rules of use, and restore rhetoric, in a new and more precise form, to its rightful place in the teaching of language.

Notes

A shortened and slightly revised version of a paper read at a BAAL seminar in Birmingham, March 1971, and published in Perren 1971.

English for Science and Technology

These three papers are concerned with how one might characterize and teach the English used in science and technology, particularly as realized in written communication. They focus on different aspects of the question and so can be located at different points on the applied linguistic spectrum. The first is directed towards the design of classroom exercises, the second discusses the relationship between such pedagogic practice and description based on theory, and the third attempts to clarify and illustrate theoretical distinctions assumed in the preceding papers.

Much of the discussion centres on two major and interrelated themes. The first of these has to do with the characterization of scientific and technical English. The argument here is that the formal linguistic characteristics of these varieties or 'registers' of English are only of interest as realizations of underlying concepts and communicative operations associated with particular areas of inquiry which go under the general name of science and technology. Scientific and technical English is thus represented not as a variety of English text but as a textualization of a variety of discourse which is itself independent of any particular language and expressive of a secondary and universal culture which scientists and technologists acquire through education.

The second theme draws out the pedagogic implications of the first. If one conceives of EST as varieties of English text, in contrast, let us say, to other varieties of text like sermons, cooking recipes, sports reports, and what have you, then there is clearly little scope for learner participation when it comes to teaching it. We are pushed towards a unilateral pedagogy in which the direction is from the teacher to the learner since the former knows the English textual forms and the latter does not. If, on the other hand, one conceives of EST as varieties of discourse textualized in English, in contrast, let us say, to other textualizations in

German, French, Russian, and so on, then, of course, the case is very different. Here the learner has a knowledge of the discourse which corresponds to his stage of learning in the area of science and technology concerned; and he can use that knowledge as a base for learning the particular textualization of this discourse in English. This way of conceiving of EST, therefore, would seem to lead naturally to a bilateral approach to pedagogy which can engage the participation of the learner by making open appeal to what he already knows.

A development of this second theme takes us on to the drafting of exercise types which might ensure learner engagement. This development is demonstrated in Paper 4 in this section and the papers in the section which follows illustrate further exploration along these lines. The first theme, that which has to do with the nature of discourse, is then taken up again in Section Four.

2 An approach to the teaching of scientific English discourse

Introduction

This paper has two complementary aims. The first relates to language teaching methodology: I want to make a number of practical suggestions as to how to approach the teaching of English to students who need to know the language in order to pursue their studies of science and technology in higher education. The second aim relates to applied linguistics: I want to make explicit the process whereby I arrived at these suggestions. All proposals about how language should be or might be taught derive from notions about the nature of language and language learning. Where these notions are not made explicit, however, it is difficult to assess the potential value of the proposals (their *actual* value can only emerge through trying them out in the classroom) or to identify which aspects are unsatisfactory. The teacher accepts or rejects them but he has no clear indication as to how they might be modified to suit his particular circumstances. He may adopt, but he may not be able to adapt.

In the first part of the paper, therefore, I shall be concerned with establishing a certain theoretical orientation to language study which I believe to be of particular relevance to the specialist English teaching purposes that have been mentioned. In the second part I shall try to show how certain principles of approach to language teaching seem to derive naturally from this orientation and how exercises based on these principles might be devised. I shall proceed, then, from theoretical considerations concerning the nature of language through certain principles of language teaching methodology to a set of practical proposals for the teaching of English to students who need the language to service their specialist studies.

I

The special English requirements of students following higher education courses in science and technology have been recognized for some time and a good deal of material has been produced to meet these requirements. It is important to notice, to begin with, that the underlying theoretical basis of most of it (though this is not always made explicit) is traceable to the concept of register. This being so, it would seem to be an appropriate point of departure for the theoretical part of my paper to consider the validity of this concept.

We may begin by examining how the notion is introduced in Halliday, McIntosh, and Strevens:

> Language varies as its function varies: it differs in different situations. The name given to a variety of a language distinguished according to use is 'register'.
> *Halliday et al 1964: 87.*

There is an underlying assumption here which I think is questionable. It is as follows: since language in general varies in accordance with the functions it is required to fulfil, then it follows that *a* language in particular must consist of different and distinct varieties. Furthermore, these varieties are defined in terms of their linguistic characteristics as subcodes of a particular language. As Halliday, McIntosh, and Strevens put it:

> It is by their formal properties that registers are defined.

I want to suggest that the argument upon which the notion of register is based rests on a double fallacy. On the one hand the fact of language variation is thought to entail the existence of separate language varieties within a language and on the other hand functional variation is thought to entail the existence of these varieties as formally distinct subcodes. It seems to me that there is a confusion here between *language* and *a language* and between *form* and *function*. In fact, variation in language (in general) need not involve the existence of varieties in any particular language and different functions need not be matched by a difference of linguistic forms.

Registers, then, are represented as formally differentiated varieties of a particular language. Thus we hear of a 'type of English' which is used for church services, or engineering textbooks, or cooking recipes. We are told that there is 'an English' of commercial correspondence or agriculture which can be described in terms of its lexical and syntactic properties. In accordance with this view of functional variation, language teachers engaged in preparing English materials for students of science and technology and other specialist areas of use have supposed that their task involves simply the selection and presentation of those lexical and syntactic features which occur most commonly in passages of English dealing with the specialist topics their students are concerned with. My view is that although such materials can serve some of the language needs for which they are intended, those, in fact, which have to do with a knowledge of the language system, they do not provide, except incidentally, for other needs, which have to do with a knowledge of the communicative functioning of the language. To meet needs of this kind I believe that we need to base teaching materials on a different theoretical approach to language variation.

What I want to suggest is that specialist uses of language, such as we find in scientific papers, technical reports, textbooks of different technologies, and so forth, are not to be associated with formally different varieties in a particular language but with certain universal modes of communication which cut across individual languages. That is to say I want to shift the theoretical orientation from particular languages to language in general and from linguistic forms to communicative functions. As a first step towards establishing this orientation let me make a distinction between *text* and *discourse*.

When confronted with a sample of language, a chapter in a chemistry textbook, for example, there are two ways in which we might describe it. We may treat it as an exemplification of the language system and point out the incidence of certain linguistic structures and items of vocabulary: in other words, we can describe its formal properties as an instance of linguistic usage. To do this is to conduct a register analysis and to characterize the sample as *text*. If we treat the sample in this way, however, there are a number of things about it that we fail to account for. In the first place it clearly does not just exist as usage, as an exemplification of the language system: it is also an instance of use; it communicates something and does so in a certain manner. If we were to ask the author or the reader to describe the sample, the likelihood is that he would characterize it as a *description* or a *report* or a set of *instructions*, or an *account* of an experiment. These terms do not refer to the linguistic properties of the sample as text, but to the communicative function of the sample as *discourse*. A register analysis of the sample as text will tell us nothing about these communicative functions of language use.

Furthermore, it will not account for another aspect of the sample. Much of the communication in a chemistry textbook is effected by other than verbal means. Apart from the purely verbal parts of the sample there will be formulae, symbols, line drawings, and tables which are an essential and intrinsic part of the communication as a whole. Since they do not exemplify the language system an analysis of the sample as text will, of course, make no reference to these communicative elements at all. An analysis of the sample as discourse, the purpose of which is precisely to characterize the communication as a whole, must take into account both verbal and non-verbal features and the manner in which they are related.

Once we shift the centre of attention from the linguistic properties of a piece of language as text to its communicative functioning (comprising both verbal and non-verbal modes) as discourse, it becomes plain that we are no longer dealing with the features of a particular language. Whether one is using English or French, Indonesian or Chinese, one is obliged, as a scientist, to perform acts, like descriptions, reports, instructions, accounts, deductions, the making of hypotheses, and the calculating of results. These are some of the basic cognitive and methodological processes of scientific inquiry and if one does not follow them, one presumably ceases to be scientific. What I am suggesting, then, is that the way English is used in science and in other specialist subjects of higher education may be more satisfactorily described not as formally defined varieties of English, but as realizations of universal sets of concepts and methods or procedures which define disciplines or areas of inquiry independently of any particular language. In other words, the 'special uses' we have been referring to are the communicative functions of language in a general sense and constitute universes of discourse which underlie the different textual features which realize them in different languages.

It is possible to reformulate the points that have been made in the previous paragraph by reference to the familiar distinction between deep and surface structure. We might say that the deep structure of, say, communication in chemistry, is the universe of discourse which consists of the concepts and procedures of this discipline, and the incidence of particular linguistic features in English chemical texts is simply the surface structure manifestation of these deep structure elements. How can this deep structure be represented? It seems reasonable to suppose that at least a part of its representation is to be found in those universal features which appear overtly as intrinsic elements in the discourse itself: that is to say, the non-verbal modes of communication like formulae, tables, diagrams, and so on. In chemical discourse, for example, whether the purely verbal part is expressed in English, Thai, or any other language, we will find devices like symbols and equations, diagrams of processes, and models of chemical compounds. Since these are drawn from a universally accepted set of conventions for representing specific concepts and procedures in chemistry they can be said to constitute part of the deep structure of chemical discourse. This deep structure, then, appears as it were, on the surface. But it can also be given a range of surface forms as it is verbalized in different languages.

Let us consider an example. The following is part of the discourse of an elementary textbook on chemistry:

$$H_2O + CO_2 \rightarrow H_2CO_3$$

These symbols and their combination to form this equation are likely to occur in any elementary chemistry textbook in any language. They are elements of a universal symbolic system. Thus, individual symbols like H, O, C, which represent chemical elements, can be regarded as the morphemes of this system, and the combination of symbols like H_2O, CO_2, which represent chemical compounds, can be regarded as the words. All of these 'words' are nominals since verbals are represented by the constants $+$ and $\rightarrow$. The whole formula constitutes a 'sentence' of this symbolic system, and the rules generate 'sentences' of this kind which are in essence the laws of chemical processes. Now this deep structure formula can be verbalized in terms of the linguistic system of a particular language. A surface form expression of it in English might be the following:

$$H_2 \quad O \quad + \quad C \quad O_2 \rightarrow H_2 \quad CO_3$$
hydrogen oxide   carbon dioxide   hydrogen carbonate
water combines with carbon dioxide to form carbonic acid

In terms of linguistic usage this is an English sentence, but in terms of communicative use it is a general statement expressing a chemical fact. The same formula can be said to underlie a different kind of communicative act such as a definition:

Carbonic acid is a compound which consists of water and carbon dioxide.

Both general statements and definitions are facts which have to do with the abstract conceptual content of a discipline, and we may say that the chemical formula we have been considering is an expression of content of this sort from which such acts can be derived. What the formula does not do is to tell us how the process takes place: it cannot, in other words, provide the underlying basis for a description of the process whereby carbonic acid is produced. This is a procedural matter. But just as we have formulae which express the *conceptual* aspects of the deep structure of chemical discourse, so we have other universally accepted non-verbal representations of the *procedural* aspects. Consider, for example, the following:

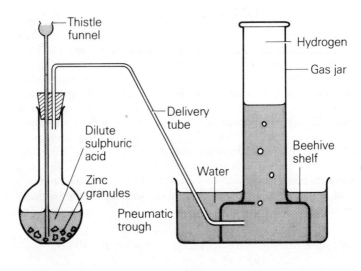

Hydrogen, H_2

$$Zn + H_2SO_4 \longrightarrow ZnSO_4 + H_2$$

zinc   sulphuric   zinc   hydrogen

acid   sulphate

Here we have a formulaic representation of a process as an abstraction from which can be derived general statements and definitions together with a conventional diagram illustrating the process as a concrete event from which can be derived such acts as instructions, descriptions, and reports. For example:

Instructions
Place zinc granules in a flask fitted with a thistle funnel and a delivery tube. Place the other end of the delivery tube in a pneumatic trough. Fill the trough with water......etc.

Description
Dilute sulphuric acid is added to zinc granules in a flask fitted with a thistle funnel and delivery tube. A chemical reaction takes place and hydrogen is given off......etc.

Report
Dilute sulphuric acid was added to zinc granules in a flask which had been fitted with a thistle funnel and a delivery tube......etc.

Let me now summarize the main points that have been made. The proposal is that we should think of 'scientific English' not as a kind of text, that is to say as a variety of English defined in terms of its formal properties, but as a kind of discourse, that is to say a way of using English to realize universal notions associated with scientific inquiry. These notions have to do with the concepts and procedures of particular branches of science which serve to define these branches as disciplines and which are expressed non-verbally in the same way, whichever language is used in the verbal parts of the discourse. In the area of science that I have chosen to illustrate this, the concepts seem to be expressed through formulae which represent the basis for such communicative acts as definitions and general statements, and the methods or procedures seem to be expressed through conventionalized diagrams which represent the basis for such acts as instructions or directions, descriptions, and reports. This may turn out, after further investigation, to be too neat a division for chemical discourse, and of course a different set of divisions may be necessary for other areas of science. But the main point is that there seems to be a universal underlying structure to different areas of scientific discourse which is neutral in respect of the different languages which are used to realize it, and that this underlying structure seems to be made overt through non-verbal modes of communicating. From this point of view, 'scientific' English relating to a particular discipline is not described formally as a type of text distinguishable from other 'registers' or 'varieties' in terms of its linguistic properties, but as the realization of a type of discourse which is defined in functional terms and distinguishable from other uses of language in general in terms of what concepts and procedures are communicated.

Let us now consider what pedagogic implications arise from this theoretical orientation to the study of language use.

II

I have argued that the English of different areas of science and technology (and probably other disciplines as well) can be regarded as particular linguistic realizations of uses of language in a general sense to express the concepts and procedures which define these areas of inquiry as disciplines. These universal defining features find a partial realization in non-verbal modes of communicating which constitute a universal set of symbolic devices for conveying the concepts and procedures of particular disciplines. Now the student entering higher education will have already been initiated into these concepts and procedures as they are realized both through his own language and through non-verbal symbolization. Thus, he already knows a good deal of how scientific communication is carried out. What he does not know is how it is carried out through the use of the particular linguistic system of English. The task of the English teacher at this point, therefore, is to extend the range of the student's communicative ability by making him aware of an alternative way of expressing the knowledge of science he already has.

One pedagogic principle that would seem to emerge from the orientation to language study that has been outlined in this paper, then, is that a course which prepares students for dealing with English use in scientific communication should present the language not as something in isolation from what the students already know but as an aspect of something with which they are already familiar. Let us now consider how we might put this principle into practice. We will assume that we wish to use chemistry as the area of science with which to associate the use of English. This does not preclude the possibility of associating English with other areas at a later stage; nor does it mean that the English which is learnt will only be relevant to students specializing in chemistry. I will return to this latter point later on. For the moment, let us suppose that we are concerned with the preparation of an English course for science students at the late secondary or early tertiary stage, that these students have had some basic grounding in science (including chemistry) and in English, and that our aim is to prepare them for their encounter with scientific communication in English such as they will find in their textbooks.

As an early, limbering-up, exercise we might require the students to make reference to, and relate, a knowledge of scientific symbols, their own language and English in the completion of a table. To complete the table they might well need to refer both to a dictionary of English and to a textbook on chemistry, and this is all to the good because such activities will.help to impress upon the student right from the start that the English he is learning has an immediate bearing on the solving of a scientific task. The following is an example of the kind of task I have in mind:

Complete the following table. Refer to an English dictionary and to a chemistry textbook if necessary.

1 symbol	2 name		3 atomic number	4 atomic weight
	L1	English		
S				
Ca				
Cl				
H				
O				
Pb				
Fe				
Cu				
Zn				
Na				

We might next present a second table representing atoms and molecules and ask the student to make simple statements in his own language based on the table and to recognize and later to reproduce comparable statements in English.

For example:

atoms	molecules
Cl	Cl_2
H	H
O	O_2
S	S_8
Fe	Fe
Pb	Pb
Cu	Cu_2

Statements in L1	Statements in English
....	A chlorine molecule consists of two chlorine atoms.
....	A molecule of chlorine consists of two atoms of chlorine.
....	Chlorine molecules consist of two chlorine atoms.
....	Molecules of chlorine consist of two atoms of chlorine.
....	A sulphur molecule consists of ....
....	A .... consists of eight atoms of sulphur.
....	Sulphur molecules .... eight sulphur atoms.
....	Molecules of sulphur ....

Other exercises of a similar kind might be introduced which gradually involve more productive participation on the part of the student, each one requiring him to realize the relationship between a symbolic representation, an expression in his own language, and an expression in English. We might, for example, go on to present a table of elements and compounds and get the student to provide names in his own language and to make appropriate statements.

Elements	Compounds	Name in L1	Name in English
Cu	CuO		
Cl	$CuCl_2$		
Fe	Fe_2O_3		
Pb	PbO		
S	CuS		

Statements in L1		Statements in English
....	Cu	Copper is an element.
....	Cu, Cl	Copper and chlorine are elements.
⋮		⋮
....	Fe	Iron ....
....	Fe, Pb	.... are ....
....	CuO	Copper oxide is a compound.
....	PbO	Lead oxide is a compound.
....	CuO, PbO	Copper oxide and lead oxide are compounds.
⋮		⋮
....	Fe_2O_3	Iron oxide ....
....	CuS	.... sulphide .... a ....
....	CuS, $CuCl_2$	.... and copper chloride .... compounds.

Consider the next exercise.

Statements in L1		Statements in English
....	$CuCl_2$	Copper chloride is a compound.
....		It consists of one atom of copper and two atoms of chlorine.
....		Copper chloride is a compound which consists of one atom of copper and two atoms of chlorine.
....		Copper chloride is a compound consisting of one atom of copper and two atoms of chlorine.
⋮		⋮
....	Fe_2O_3	.... is a compound.
....		.... consists of .... and three ....
....		.... oxide is a compound which consists of .... of iron and .... of .... a compound .... two atoms of iron and ....

As a development of the last two exercises, we might now ask the students to understand first and then write out two statements followed by a single statement which combines the two.

So far the communicative acts which we have required the student to understand and perform might be characterized as simple classifying statements like *copper is an element, copper oxide is a compound*, general statements or generalizations concerning composition like a *chlorine molecule consists of two chlorine atoms* and combinations of these two acts which yield defining statements, or definitions, like *copper chlorine is a compound which consists of one atom of copper and two atoms of chlorine*. We may now proceed to other uses of English: to simple statements about processes, for example. To do this we might present a set of equations such as were referred to in part I of this paper and derive appropriate statements from them in the following manner:

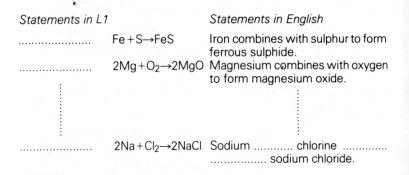

Statements in L1		*Statements in English*
....	$Fe + S \rightarrow FeS$	Iron combines with sulphur to form ferrous sulphide.
....	$2Mg + O_2 \rightarrow 2MgO$	Magnesium combines with oxygen to form magnesium oxide.
⋮		⋮
....	$2Na + Cl_2 \rightarrow 2NaCl$	Sodium .... chlorine .... sodium chloride.

It should be noted that the focus of attention in all of the exercises that have been suggested is on the way English functions in the performance of certain acts of communication which are central to scientific inquiry in general, although exemplified in this particular instance by chemistry. But although the focus is on use, the students are, of course, being given practice in usage at the same time: that is to say they are exercising their ability to compose correct sentences in the process of performing appropriate acts of communication. What this approach enables us to do is to bring together sentence patterns which have been learnt in separation in different parts of a school course and to show how they can be associated as realizing the same communicative function. In this way we draw on the student's previous knowledge and give it a new significance so that its relevance to scientific study becomes apparent.

The kind of communicative acts we have dealt with so far are those which are expressive of some of the concepts of chemistry and these acts (classification, generalization, definition) are of course expressive of concepts in other scientific disciplines as well and can be regarded as features of the basic rhetoric of science. Thus what the student is learning is not simply how the concepts of chemistry are expressed but a set of communicative acts which have a much wider range of employment. We might, at this stage, wish to bring this home to the students by illustrating the use of these acts in the expression of the conceptual content of other scientific areas.

From communicative acts based on formulae and equations relating to concepts we might next proceed to communicative acts based on diagrams relating to procedures. For example, an equation like the following:

$$Zn + H_2SO_4 \rightarrow ZnSO_4 + H_2$$

provides a basis for general statements of fact like:

> Zinc combines with sulphuric acid to form zinc sulphate and hydrogen is given off.
> When zinc combines with sulphuric acid, zinc sulphate is formed and hydrogen is given off.

and so on. The equation provides a basis for making factual statements to the effect that a certain reaction takes place: it does not provide a basis for the description of how we must proceed to bring about such a reaction. The kind of non-verbal device which does provide such a basis is a diagram of the kind which was illustrated in the first part of this paper. As was pointed out there, from such a diagram can be derived acts like instructions, descriptions, and reports and these acts can be realized as before, both in the student's own language and in English. Again, it should be noted that these acts can relate to a much wider range of procedures than those specifically associated with chemistry and exercises drawing on other scientific areas may be devised accordingly.

The shift of attention from acts relating to concepts to acts relating to procedures also tends to involve a transition from structurally simple acts consisting mainly of one utterance to more complex ones consisting of a combination of utterances. We now begin to approach the kind of discourse which the students will encounter in their text-books. At the same time, we might wish to withdraw the help given by the use of the L1 and place an increased emphasis on the use of English. We still maintain the principle that what is to be learnt should be related to what is already known, but what is already known is now the knowledge of English and its operation that the course itself has developed. With the removal of the L1-English link, more reliance will have to be placed on the relationship between English and non-verbal representations and these can be exploited more fully to give meaning and point to the language being learnt. Let us now consider how this might be done.

In the exercises that have been suggested so far, statements in English have been associated with statements in the L1 and with non-verbal representations of one kind or another. The student's task has been initially to recognize the value of the statements and subsequently to participate in making statements of a similar kind. Another way of exploiting these representations which could follow on from this would be to have students derive an appropriate representation from a statement or a set of statements and the reverse. For example:

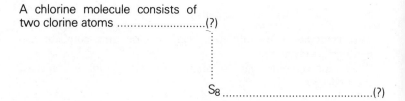

Here, the student is required to provide the formula Cl_2 to correspond with the first statement and the statement *A sulphur molecule consists of eight sulphur atoms* to correspond with the formula which is given. The degree of similarity of the two formulae controls the extent to which the first statement (the one which is given) serves as a model for the statement which the student has to provide for himself. This simple scheme allows for reception and production (comprehension and composition) to be related in a controlled way as aspects of the same language learning process.

Now when we come to the teaching of acts relating to procedures like descriptions, reports, and instructions without recourse to an overt relationship with the way these acts are realized in the L1, we can exploit this scheme more fully. For example, a description of an experiment might be given and the student required to label or complete a diagram, or draw one, which illustrates what is described. This is a comprehension task. Next, the student is given a diagram comparable to the one he has completed or drawn and is required to derive a description from it which will be correspondingly similar to the original description, which serves therefore as a model. Deriving a description from a diagram is, of course, a composition task. We can represent these proposals more generally as follows:

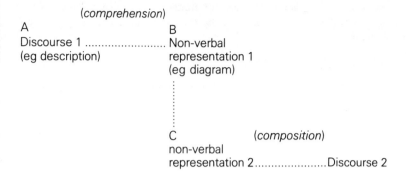

In this diagram (and in the previous one), the dotted lines (both vertical and horizontal) represent where control can be exerted. It can be exerted between A and B by varying the degree of difficulty of the task given to the student. He may be presented with a partially labelled diagram, for example, or a diagram with no labels, or an incompletely drawn diagram, or no diagram at all. Similarly, the task of moving from C to D can be made more or less difficult: the student can be provided with certain key words or phrases, or be asked to complete a discourse by filling spaces, or be asked to compose the discourse without any clues at all. The control between B and C has to do with the degree of similarity of the non-verbal representations: and this will determine, of course, the extent to which Discourse 1 can serve as a model for Discourse 2.

Conclusion

In this paper I have tried to show how the adoption of a certain view of the nature of language and how it is learnt can lead to proposals for language learning exercises. I have suggested that if one considers the way English is used in science as the realization of universal modes of thought and practice and not as a formally defined 'register' of English then it follows that it should be presented in association with corresponding uses of the first language and with those non-verbal means of expression which realize the concepts and procedures which define different scientific disciplines. I am not claiming that the exercises that have been proposed are in any way definitive: I have no doubt that they can be improved upon and that they might well require extensive modification in the light of practical classroom experience in different teaching circumstances. What I would like to claim, however, is that although they may be faulty in design they are sound in intention. They are meant to develop in the student an awareness of how English is used to communicative effect in scientific discourse. And whatever exercises in English are devised for students of science and technology their ultimate justification must be the extent to which this intention is realized.

Notes

First published in *RELC Journal* (Singapore), Vol. V No 1, June 1974.

3   EST in theory and practice

Over the past few years two developments have been apparent in the methodology of English teaching. One of these has been an increased concern with the problems of learners in further and higher education who need to know the language to pursue their specialist studies, in particular in the fields of science and technology. The second has been the recognition, provoked by recent work in sociolinguistics and philosophy, that the ability to use the language as a means of communication does not follow as a necessary consequence of learning the language as a formal system but has to be developed by teaching in some way. One development has extended from ELT to ESP/EST and the other has extended from linguistic structures to communicative activities. The developments are not, of course, unconnected. When English is taught in the context of general primary and secondary education there is no immediate means of checking on the assumption that communicative abilities will naturally emerge from a knowledge of the language system when the need arises. Aims are defined internally by reference to examination requirements. When aims are defined externally by reference to specific purposes, however, as they are in ESP/EST, an immediate return on teaching investment is expected in the form of effective communicative ability. A concern with ESP/EST necessarily entails a concern with communicative competence.

I do not think that it will be seriously disputed that there is a need to devise teaching programmes which will develop the communicative ability to handle scientific and technical discourse in English. The question at issue is how we might set about doing it and in this paper I want to explore this question and try to make clear in my own mind what problems are involved. The exploration will be tentative because I am uncertain of the ground and there are no reliable maps to guide us. I shall be feeling my way.

I will begin with a general observation and then explore its implications in detail. It seems to me that there are currently two ways of thinking about EST. One of them would appear to take the view that we already have the means of devising EST programmes and that our problems are essentially operational ones within the scope of pedagogy involving the appropriate application of what we already know. On the other hand there is an opposing school of thought which takes the view that we have very little to apply, that we know little or nothing about the nature of scientific and technical communication, and that the design of effective teaching programmes depends on the findings of research which has yet to be undertaken. In this view, the problems are essentially theoretical and come within the compass of linguistics broadly defined. My own feeling is that the first school of thought over-simplifies the situation and that the second over-complicates it. In this paper I should like to try to give substance to this feeling and thereby to work my way towards a formulation of what I see to be the principal problems in EST. In doing so I shall be trying to reconcile the operational and theoretical views, to mediate between pedagogy and linguistic theory in a broad sense. This paper is intended, therefore, as an exercise in applied linguistics.

I think that those who take the operational view believe that scientific and technical English can be characterized and taught as a register or group of related registers defined in terms of formal linguistic properties. To devise an EST programme, therefore, one would proceed in the following way: conduct a statistical survey on a sample of English of the kind one wishes to teach and establish the relative frequency of occurrence of the lexical and syntactic units in it, then devise language teaching materials which will give relative weighting to these linguistic elements in accordance with their importance as measured by frequency. This, of course, is one of the basic procedures employed for selection in structural syllabuses of the conventional kind. In this view, EST simply involves the application of an already existing approach to a more restricted sample of language data. Presentation as well as preparation procedures are also conceived in conventional terms and in a good deal of existing EST material we find structural exercises and comprehension questions which only differ from those in general ELT material by being associated with language data which is scientific and technical in referential content.

I have expressed elsewhere my doubts about the efficacy of the structural approach in general and about its appropriateness for the teaching of science and technology in particular (Widdowson 1968). Perhaps I might briefly summarize my position here. A register analysis, as generally understood and practised, takes samples of actual discourse and breaks them down into their constituent linguistic elements. What counts as a linguistic element for the purpose of the analysis will be determined by the model of description being used and the largely *ad hoc* decision as to which elements are likely to be easiest to recognize and count and which are likely to yield a significant characterization of the sample. A taxonomic model, for example, will reveal no deep structure elements; inter-sentential relations involving cross-reference might be significant but difficult to recognize and count; certain forms (*on, by, to,* for example) would be easy to recognize and count but carry little information in isolation from the syntactic environments which indicate their functional significance. But quite apart from these design faults there is the more radical question of the nature of the information that emerges from this kind of formal analysis. What we get is a quantitative statement about the frequency and types of those linguistic elements which are specified in the model of analysis. Since the analysis isolates these from context it cannot indicate how they function in relation to each other in the discourse as a whole. It may reveal the relative frequency of tokens of certain clause types, for example, but it cannot indicate any variability in their communicative value; it may reveal a high incidence of passive verb forms but it cannot indicate the different kinds of statement which these forms are used to make. In brief a register analysis which atomizes discourse into linguistic elements characterizes a sample of language quantitatively as a manifestation of the language system. What it does not do is to show how the language system is realized qualitatively in particular instances as communicative activity. It accounts for samples of language as instances of linguistic usage but not as instances of communicative use.

It is of course precisely the manifestation of the language system as usage which the structural approach as commonly practised in general ELT is primarily designed to teach. Thus the operational view which sees the problem of EST as having to do with the application of the findings of register analyses in effect does not recognize the connection between the two developments which I mentioned in the introductory paragraph. The transition from ELT to EST does not correspond with a transition from linguistic forms to communicative functions: the assumption is still that once the usage characteristic of scientific and technical English is learned then students will automatically know how the language is put to use in those communicative activities which characterize science and technology as fields of inquiry. I do not believe that this is so and it is for this reason that I think that the school of thought that holds such a view over-simplifies the situation. I do not believe that a knowledge of how English is used in scientific and technical communication can arise as a natural consequence from the learning of the sentence patterns and vocabulary which are manifested most frequently in samples of communication of this kind. We need to set up conditions which will lead students to make the transition from usage to use.

But if EST is to be concerned with the teaching of use where can we find descriptions of use upon which teaching programmes can be based?

The short answer is: nowhere. At this point we come to the second school of thought. The view here might be expressed as follows: EST must be centrally concerned with developing the ability to process scientific and technical communication. This involves a recognition of how the concepts and procedures of science and technology are expressed through communicative acts which are related in an intricate way to form structured discourse and how this complex structure of acts is realized through the particular medium of English. In brief, the effective design of EST programmes is thought to depend on descriptions of use based on a comprehensive model of discourse. Whereas the operational view represents the task of teaching EST as straightforward and within the competence of the practising teacher, this view represents it as enormously complex: a matter for research in an area of inter-disciplinary inquiry which at present is the scene of a great deal of busy activity in the form of tentative exploration with everybody staking claims but where nothing is known with any certainty. A pioneer's delight but a nightmare for anyone with a liking for law and order.

It might be edifying to consider briefly the kind of difficulties which have arisen in this field of research. So long as the systematic study of language operates at a level of idealization which excludes variation and context, it is possible to specify the properties of a language in terms of well-defined linguistic units. But once this idealization is relaxed to allow consideration of the fact that people use language to communicate with each other in social settings, the ordered arrangement of this neat conceptual universe begins to disintegrate. Philosophers in their speculative way talk about speech acts and linguists, naturally inclined to value speculation, feel compelled to take note of how sentences are used in the performance of such acts. In consequence, certain basic distinctions lose their clarity. The classic dichotomies upon which so much of modern linguistics depends: *langue/parole*, competence/performance, sentence/utterance, semantics/pragmatics, are called into question. At the same time, the linguistic order is being undermined from another quarter: those scholars who adopt a sociological perspective on the study of language point to the regularity of variation and its significance in accounting for social meaning. They show how the systematic study of actual language data can reveal system, that by widening the scope of linguistic inquiry one can establish regularity without having to postulate homogeneity, that system can be dynamic and variable and does not have to be static and well-defined.

It should not be supposed that the current uncertainty in linguistics betokens a decline. Theoretical principles must, like everything else, be subject to change. All systematic inquiry must be based on idealization of one sort or another, and idealization of one sort provides the opportunity of developing insights which are different from those which idealization of another sort might allow. The fact that linguistics is currently undergoing a reappraisal of its principles and a realignment of its theoretical position should not make us forget the immensely important advances which were made under the formalist, and more particularly, the transformational-generative régime. On the other hand it should make us aware of two points which are of relevance to our discussion of EST.

The first relates to the operational school of thought which I spoke about earlier. It is this: there is no model of linguistic description that has a patent on the truth and so there is no model of linguistic description which should command complete allegiance. The language teacher necessarily looks to the linguist for guidance and it is obviously tempting to seek security in one view of language rather than to range restlessly over several. But it seems to me that the second alternative is the one that is to be preferred. The language teacher should be adept at drawing insights from a wide spectrum of inquiry and to exploit them for his own purposes in order to arrive at a synthesis based on pedagogic principles. Only if he has this flexibility will he be able to adjust to the kind of teaching needs which EST, for example, brings to light by taking new developments in linguistic thinking into account. As I have already suggested, the operational view is inadequate because it adheres too closely to a particular model of description.

The second point that arises in connection with the current state of linguistics relates to what I have called the theoretical view of EST. The problem here is that those who espouse it are in a sense too much involved in recent developments. Whereas the first view is not sufficiently informed by theory, the second is not sufficiently informed by practice. Let us consider this view more closely. In standard generative theory there is an assumption that the underlying cognitive processes which inform language behaviour can be captured by a set of algebraic rules: an equation is set up between linguistic description and linguistic knowledge and the term generative is used to refer both to the production of formal objects in a grammar and the production of mental constructs which are represented as underlying the utterance of pieces of language when the occasion for utterance arises. This equation is now being questioned. Sociolinguists in particular are saying that a good deal of what a speaker knows about his language cannot be incorporated into a generative grammar so that the linguistic description it presents cannot be equated with linguistic knowledge. The question is, of course, what kind of description *can* account for this knowledge? Is there any way of saving the equation? It is precisely this question which is exercising linguists at the moment and which lies behind their concern with illocutions, speech functions, presuppositions, text grammars, discourse analysis, and all the rest of it. It is a crucial question for the development of linguistics, but is it a crucial question for the development of language teaching, and in particular for the development of EST? The theoretical view believes that it is: that we cannot teach communicative competence, the ability to handle English use in discourse, until we have a description of it, that teachers cannot proceed to develop this knowledge in their students until the linguists have described it for them. I myself believe that this view is wrong and that it over-complicates the issue. Moreover, I think that it shows just as mistaken a concept of the relationship between linguistics and language teaching as does the operational view.

So far I have done a good deal of criticizing, but I have now come to the point at which I must suggest an alternative way of looking at these matters: one which mediates between teaching and research and which brings developments in EST within the scope of practical methodology. The theoretical view is basically that we cannot effectively teach what we cannot explicitly describe and since we cannot describe the way English is used in scientific and technical discourse, our attention must be directed towards doing so as a preliminary to the design of EST programmes. This leaves the language teacher with nothing to do but to stand and wait. But although we are not in a position to describe discourse in a systematic way, the language user himself knows how to create and understand discourse of different kinds expressed in his own language. This knowledge has not been made explicit in exact descriptions of the kind the linguist would find satisfactory but do we so completely depend upon such a description for developing means of guiding students to an acquisition of this knowledge? I do not think so.

Let us consider what a practical knowledge of EST might involve. I think that the first point that has to be made is that EST is at one and the same time a variety of English usage and the particular linguistic realization of a mode of communicating which is neutral in respect to different languages. That is to say, EST does indeed manifest the system of English in a certain way but the significance of this is that it does so in the expression of concepts and procedures which characterize different technologies and scientific disciplines, and which might be said to constitute their basic communicative system. What I am suggesting, then, is that fields of inquiry in the physical and applied sciences, as these are generally understood, are defined by their communicative systems, which exist as a kind of cognitive deep structure independently of individual realizations in different languages. I think that this communicative deep structure frequently emerges on the surface as mathematical expressions, formulae, graphs, charters, conventionalized diagrams, and so on, which take the same form irrespective of the differences of the verbal context in which they occur. We can define scientific discourse, then, as the verbal and non-verbal realization of the communicative system of science. Now this system *has* been described under the name of the philosophy of science, and any systematic description of scientific discourse in English must therefore take account of this philosophy, which represents the basic principles of scientific inquiry. But does this mean that the teacher must also take account of it in his teaching of EST? This question worries many English teachers: they feel that they cannot possibly teach EST because they are not scientists. It is a question, therefore, which we must consider carefully.

The philosophy or communicative system of a science defines that science as a discipline. The science teacher's task is to develop teaching techniques and materials which will guide his students to acquire a knowledge of this system. In other words, the principles of the discipline are pedagogically processed to fashion a subject for teaching. The teacher of EST is not generally called upon to teach the English discourse of science as a discipline, but the English discourse of science as a subject, as this has been designed through the pedagogy of science. It is not the English teacher's task to design science teaching programmes. He might find it of interest to investigate the philosophy of science as a discipline but what he needs to know something about is the pedagogy of science as a subject. The reason for this is that the closer the English teacher's methodology can be made to approximate to that of science teaching, the more successful he will be in integrating the two areas of knowledge whose synthesis constitutes relevant English use. I shall return to this point presently.

Meanwhile, let us consider the question of what is involved in a practical knowledge of EST. If what has been said in the preceding paragraph is accepted, it will be evident that what students need to know is how English is used to realize the discourse of that level of scientific instruction that they have arrived at. I have already suggested that the communicative systems of different scientific disciplines are independent of any particular linguistic realization. Can we also say that the pedagogic methodology associated with different scientific subjects is similarly universal? I think that perhaps we can. I think that it is likely that scientific textbooks written in different languages express essentially the same methodology. Moreover, as with the communicative system of the discipline, I think that this methodology is reflected in certain non-verbal devices of exposition which are common to all textbooks. Now if this is so, then students will have already acquired some knowledge of the communicative systems of science which appear, pedagogically processed, in scientific subjects. How much they know will depend on the stage they have reached in their studies, but they will know something. This knowledge may hitherto have been acquired only through their own language. The English teacher's task is not to develop this knowledge but to demonstrate how it is realized through the medium of a different language. How can this best be done?

The operational view would presumably be that we teach the vocabulary and structures which are manifested most commonly in English scientific discourse in general. The theoretical view would be that we must first describe and then teach how the communicative systems of the discipline in question are realized uniquely in English. Underlying both points of view are two assumptions, both of which seem to me to be mistaken. First, it is assumed that the learner has little or no previous knowledge of how language is used in scientific communication. EST is represented as in some sense a separate learning task. The second assumption is that what is to be learned has to be explicitly taught, that knowledge is a kind of model that has to be constructed in the learner's mind rather than a dynamic process which develops of itself. Here EST is represented as in some sense a complete and well-defined learning task. I think that both of these assumptions are wrong and misrepresent the kind of knowledge which students of EST must acquire.

Let us consider the case of a student who enters higher education to study a scientific or technical subject, and who has to read textbooks in English. In his secondary schooling he has, we will assume, acquired knowledge of two kinds. In the first place, he will have some knowledge of English usage, conveyed to him by means of a structural syllabus of the familiar kind. Secondly, he will have learnt some science and in consequence he will have some knowledge of how his own language is put to communicative use in scientific discourse of an instructional sort. This learning of science will, of course, have drawn upon the student's more general awareness of how his own language functions as communication. The situation is, then, that the student has some knowledge of English usage and some knowledge of how his own language is put to use in scientific discourse. The task for the teacher of EST is to relate these two kinds of knowledge, to convert usage into use by reference to the student's existing communicative competence in his own language. EST is best considered not as a separate operation but as a development from, or an alternative realization of, what has already been learnt, that is to say existing knowledge. Its first objective is to change the student's concept of English from that which represents it as a separate set of facts about words and sentence patterns and grammatical rules to that which represents it as a means of communication similar in nature to his own language. It is not easy to persuade a language learner to see a foreign language in this light in the context of general education since so many of the situations which are set up to give meaning to the language are obviously contrived for that sole purpose. In the context of EST, however, it is not difficult to convince the student of the communicative reality of the language. What the EST programme has to do is to show him how to cope with it.

I have discussed elsewhere one way in which this might be done. It involves making use of those non-verbal devices which are, as I have already suggested, the universally conventionalized expression of the underlying communicative systems of science. Now since these non-verbal modes of communicating represent some of the basic concepts and procedures of different scientific subjects, they can serve as a point of reference for verbal realizations in the student's own language and in English. What I am suggesting is a translation procedure but as a three-cornered operation. Translation, as it is commonly conceived, converts one structure into another which is thought to have the same meaning by virtue of the semantic equivalence of its linguistic elements. The use of non-verbal devices enables us to relate three ways of expressing the same basic concepts and procedures. In this way, the student can be shown in general how English is used in the same way as his own language and in particular how it is used in the performance of specific acts of communication relating to the communicative system of science. Thus a knowledge of EST can derive from what the student knows of science and the functioning of his own language in association with what he has learnt of English usage. This three-way translation procedure can be controlled for difficulty, as it must be of course if it is to function effectively as a teaching device.

Exercises of this three-way translation type can prepare the way for exercises in which the support of the student's own language is withdrawn and the relationship to be established is made directly between non-verbal representations and English use. In exercises of this information transfer type, we have two instances of English use related to the same type of non-verbal device. In the case of three-way translation, we have the following situations:

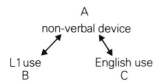

When the non-verbal device is given with the instance of English use, $(C \rightarrow A)$ the provision of the translation is essentially a comprehension task. When the non-verbal device is given with the instance of L1 use (B→A) then the provision of the translation is essentially a composition task. We might show this as follows:

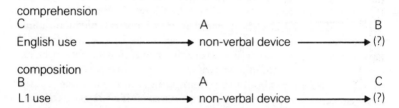

comprehension
C   A   B
English use ——————————→ non-verbal device ——————————→ (?)

composition
B   A   C
L1 use   ——————————→ non-verbal device ——————————→ (?)

In the case of information transfer exercises, there are two instances of use again but both are in English, and we present two instances of non-verbal device of the same type. For example, we might give a brief description of an experiment, a mechanical device, a piece of equipment, and so on. This would be the first instance of use. We might then require the student to label a given diagram, or draw a diagram of his own which represented the facts of the description. This would be the first instance of a non-verbal device. The transfer here is essentially a comprehension task. Next we present a second diagram which represents the same kind of information (realizes the same type of concept or procedure) as the diagram that the student has already completed and we now require him to derive a description from it which will be correspondingly similar to the original description, which, of course, acts as a model for this second instance of use. The transfer from the second instance of verbal device to the second instance of use is essentially a composition task. We might represent the process of information transfer as follows:

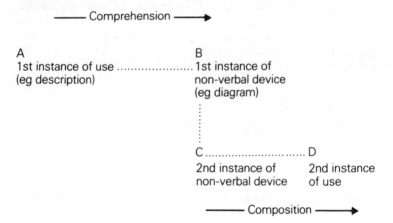

————— Comprehension —————→

A   B
1st instance of use .... 1st instance of
(eg description)   non-verbal device
                                    (eg diagram)

                                    C .... D
                                    2nd instance of   2nd instance
                                    non-verbal device   of use

                                    ————— Composition —————→

The dotted lines in this scheme show where control can be applied. It can be applied between A and B by varying the degree of difficulty of the task the student has to undertake: he may be given a partially labelled diagram, or an unlabelled diagram, or an incomplete diagram, or no diagram at all. Control can also be applied between C and D in a similar way: the student might be given key words or phrases, or be asked to assemble an assortment of sentences into a well-formed discourse, or be given no help at all, except of course the possibility of referring to the first instance of use as a model. The control between B and C has to do with the degree of similarity that holds between the instances of non-verbal device, and this will in turn determine the extent to which the first instance of use can be used as a model for the second.

I should like to make two points about the procedures that have been outlined and partially illustrated here. The first of them has to do with the comment I made earlier about the desirability of the English teacher knowing something about the methodology of science teaching. It is obviously central to the purpose of these exercises in mediated translation and information transfer that the language presented and produced should be instances of use and not instances of usage. The students must feel that they are involved in meaningful communicative activity and not just doing a language exercise. This means that the problems they have to solve should as far as possible make appeal to the kind of cognitive processes which it is the purpose of science teaching to develop. What this involves in general is an exploitation of science teaching methodology. The suggestions I have made give only a hint of how this might be done, but I believe that the teacher of EST would be best advised to seek methodological guidance not from the linguist or the philosopher of science but from the science teacher. His best source of reference is likely to be (at least in our present state of theoretical and descriptive uncertainty) textbooks of science and the experience of his science teaching colleagues. In short, it seems to me that if EST is to be concerned with the teaching of use, then it must be conducted not as a separate operation but as an extension from science education.

My second point relates to the second assumption that I referred to earlier, and here I move on to very uncertain ground with only my intuition to guide me. The exercises I have suggested do not direct the student's attention to features of language in any explicit way: they provide an opportunity for the student to induce meanings by reference to his own knowledge. The focus is on the communicative function of use and not on the linguistic forms of usage. The underlying assumption is that usage will come into focus, that is to say, will conform to norms of correctness, as a consequence of practice in appropriate use. This, of course, is the reverse of the commonly held view that correctness should be of primary concern. But I would like to take a more radical departure from established opinion. The exercises concentrate on use but they do not do so in any very exact way: the student is largely left to work things out for himself within the controlled specification of the problem. Now there is a good deal of talk these days in language teaching circles of the importance of teaching communicative competence and there is a general assumption that this competence can and should be described with the same degree of precision as linguistic competence is described in grammars as a preliminary to really effective teaching. It is this assumption that informs what I have called the theoretical approach to EST. Thus both the operational and the theoretical views suppose that precise description is a prerequisite for effective learning, that what is taught and learnt has to be specified in advance as a set of structures or lexical items or communicative acts which are, as it were, stored in the mind for use when required; that once these have been transferred to the store the learning task is done and the rest is a matter of applying this existing knowledge as the occasion arises. This view seems to me to be intuitively wrong. It does not seem to explain the way in which language users create discourse *extempore*, how they make sense of language use even when it does not conform to norms of correct usage. It does not seem to explain how language develops in the individual and changes in society. What we need, I think, to account for these phenomenon is a model of use which deals not in precise rules but in more general strategies and which represents the communicative process not as a matter of correlating what one perceives with already acquired schemes of knowledge but as an 'ongoing accomplishment' (the term is Garfinkel's (see Turner 1974)) whereby one realizes as much meaning from instances of use as seems necessary for one's purposes.

What I am suggesting is that descriptions of use in terms of precise rules may give an inaccurate picture of how people use language, that accuracy cannot be achieved by exactness because exactness is not a feature of normal communication. This does not mean, of course, that it is not a valid research aim to devise means of describing use, but I believe that these means will not satisfactorily be found in the postulation of precise rules which will generate discourse structures in the same sort of way as sentences are generated by a grammar. Most linguists think of discourse analysis as an operation on existing data to discover patterns of form or function which can be reduced to rule. I would suggest that we are likely to arrive at a more convincing account of discourse by looking not at the finished object, a piece of existing text, but at the process which creates and interprets it by a combination of knowledge, imagination, reason, common sense, and other attributes of the human mind. I cannot help feeling, outrageous though the feeling might seem to be, that literary critics have come closer than linguists to an understanding of the communicative function of language and the ways in which discourse is made. Their approach to language acknowledges at least that meanings in discourse are to be worked out by active interpretation and are not a simple function of correlation, that this interpreting ability depends on more than just a knowledge of preformulated rules. The literary approach to discourse analysis is, in fact, not unlike that of the ethnomethodologists: both stress the elusiveness of exact meaning, the creative aspect of interpretation, the importance of involvement.

The concept of precision has, of course, been carried over from linguistics to language teaching. The teaching of the structural syllabus is generally carried out in a systematic step-by-step fashion with the intention that each linguistic unit should be thoroughly learnt before proceeding with the next, and there is a generous provision for repetition to ensure that it is. No allowance is made in the actual teaching, however, for the relative communicative value of these units as they occur in discourse, so that when it comes to reading comprehension, learners attempt to be too precise, to focus their attention myopically on the meaning of individual linguistic units. The practised reader, however, ranges selectively over discourse and draws from it just such meaning as will satisfy his expectations before he begins to read and the predictions which are set up as he reads. He develops a changing cognitive map, as it were, and takes note of what is of relevance to it and lets pass what is not, using his knowledge of the communicative system of different universes of discourse as a general prompt but not as a script. Many native speakers would fail miserably on comprehension tests of the conventional kind (unless they were given advance warning) because such tests require a close scrutiny of detail which the reader would not normally submit to what he reads, and which would, indeed, interfere with his normal reading process. Comprehension tests are often designed in such a way as to prevent rather than to develop an effective reading ability. They focus too much on detail; they are too precise.

These very tentative observations lead me to conclude that the description of discourse and the interpretative strategies of language users (whether they are applying these strategies in production or reception) should not be distinct. The task for theory and description is to devise a model of interpretation which will capture its systematic and *extempore* character and show how the static knowledge of rules is converted into communicative activity. I have no idea what a model of this kind would look like, but among current explorations into language use I suspect it would bear a closer resemblance to the work of ethnomethodologists and literary critics than to that of linguists.

Meanwhile, the language teacher does not have to wait for such a model to be devised. He can treat the kind of speculations I have presented here as initial hypotheses and develop teaching materials to test them for pedagogic potential. With regard to EST in particular he can devise exercises of the kind I have suggested which draw on the student's ability to interpret his own language as use and encourage him to apply the same process to English.

As time goes by, academic research will no doubt yield more insights about language use in discourse in general and about English use in particular. But the devotees of disciplines do not have a monopoly on research: it can also be done by practising teachers drawing their inspiration from ideas already in circulation. The development of EST depends on a reconciliation between the operational and theoretical views as I have described them, on a recognition that theory and practice in language teaching are aspects of the same single, if complex, activity.

Notes

First published in *English for Academic Study*, an ETIC Occasional Paper. The British Council, April 1975.

4 The description of scientific language

In this paper I want to discuss three ways of approaching the description of scientific language. The title is vague and it might seem desirable to formulate my theme in more precise and less ambiguous terms with a title like 'The grammar of scientific discourse'. But the ambiguity persists here in perhaps more pernicious form. Both the terms 'grammar' and 'discourse' are open to a range of different interpretations. I am not sure to begin with how far the approaches I shall be considering can be said to be contributions to grammar. It all depends on what is intended by the term. Certainly I do not want to commit myself to the belief that the general conventions which regulate the way scientists communicate can in some significant sense be accounted for by postulating a system of formal linguistic rules analogous to them devised for the generation of sentences. What I have to say is in the nature of a preliminary survey of the field taken from three different perspectives. I do not want to prejudge the issue and prejudice the discussion by calling them grammatical. The term 'description' is suitably neutral and imprecise.

I have discussed the ambiguities attaching to the term 'discourse' elsewhere (Widdowson 1973). I want to avoid it in my title because of the three approaches to description that I shall now review, one of them does not come within my sense of the term at all. That being so, I had better begin by making it clear how I understood the notion 'scientific discourse'.

I assume that the concepts and procedures of scientific inquiry constitute a secondary cultural system which is independent of primary cultural systems associated with different societies. So although for example, a Japanese, and a Frenchman, have very different ways of life, beliefs, preoccupations, preconceptions, and so on deriving from the primary cultures of the societies they are members of, as scientists they have a common culture. In the same way, I take it that the discourse conventions which are used to communicate this common culture are independent of the particular linguistic means which are used to realize them. Thus, for example, the expression of cause and effect relations and the formulation of hypotheses are necessary rhetorical elements in scientific discourse, but they can be given a very wide range of linguistic expression. So I would wish to say that scientific *discourse* is a universal mode of communicating, or universal rhetoric, which is realized by scientific *text* in different languages by the process of *textualization*. We can represent these three notions in a simple diagram as follows:

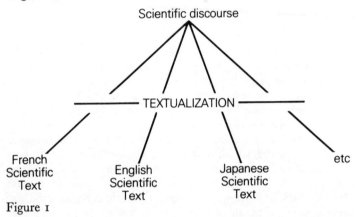

Figure 1

It should be noted that this diagram simplifies the situation in (at least) two ways. Firstly, it suggests that scientific discourse is homogeneous whereas the term can cover a whole range of different kinds of communicating. The discourse of scientific instruction, of science as a subject, such as appears in textbooks, for example, is different from the discourse of scientific exposition, of science as a discipline, such as appears in research papers. I think we can account for these differences by ranging them on a single rhetorical scale which connects the primary culture with the secondary culture of science. What I mean by this is that scientific instruction at different levels introduces both the concepts and procedures of scientific inquiry and at the same time, as a necessary concomitant, the rhetorical principles of scientific discourse. Instruction at the early stages makes reference to the learner's own experience and so relates to his primary culture but as instruction proceeds the secondary culture is developed, and the student gradually approximates to a scientist. Thus the discourse of science as a subject is a means of presenting the discourse of science as a discipline. The term 'scientific discourse' is sometimes also used to refer to treatments of scientific topics such as are found in popular journalism. Whereas scientific instruction develops the secondary culture from the primary, scientific journalism operates in the reverse direction and recasts the findings of the secondary culture into primary culture terms, making appeal, and making concession, to social beliefs, attitudes, views of the world. The discourse of scientific journalism is informed by very different rhetorical principles from those which define scientific discourse proper. We might summarize the above discussion as follows:

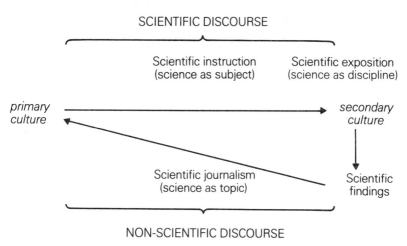

Figure 2

The second way in which Figure 1 is a simplification is that it suggests that scientific discourse is only realized by text, which is by definition verbal. But this is, of course, not the case. It is also realized non-verbally in a variety of different ways. Let us consider a simple example:

$$S + O_2 \rightarrow SO_2$$

This is the statement of a chemical law and an example of scientific discourse but it is expressed by means of a symbolic system which avoids the problem of alternative textualizations in different languages. We can render the statement by means of an English sentence:

Sulphur combines with oxygen to form sulphur dioxide.

The formula and the English textualization of it can be said to be expressions of the act of general statement, universal on the one hand and particular on the other. Neither serves as an act of description of how the law that is stated can be exemplified by experimental procedure. A (partial) description in English might take the following form:

Sulphur is placed in a deflagrating spoon and ignited. It is then placed in a vessel containing oxygen.

But this description too can be non-verbally represented:

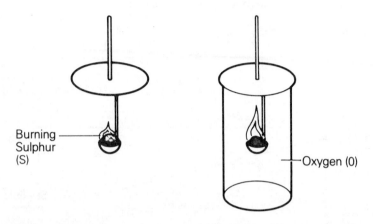

Figure 3

These diagrams are also examples of scientific discourse and like the formula to which they relate are independent of any particular textualization. Such non-verbal modes of communicating can be said to bear witness to the universality of scientific discourse, and the independence of science from primary culture systems as reflected in different languages. One might indeed argue that non-verbal modes of communicating (formulae, diagrams, charts, graphs, and so on) to some degree, at least, represent the basic elements, or the 'deep structure', of scientific discourse of which different linguistic textualizations are the surface variants.

We can now turn to a consideration of the three approaches to the description of discourse that I mentioned at the beginning. With reference to Figure 1, the first I shall deal with focuses attention on text, the second on textualization, and the third on discourse.

The first approach is that which is outlined in Halliday, McIntosh, and Strevens (1964). Here the point is made that language varies in relation to the different people who speak it and in relation to the different purposes to which it is put. This is a common enough observation. But then the authors conclude, with rather elusive logic, that since there is variation in language there must be different and distinct varieties of particular languages. These, it is claimed, divide into two types: one is associated with different users and these are dialects, while the other is associated with different uses and these are registers. Both types are said to be defined by reference to their formal linguistic properties. That is to say, they are, types of text in my terms. Thus scientific English, and its various subdivisions, are represented as distinct registers of English varieties of language behaviour (*parole*) which can be characterized in terms of how the language system (*langue*) is manifested.

With reference to the instances of scientific discourse mentioned earlier, this approach could only describe them as types of text. By noting the incidence of, for example, the universal present tense and the passive voice, and the collocation of lexical items like *sulphur*, *oxygen*, *vessel*, *ignited*, and so on, it might characterize these items of language as belonging to the register of scientific English. We might represent this text-based approach diagrammatically as follows:

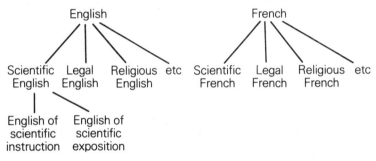

Figure 4

It should be noted that this approach cannot indicate rhetorical relationships between different varieties, either within or between languages. Scientific instruction and scientific exposition, for example, may be widely different in the way they manifest linguistic properties and so they necessarily become widely different registers with no connection between them. And of course, there can be no possibility of a link between scientific English and scientific French in spite of the fact that they realize the same discourse. A paper on physics in English and its translation into French would be instances of totally different varieties of language.

This approach, as I have described it (fairly, I think, although one can never be sure), has been extremely influential in language teaching and in particular in the fashionable area of the teaching of English for Special Purposes (ESP). It is all the more important to realize, therefore, that, as it stands, it can tell us nothing whatever about scientific discourse, or about any other kind of discourse for that matter. What it does is to describe the indexical features of different ways in which a language system is manifested, but it tells us nothing about how the language system is realized as communicative activity. The fact that scientific English text exhibits a relatively high proportion of certain syntactic features and a relatively low proportion of others may be useful for identifying scientific English texts should we ever wish to do such a thing. In fact this approach has proved useful for establishing authorship; it can reveal, with the help of a computer, who wrote what. But it cannot reveal the communicative character of what was written. It cannot of its nature deal with discourse.

This first approach then is concerned with the quantitative linguistic analysis of text. I have represented it as rather a crude way of indexing different registers by reference to formal properties. But it can be more discriminating than that. Labov has shown (Labov 1972a) that variation in social dialect can, to some degree at least, be described in terms of the frequency of linguistic forms as constrained by situational factors. This shows, incidentally, that variation according to user and variation according to use are not in fact as clearly distinguishable as Halliday *et al* would seem to suggest. What is of interest in the present discussion, however, is the possibility that the Labovian approach might be applied to registers as well as to dialects. Halliday *et al* talk of three dimensions of situation by reference to which language variation can be described; they call these (quite appropriately) field, mode, and style of discourse. Let us suppose that we are dealing with written scientific discourse in English. We should be able to discover how far dimensions of field, and style constrain the selection of particular textual features. We might take samples from three styles: expositional, instructional, journalistic; each of which deals with three fields: say, physics, engineering, and economics. We might then feed these samples into a computer which was programmed, for example, to record tense and aspect. Then the relative occurrence of, say, the passive might (after the manner of Labov) be shown in the following way:

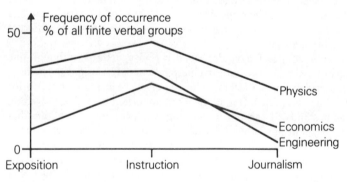

Figure 5

One might be able to discern quite interesting regularities and trends from a graph of this simple sort, and bring these into more exact focus by adjusting and refining the variables. One might even be tempted to write variable rules of the quantitative Labovian kind to give such findings formal expression; to make a start, indeed, on a partial grammar of scientific English. If the information recorded in Figure 5 were true (and not, alas, just a figment of my imagination for display only) then we would be able to specify that the occurrence of the passive correlated with different styles rather than with different fields and essentially had nothing specifically to do with scientific English at all. And we would be able to formulate a rule with a built-in style factor to account for the probability of occurrence.

From an approach which focuses on text we now turn to one which focuses on textualization. Whereas the first indicates only how the language system is formally manifested, the second indicates how it is functionally realized. Whereas the first is quantitative and tells us what linguistic forms occur and how frequently, the second is qualitative and tells us what the forms count as communication, how they express elements of discourse. To illustrate these differences we can consider again the matter of tense and aspect. In Lackstrom, Selinker, and Trimble (1970, 1972) there is an attempt to associate the occurrence of these formal features with the expressions of degrees of generality. That is to say, they discuss these features as ways in which the rhetorical activity of generalization in scientific discourse is textualized in English. They consider the following three statements:

1 A plant to convert cellulose of pine sawdust into fermentable sugar and that into ethyl alcohol *failed* because a sawmill *couldn't* sell as much lumber as plans *called for*, and thereby *curtailed* the alcohol plant's raw material supply.

2 Plants to convert cellulose of pine sawdust into fermentable sugar and that into ethyl alcohol *have failed* because sawmills *haven't been able* to sell as much lumber as plans *have called for*, and thereby *have curtailed* the alcohol plants' raw material supply.

3 Plants to convert cellulose of pine sawdust into fermentable sugar and that into ethyl alcohol *fail* because sawmills *can't* sell as much lumber as plans *call for*, and thereby *curtail* the alcohol plants' raw material supply.

If we consider these as instances of text, we would treat them as *sentences*, and note their formal linguistic properties. But in terms of textualization, what we are interested in is how the choice of certain linguistic features effects what kind of *statement* is made in each case.

Lackstrom *et al* make the following comments:

> The choice of the present, present perfect, or past tense in 1, 2 and
> 3 respectively is not a choice based upon the time of the ethyl-alcohol
> plant failures, but upon how general the author believes this phe-
> nomenon to be. To put it another way, the author will choose one or
> another of the tenses depending upon how many instances of
> ethyl-alcohol plant failures he knows about. If he has knowledge of a
> large number of cases, he will use the present tense. If he knows of
> fewer cases, he will use the present perfect. If he knows of only one
> case, the past tense will be used.
> *Lackstrom et al 1970: 109.*

In another paper (Lackstrom *et al* 1972) there is a suggestion that in
scientific and technical writing, the past tense is used to describe
experimental apparatus which is temporary, set up, perhaps, solely for
the particular experiment being reported, whereas the present tense is
used to refer to apparatus which is permanent. What is significant about
these tenses from the textualization point of view, then, is not that they
appear with a certain frequency, but that they are used to make statements and descriptions of different kinds which are part of the discourse
of science.

Another example of what I have called the textualization approach is
to be found in Swales (1974)—an important but, unfortunately, not
easily accessible paper. At one point in his discussion, Swales discusses
the function of the pre-modifying participle *given* in such expressions
as *a given reaction, a given element,* and so on. He points out that
expressions of this kind are very common in scientific writing in
English and then, moving from this observation about text, he explores
what rhetorical value the participle has, that is to say, what elements
of discourse it textualizes. He suggests that it has two principal functions. The first of these relates to the act of exemplification, as illustrated
by:

> A given bottle contains a compound which upon analysis is shown to
> contain 0·600 gram-atom of phosphorus and 1·500 atom-gram of
> oxygen.

Here the participle *given* is used to indicate that the nature of the
bottle referred to is of no relevance, that the normal exactitude in
scientific description is not required. As Swales points out:

> In science, attribution is an important convention. The role of
> *given* . . . is, therefore, to signal unmistakably that the convention is
> being suspended.
> *Swales 1974.*

Thus *given* (in association, it will be noted, with our old friend the present tense) serves to realize the discourse function of exemplification. The second function of this participle relates to the act of general statement, as illustrated, for example, by:

Figure 9.5 shows how the vapour pressure of a given substance changes with temperature.

The function of the preposed *given* here is, as it were, to express definiteness without commitment to specificity which it seems one only needs to do in discourse of a scientific or technical kind. If one attempts to rephrase the statement in different terms, one makes it either too particular in reference:

Figure 9.5 shows how the vapour pressure of a certain substance varies with temperature.

or too general in reference:

Figure 9.5 shows how the vapour pressure of any substance varies with temperature.

I have been reviewing what Swales says about a particular past participle which commonly occurs in scientific English text. The *present* participle, as has often been noted, also occurs with high frequency in this kind of English. This fact on its own is of little interest, as far as I can see. What would be interesting, however, would be some indication of how this participle functions rhetorically in the realization of scientific discourse. Let us, then, consider the matter for a moment. The function which the present participle appears to have when it occurs in non-finite co-ordinate clauses in scientific and technical writing is the expression of what might be called causal co-occurrence. Consider the following:

Basil read the letter, pacing up and down the room.
Basil tripped over the carpet, striking his head on the floor.

The first of these statements represents the events referred to as co-occurrent, but not otherwise connected. The second, on the other hand, represents them as consecutive, and causally related. Now very frequently in scientific and technical descriptions we find statements which seem to combine these two functions. Here are two examples:

Nitrogen oxide dissolves in water, forming a mixture of nitrous and nitric acids.
The moulding box is now inverted on the moulding board, exposing the pattern face in the sand.

In both of these cases, the events, or states of affairs, are co-occurrent and interrelated causally: thus, a mixture of nitrous and nitric acids is formed at the same time as nitrogen dissolves in water and as a consequence of nitrogen dissolving in water. They can, indeed, be regarded as aspects of the same event.

The examples I have discussed here represent attempts to specify the restricted values which certain linguistic elements of English take on in the expression of the rhetoric of scientific discourse. Work of the same kind can be (and for all I know has been) carried out on the way textualization is effected through other languages. In such work, as we have seen, assumptions are necessarily made about the nature of scientific discourse in general; references are made to such rhetorical acts as descriptions, exemplifications, generalizations, and so on. In the third approach I mentioned, the focus of attention shifts to the characterization of acts of this sort, and the manner in which they combine to form coherent stretches of discourse. The concern here is with the universal features of scientific discourse which are variously textualized through different languages.

A consideration of these features takes us into the territory of the philosophy and methodology of science, which defines the discipline, and the related pedagogy of science, which defines the subject (see Figure 2). Consider, for example, the following quotations from an introduction to the logic of science:

> A *nominal* definition asserts a determination to use a certain expression as an exact equivalent and substitute for another expression. In this kind of definition the meaning of the *definiendum* depends solely upon that of the *definiens*; the definition gives the entire meaning of the expression defined . . .
> A *real* definition states that two expressions, each of which has an independent meaning, are equivalent to one another.
> *Alexander 1963: 89–90.*
> It is useful to distinguish between a *general statement* and a *generalization*. Calling a statement a 'generalization' suggests that it was in fact arrived at by generalizing, by arguing from particular instances to a statement about all instances of the same thing, whereas calling it 'general' does not suggest anything about the way it was reached . . .
> Calling a statement 'general' is saying something about the range of its applicability, whereas calling it a 'generalization' is *also* saying something about how it was reached.
> *Alexander 1963: 104–105.*

What we have here are characterizations of certain illocutionary acts of scientific discourse, which would be recast in the more precise form of specific conditions in the manner of Searle's definition of the act of promising (Searle 1969). I assume that the distinctions that Alexander is making here are required for effective scientific communication but are not necessarily valid for other kinds of discourse. Furthermore, although we might illustrate these distinctions by citing instances of such acts as textualized in English, or French, or any other language, they do not depend on such textualization for their existence as elements in scientific rhetoric. They are, as it were, part of the ethnography of science as a secondary culture.

But the description of the rhetoric of science does not consist only in the specification of separate illocutionary acts of the kind we have been considering, derivable from the philosophy of science. It has to do also with the organization of larger stretches of discourse which relate to the methodology of science as well. It has to do, for example, with the accepted format for the reporting of experimental findings involving the combination of such constituent acts as statement of hypothesis, description of procedure, statement of findings, summary, and so on. Scientific exposition is structured according to certain patterns of rhetorical organization which, with some tolerance for individual stylistic variation, imposes a conformity on members of the scientific community no matter what language they happen to use. As Figure 2 indicates, scientific instruction is a means of secondary socialization whereby this conformity is transmitted. And as I suggested earlier, this conformity is reflected in the universal conventions associated with non-verbal modes of communicating.

I said at the beginning of this paper that I was uncertain as to whether the discussion could be regarded as a contribution to grammar. But perhaps grammar might make a contribution to the discussion by providing us with an analogy. This might help to clarify and summarize what has been said. We can think of scientific discourse as analogous to universal deep structure, texts as analogous to surface variants in different languages, and textualization as analogous to transformational processes which mediate between the two. So we can compare the discourse approach with the grammarian's search for language universals underlying a variety of language systems, the textualization approach with a study of language-specific transformations which enable us to treat different linguistic forms as expressive of universal categories, and the text approach with the study of these forms as such in the manner of the taxonomic grammarians with regard to their outward appearance but without regard to what significance they might have as realizations of more general features of natural language.

Notes

First published in a French version in *Le Français dans le Monde*, No 129, May/June 1977.

SECTION THREE

Exercise types

The focus of attention here is on the types of exercise which might be devised to translate general ideas about communicative language teaching into classroom procedures. Both papers in this section take up the principle expressed in the one preceding that teaching materials should engage the learner's active participation by making overt appeal to what he already knows; and both apply this principle to the business of practical exercise design. Notice that by participation I do not mean the conducting of orchestrated responses from a class under the direction of the teacher, which is a familiar feature of current pedagogic practice, but a real exercise of learner initiative in bringing his own knowledge and experience to bear on the learning process.

These papers, then, are attempts to think certain ideas through to their practical consequences. Unless one makes this kind of attempt, one is easily led astray by the allure of the ideas themselves, made all the more attractive by their apparent novelty. An awareness of this danger underlies the discussion in the first paper of this section. It was written at a time when the concept of communicative or notional syllabuses was beginning to take on the character of a new creed. It seemed to me then, and it seems even more to me now, that such a concept was only a stimulating speculation with which to open a debate (see Paper 19 in Section Eight below). Unfortunately, it has been widely adopted as a conclusion and people are busy not investigating but implementing it. Most of the real problems of applying a communicative approach are, in consequence, left unexplored. The papers here reflect my feeling that one is less likely to be misled into zealotry if one begins not at the selection stage but at the presentation stage of the language teaching process. Apart from anything else, this provides the context where one actually encounters the learner.

5 Two types of communication exercise

The title of this conference is testimony to a growing conviction among applied linguists and language teachers that teaching a language should involve not simply the teaching of its grammar but also the teaching of how the grammar is used in the business of actual communication. A new orthodoxy is emerging which defines the 'content' of language teaching in terms of function rather than form and which represents the learner's terminal behaviour as communicative rather than grammatical competence.

Some people (myself included) have suggested that it should be possible to apply the procedures of selection and grading not to grammatical units in the manner of structural syllabuses of the familiar sort but to communicative units of one kind or another (Candlin 1972, Wilkins 1972, 1974), and these writers have demonstrated how 'notional' or 'communicative' syllabuses might be devised. I find these demonstrations convincing and I am very much in sympathy, of course, with the approach they exemplify. But at the same time I think we ought to be careful of assuming too readily that syllabuses of this kind are universally appropriate. Part of the purpose of this paper is to suggest that in some circumstances there might be difficulties involved in applying communicative principles to selection and grading. Another part of its purpose is to suggest that in such circumstances it might be more feasible to apply such principles to presentation procedures at a later stage of language learning. The two types of communication exercise mentioned in my title are offered as examples of these procedures.

Possible difficulties with the communication-orientated syllabuses that have been proposed emerge when one considers how the notional categories they contain would be actually taught in the classroom. I should make it clear that I am not thinking of what Wilkins refers to as 'semantico-grammatical categories'. These are elements from the language system and relate to what Halliday calls the ideational and inter-personal functions of language as they are 'reflected' in the structure of the code itself (Halliday 1967/1968, 1970a). Such intrinsic functions have traditionally been part of the content of language teaching: what the notional syllabus does is to group them in such a way as to make their meaning potential more evident. In this respect this kind of syllabus does not represent a departure with regard to content—it still deals with grammatical categories—but with regard to methods whereby these categories are arranged. What Wilkins calls 'categories of communicative function', however, are a different matter. These are not semantic but pragmatic elements and relate not to the intrinsic functions of the language system but to the extrinsic functions of language use. To include this kind of category in a syllabus is not to present aspects of language of a familiar kind in an unfamiliar way but to present aspects of language which have generally speaking not been included in syllabuses at all. The kind of difficulties I want to discuss arise because one is asking the teacher not only to adopt new methods but also to change his concept as to what the content of language teaching should be.

Let us consider what the teaching of communicative acts might involve. The first thing we have to recognize is that the names we give to these acts – promise, greeting, apology, praise, criticism, complaint, and so on—are labels we use to identify forms of social behaviour. Our ability to use such labels derives from our knowledge of the way our society is organized, of the way rights and obligations are associated with certain roles, and so on. In other words, communicative functions are culture-specific in the same way as linguistic forms are language-specific. Just as what we call present tense or perfective aspect will not necessarily correspond directly with grammatical categories in another language, so what we call a complaint or a promise will not necessarily correspond directly with 'categories of communicative function' in another culture. Asking for a drink in Subanun is not at all the same thing as asking for a drink in Britain (Frake 1964). The teaching of communicative functions, then, necessarily involves the teaching of cultural values. This may not pose much of a problem when there is close affinity between the cultures concerned, but difficulties are likely to arise when the values associated with the communicative functions of the language being learnt are remote from those of the learner's own culture. Wilkins' syllabus is designed specifically for Western European learners and the notional categories it includes are represented as communicative universals. It is important to recognize, however, that they are only universals in relation to the shared cultural values of Western Europe. How far, then, is a syllabus of this type exportable outside Europe?

I think we have to accept the possibility that it might not be, at least not in its present form and if it is intended, as I assume it is, for initial rather than remedial teaching (a remedial syllabus has to meet different conditions of adequacy, some of which will be implied in what follows).

Let us suppose that we wished to teach a particular communicative act in an Asian or African classroom. There are a number of ways in which we might set about doing this. We might, for example, simulate a real-life situation in which two or more people were engaged in a conversation which included the performance of the communicative act in question. The difficulty of this procedure is that the learners have somehow to separate out from the situation as a whole just those features which serve as the necessary conditions whereby the act is effectively performed. This is a general difficulty with the situations devised to create a context for language in the classroom: language items are associated with the situation as a whole and not with those factors in the situation which are relevant in the realization of the communicative value of these items. Classroom situations may be effective for teaching the semantic signification of sentences and their constituents but they generally fail to teach the pragmatic value of utterances.

Somehow or other, then, the learner has to be made aware of what conditions have to be met for the utterance of a sentence to have a particular communicative effect. Simply presenting the sentence in a situation will not do since the learner has still to know which features of the situation are relevant and which are not. Furthermore, no matter how the teacher exemplifies the act he must represent the person performing it as having a certain role which makes him an appropriate performer of the act. But of course a role in the learner's own culture which appears to be comparable may not be associated with the kinds of rights, obligations, and so on which are required for this role to meet the necessary conditions for the act in question to be performed. The teacher could of course actually explain the set of conditions associated with each of the communicative categories he introduced and perhaps make overt cross-cultural comparisons, but to do this he naturally has to know what these conditions are.

At this point we make contact with a further difficulty. The adoption of a notional or communicative syllabus requires the teacher to be familiar with rules of use as well as rules of grammar. But how does he acquire this familiarity? His own education will have acquainted him with grammatical rules, and these make explicit and, as it were, exteriorize his own intuitive knowledge of the system of English and thereby provide in some degree for his ability to teach this system. There are, however, no such explicitly stated rules of use to which he can make reference in a similar way. It seems to me that the provision of such rules is an applied linguistic task which logically precedes the design of communicative syllabuses. What is urgently needed is a taxonomic description of communicative acts characterized in terms of the conditions that must be met for them to be effectively performed, and grouped into sets according to which conditions they have in common (cf. Candlin 1973). The kind of formulae presented in Searle (1969), Labov (1970), and Fillmore (1971) suggest ways in which such a description might be developed.

What I have in mind is a kind of pedagogic rhetoric which will serve as a guide to rules of use in the same way as a pedagogic grammar serves as a guide to grammatical rules, an exteriorization of knowledge which the teacher can use as a link between his own learning of the language and his teaching of it to others. I think that it is possible that rhetorics of this kind done for different languages would reveal certain 'social universals' in the conditions on different communicative acts. If this were so, they would provide a basis for comparison across cultures, and this would obviously give an indication as to how the content of a communicative syllabus might be selected and graded for learners in communities very different from our own.

But all this is in the future. Meanwhile English teachers have no guidance as to how a notional syllabus is to be interpreted in terms of classroom teaching, and where guidance is necessary I think it would be a mistake to attempt to impose such a syllabus upon them. Let me say again that I am referring to that part of notional syllabuses which has to do with categories of communicative function. The reform of syllabuses with reference to Wilkins semantico-grammatical categories would seem to be perfectly feasible because it does not involve a fundamental alteration in concept of content. I do not wish to appear reactionary but I believe that we should be wary of recommending radical change. English teaching has suffered badly in the past by the imposition of pedagogic dogma: all too often an approach to teaching applicable to one set of circumstances has been given the status of a universal creed. The usual consequence of this has been that teachers have been led to renounce their faith in their own methods in order to embrace principles which they cannot practise.

I have tried to suggest certain difficulties which cast doubt on the wisdom of adopting it as a universal principle that syllabuses for initial language learning should be devised by selecting and grading their content by reference only to communicative criteria. I hope that it is understood that in saying this I am not questioning the importance of notional syllabuses for the teaching of European languages in Europe, nor the need for a communicative approach to the teaching of language in general. But I think that we have to accept that in many countries and for some considerable time to come English teaching will continue to be based on the familiar structural syllabus, though perhaps modified, wherever local circumstances permit, along the lines suggested by the semantico-grammatical component of Wilkins' syllabus. If we accept this, however, we must look for some other way of making the

learner aware of the communicative functioning of the language. I now
come to the second part of my paper.

Given that in many countries English teaching in schools will
continue to focus on the language system, and given that such teaching
leads learners to acquire some knowledge of sentences, the problem is
how to develop in the learner an awareness of how sentences can be
used in acts of communication. What we need to do is to alter his
concept of English from one which represents the language as a set of
patterns to be manipulated for their own sake to one which represents
it as a means of conveying information, ideas, attitudes, and so on and
whose functions are comparable to those of the learner's own language.
To use Halliday's term, we want to provide him with a new 'model' of
English (Halliday 1969). I think we can do this by devising exercises
which draw upon two kinds of knowledge and which then relate them,
it being in the relationship between them that the communicative value
of linguistic forms is realized. The first kind of knowledge is what the
learner knows of the formal properties of English, incomplete and
imperfect though this may be. The second kind of knowledge is that
which he has acquired in other areas of his education: knowledge, for
example, of geography, history, general science. In his learning of these
other subjects he has quite naturally experienced language as a means of
communication: indeed learning *how* information is conveyed in these
different subjects is just as much a part of the subjects as learning *what*
information is conveyed. So although his English lessons may not have
taught the learner the communicative functions of English, his lessons
in other subjects will necessarily have taught him the communicative
functions of the language which is used as a medium for teaching them.
In other words, at the end of, say, three or four years of secondary
schooling, he already knows a fair amount about the functions of
language in use. What he does not know is how *English* is used to fulfil
these functions. The proposal I am making, then, is that after three or
four years of secondary schooling (though this stage and period of time
will obviously vary in different circumstances) we should present
exercises which establish a relationship between these two kinds of
knowledge which the learner has acquired in isolation from each other
and so realize the potential of English sentence patterns as a medium
of communication. In making this proposal I am simply following what
I take to be a fundamental pedagogic principle: that wherever possible
new learning should be an exploitation of what the learner already
knows.

What kind of exercises? I want to approach this question by considering two general aspects of communication which the learner's
own experience of language use will have exposed him to. The first of
these is quite simply that communication is multi-functional. There is

no need for me to dwell on this aspect of communication since we are all familiar with recent attempts to formalize it in terms of speech functions, illocutionary acts, and so on to which reference has already been made in this conference. It is of course this multi-functional character of communication which the notional syllabuses I have been discussing are designed to teach and which, I have argued, learners will have been made aware of in their 'subject' lessons. They will have recognized in their learning of science, for example, that language does not simply express propositions, but is used to define and classify, to give instructions, to make generalizations, to set up hypotheses, and to deduce rules from particular instances. Learning these functions will have been part of the learning of science.

My first type of communication exercise would aim at making explicit the multi-functional nature of language use and at exemplifying this with reference to English. Its purpose would be to show how English can be used to fulfil the different functions previously associated with the language through which the other subjects in the curriculum have been learnt. In science, for example, the learners will be familiar with sets of *instructions* as to how an experiment is to be carried out, with *general accounts* of how experiments are conducted and of what results are obtained, and of *reports* of particular experiments and their findings. We might then devise an exercise in what has been called elsewhere *rhetorical transformation* (Allen and Widdowson 1974b) whereby learners are required to transform a set of propositions into an appropriate communicative act, or transform one communicative act into another. Let us continue to suppose that the subject which we are making use of is general science. We might provide the learner with a set of simple sentences whose propositional content has to do with the process of electrolysis, with which we will assume they are already familiar. One such set of simple sentences might look something like this:

We weigh two copper plates.
We place the switch in the 'on' position.
The current flows through the circuit for about half an hour.
We place the copper plates in copper sulphate solution.
We connect up the copper plates to a battery and a switch.
etc.

The learner is then required to transform this set of sentences into, say, a set of instructions for carrying out the experiment in question. This involves rearranging the sentences, perhaps conjoining and embedding some of them, and making certain structural changes. One could also, at a later stage, deliberately omit sentences referring to necessary stages in an experiment and get the learner to provide the missing information from his own knowledge. Notice that an exercise of this type would combine the purposes of reading comprehension and guided composition by directly associating language use with an area of familiar knowledge. A set of instructions derived from the simple sentences cited above might look something like this:

Weigh two copper plates and place them in copper sulphate solution.
Connect up the plates with a battery and a switch.
Place the switch in the 'on' position.
Allow the current to flow through the circuit for about half an hour and then remove the plates.
etc.

Further rhetorical transformation operations can be carried out to change these instructions into, say, a general account, or into a report keeping the propositional content constant. Examples of these two communicative acts would be something like the following:

Two copper plates are weighed and placed in a copper sulphate solution. They are then connected up to a battery and a switch. The switch is placed in the 'on' position and the current is allowed to flow through the circuit for about half an hour. The plates are then removed from the solution.
etc.

Two copper plates were weighed and placed in copper sulphate solution. They were then connected up to a battery and a switch, and the switch placed in the 'on' position. After the current had been allowed to flow through the circuit for about half an hour, the plates were removed.
etc.

I have given different ways of organizing the propositional content of these acts to show how this kind of exercise can be further exploited to develop the learner's awareness of the devices available in English for giving differential 'rhetorical prominence' to the different elements of information being presented. These devices are of obvious relevance in the description of processes, where the order in which information is presented is frequently different from the sequential order of the actual events.

It is easy to see that this type of exercise can be used to cover a wide range of functional uses. There are two further advantages I would wish, tentatively, to claim for it. Firstly, it automatically provides practice in the manipulation of linguistic structures and in this respect is remedial. But notice that the formal operations are not being undertaken for their own sake but as part of the process of meaningful use. Secondly, communicative acts are not represented as isolated units isomorphic with sentences, but as units of discourse extending over a combination of sentence-like elements. One of the possible limitations of the notional syllabus is that grading constraints require that it associates communicative functions with sentences as self-contained units of meaning. This leaves the problem of how we are to teach the way functions are actually realized in use—not by independent utterances but by utterances in combination. In other words, we still have to make the transition from system to use, from the learning of units separated out for teaching purposes to the learning of how they are used in actual discourse. I would suggest that the exercises in rhetorical transformation that have been proposed do help to make this transition by focusing on the way functions operate over a set of utterances which constitute a discourse precisely because of the functions they fulfil.

My first type of exercise, then, attempts to develop in the learner a sense of the multi-functional nature of linguistic communication as this is realized through English by bringing into association the learner's knowledge of English structures and his knowledge of other subjects in the school curriculum which incorporates, however implicitly, a knowledge of how language functions in use. The second type of exercise also draws on these two kinds of knowledge but this time it focuses on a different aspect of communication: the fact that it fulfils not only a range of functions of which the expressing of propositions is only one, but also takes a range of forms, of which the verbal is only one.

It has been pointed out often enough that in spoken interaction meanings are conveyed not only by verbal means but also through such paralinguistic phenomena as gesture, posture, facial expression, and so on (Laver and Hutcheson 1972). What has perhaps been less often pointed out is that paralinguistic features occur in written discourse too. An instruction leaflet, for example, will characteristically include diagrams, a tourist brochure will include maps, and in both cases the non-verbal devices may, like gesture, either supplement the verbal message or replace it. The kind of written communication which the learners I have in mind have had experience of will include a wide range of non-verbal devices: maps, charts, tables, graphs, line-drawings, and conventional diagrams. A glance at any elementary science textbook for example, will reveal that a large part of the information contained in it is conveyed through non-verbal means, and in the learning of science the student will be learning the conventions associated with this mode of communicating. He will be learning the relationship between verbal and non-verbal means of presenting information, of how to interpret a graph, or a diagram, or a flow-chart with and without direct reference to verbal messages, and of how to use these devices to present information originating from a verbal source. In other words, his learning of science, geography, mathematics, and so on will naturally have involved practice in what might be called *information transfer* (Allen and Widdowson 1974a, Widdowson 1973).

The second type of exercise that I want to propose attempts to exploit this knowledge of the multi-formal operation of communication by having the learners use English as the verbal means which is associated with non-verbal means of conveying information in the total communication process. It requires the learner to transfer information from one mode into another. For example, one might provide a short passage describing an instrument or a machine of some kind and instead of asking comprehension questions of the traditional type get the learner to complete or label a diagram by reference to the information contained in the passage. Similarly one might ask him to express a set of facts in the form of a table, or a graph.

Transferring information from a verbal to a non-verbal mode is an exercise in comprehension. Transferring from a non-verbal to a verbal is an exercise in composition. This suggests that information transfer can serve as a transition between receptive and productive abilities in handling written language. Once the learner is practised in the completing or drawing of diagrams, tables, graphs, and so on based on verbally expressed information, these non-verbal devices may be used as prompts for verbal accounts. Thus, for example, one might present a verbal description of a chemical experiment and require the learner to label a diagram, or draw a diagram of his own which expressed the same information. A diagram showing a similar experiment might then be presented and the learner required to produce a verbal description, which would to some degree match that of the original descriptive passage. Simple information transfer exercises of this kind could of course be graded for difficulty by increasing the complexity of the verbal and non-verbal accounts, by withdrawing prompts, and so on. (For examples see Allen and Widdowson 1974a, Glendinning 1975.)

In the first part of this paper I pointed to certain possible difficulties about applying communicative criteria to selection and grading as a universal principle of syllabus design and suggested that in some circumstances the approach to language study it assumes might be more effectively applied at a later stage in the learning process. In the second part I proposed two types of exercise as examples of such an application. These, it was argued, deal with two fundamental aspects of communication, which learners at a certain stage of their schooling might be expected to be familiar with through their experience of language in association with other subjects in the curriculum. These exercises in rhetorical transformation and information transfer attempt to link up the learner's knowledge of the multiple functions and forms of communication with his knowledge of English structures. They focus not on communicative acts as independent functional units formally made manifest as sentences, but on stretches of discourse where function ranges over a number of sentence-like elements. Furthermore, they attempt to develop comprehension and composition not as separate activities but, more naturally, as two aspects of the same communicative process.

Notes

Paper presented at a BAAL seminar in Lancaster called 'The Communicative Teaching of English', March 1973.

6 Gradual approximation

What I want to do in this paper is to suggest ways in which we might make use of the learner's existing knowledge and experience in designing language teaching procedures which, by a process of gradual approximation, will guide him towards an ability to handle English discourse. More specifically, I want to consider the case of a learner who needs English for reading textbooks which are necessary for him in following an academic course of study at college level. But I also have a more general purpose. This is to provoke discussion on what I see as a basic problem in language teaching pedagogy: how to reconcile the necessarily contrived nature of teaching procedures with the need to prepare learners for the reality of actual communication.

Language teaching methodology in the past has not been notable for its recognition that learners have knowledge and experience which they can bring to bear on their task in acquiring another language. Often the assumption has been that the teacher is presenting something entirely new and the learner is actively discouraged from associating it with what is already familiar to him by transferring his experience through translation. That is to say, he is not supposed to exercise the normal learning strategy of relating new experience to existing conceptual and behavioural patterns. Thus the techniques of the teacher have sometimes tended to isolate the learner and to put him at one remove from his own experience of language. He makes reference to it surreptitiously all the time, of course, but this natural strategy is not pedagogically sanctioned. This assumption of learner ignorance in fact can result in a representation of language which is at variance with the learner's own concept of what language is and how it operates. He is likely to be presented with language data which serves only the metalinguistic purpose of demonstrating the formal properties of the foreign language system but which has little or no implication of utterance. He is then very commonly required to learn these instances of usage as new information and to manipulate them in detachment from the actual contexts of use which provides the knowledge of the system of his own language with its communicative relevance.

I do not wish to suggest that the teaching of usage should be avoided.

Indeed it cannot be avoided. Clearly, the language learner has to acquire knowledge of the system of the language he is learning: he cannot hope to communicate without a code. But to present it in isolation is in some degree to misrepresent it since in actual language behaviour the system is not simply *manifested* but is *realized* as meaningful communicative activity. The learner knows this well enough as a competent user of his own language. Too exclusive a concern for the peculiarities of the system of the language he is learning, however, allows him little opportunity to bring this knowledge to bear. The teacher in these circumstances is in complete control and knows everything, whereas the learner knows (or is supposed to know) only what the teacher permits him to know: there is a one-way traffic of information directed entirely by the teacher. We have a pedagogy of imposition rather than of participation. My reason for thinking this to be unfortunate is not because I believe that teacher/learner relations should as a matter of principle be based on equality (whatever that may mean), but simply because I believe that a pedagogy that does not involve learner participation is not likely to be as effective as one that does.

In order to ensure participation we need to engage the learner's existing knowledge and experience. I want now to consider how we might bring this about in our teaching of English as a second language to college students who need the language primarily as a reading resource. Let us suppose that we are dealing with students in the first year of tertiary education who have undergone a course of instruction in English in their secondary schools. We will assume that as a result of this exposure they have some knowledge of English grammar and vocabulary and have acquired some ability in manipulating English sentences. They are also likely to have some knowledge relating to their subject of study. And, of course, as competent communicators in their own language they have a good deal of knowledge of how language in general operates in normal contexts of use, though, as I have already intimated, they may not have been encouraged to bring this knowledge to bear on their learning of English. Our task now is to devise teaching procedures which will exploit these different kinds of knowledge in order to extend the learner's experience of language to include a communicative competence in English for his specific study purposes.

I want to propose under the heading of *gradual approximation* a general strategy which I think might help towards achieving these aims. I do not wish to pretend that the exercises I shall suggest are in any way definitive. They are illustrative of a strategy which might serve as a general guide, but they do not preclude the necessity for planning tactical manoeuvres to meet the exigencies of particular situations. Gradual approximation begins by providing exercises within the scope of the learner's (limited) linguistic competence in English and then gradually realizes its communicative potential by making appeal to the other kinds of knowledge that the learner has. Thus the starting point is the sentence and the end point is discourse, the progress from one to the other being mediated by an integration on the part of the learner of the different kinds of knowledge that I mentioned earlier. We now need to consider an example.

Let us suppose that the following is representative of the kind of discourse which the learners in our charge will ultimately have to deal with in their reading.

Discourse sample

The skin is composed of several layers. There are two basic ones, the *epidermis*, which is the outside layer, and the *corium*, which is the inside layer, but both of these could be further subdivided.

The epidermis is composed of a hard and dry outer layer, which is continually being worn away. The scurf which is found on an animal is composed of the dead cells of this layer. The second layer of the epidermis is moist and deeper and consists of several layers of cells which are used to replace the ones which are worn away. It is this inner layer which possesses the pigment which gives the skin its colour. There are no blood vessels in the epidermis but there are small nerve endings.

The corium is a mixture of fibrous tissue and elastic fibres which allow the skin to stretch but, at the same time, keep it in place. This is the layer of skin which contains the sweat glands, the *sebaceous* glands (or glands producing oil), the *hair follicles*, and a complex system of small blood vessels and nerves which are associated with sensations such as pain, temperature, and touch. In addition it possesses a certain amount of *muscle fibre*.

Our task is to bring our learners to the point of being able to respond to passages of this kind in an authentic way. That is to say, we have to make him aware of how English can be put to use, just as his own language is, in the reasoning processes which realize meaning in discourse.

A very general problem we have to try and resolve is that in the normal circumstances of communication people are not suddenly confronted with short passages of prose which they are required to read and comprehend to order. The very presentation of 'reading passages' as such creates abnormal conditions. Reading is not normally a detached activity carried out for its own sake but an integrating activity, as one of the means whereby we adjust our knowledge of the world to incorporate new information. We read to extend what we know and before we begin we assemble our thoughts and project them forward in prediction. We are primed to interact with what we read, to participate in the communicative process. To get the learner to adopt the same approach to his reading, we need to persuade him to participate instead of being imposed upon, to prepare him by means of some kind of priming device. One possibility available to us in the present case is to begin by presenting information in the form of a diagram and appealing to the learner's knowledge or interest in the subject matter in disassociation from its linguistic expression in English. Note that a description of the kind we are considering would quite naturally appear in conjunction with a diagram in a textbook (as indeed it does appear in the textbook from which the passage was taken) so that our diagram is not simply a language teaching 'visual aid' but a genuine communicative device in the kind of discourse we are preparing the learner to handle, and which he has perhaps already handled as realized through his mother tongue. In this respect it is a part of the learner's world.

We may begin, then, by presenting the learner with a diagram like the following.

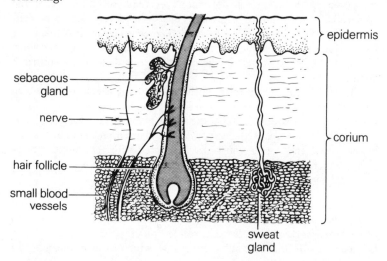

What we now need to do is to devise gradual approximation exercises which will involve the learner in the discovery of how the information presented in the diagram can be expressed verbally in written English discourse of the kind represented by our specimen passage. The first step is for the teacher to decompose this passage into a set of constituent propositions. For example:

Discourse decomposition

1 The skin is composed of several layers.

2 There are two basic layers in the skin.

3 The outside layer of the skin is called the *epidermis*.

4 The inside layer of the skin is called the *corium*.

5 The layers can be further subdivided.

6 The epidermis has an outer layer and an inner layer.

7 The outer layer of the epidermis is hard and dry.

8 The outer layer is being continually worn away.

9 Scurf is composed of the dead cells of the outer layer.

10 Scurf is found on animals.

11 The second layer of the epidermis is deeper than the outer layer.

12 The second layer of the epidermis is moist.

13 The second layer of the epidermis consists of several layers of cells.

14 The cells in the second layer of the epidermis are used to replace other cells.

15 Cells in the outer layer of the epidermis are worn away.

16 The second layer of the epidermis possesses pigment.

17 Pigment gives skin its colour.

18 There are no blood vessels in the epidermis.

19 There are small nerve endings in the epidermis.

20 The corium is the inside layer of the skin.

21 The corium is a mixture of fibrous tissue and elastic fibres.

22 The elastic fibres allow the skin to stretch.

23 The elastic fibres keep the skin in place.

24 The corium contains the sweat glands.

25 The corium contains the sebaceous glands.

26 The sebaceous glands produce oil.

27 The corium contains hair follicles.

28 The corium contains small blood vessels.

29 The corium contains nerves.

30 Small blood vessels and nerves make a complex system.

31 The nerves are associated with sensations.

32 Pain, temperature, and touch are sensations.

33 The corium contains a certain amount of muscle fibre.

The object of this operation is to separate out the different propositions which are contained within the passage and to make them explicit. This involves assigning full lexical value to different proforms and giving independent status to conjoined and embedded sentences. But that is not all: it also involves emendment and addition to the propositional content in order to bridge presuppositional gaps in the original, and to resolve any possible ambiguity. P(roposition) 5 is an example of emendment. The sentence in the original reads: *both of these* (basic layers of skin) *could be subdivided*, which would normally carry the implication that they will not be subdivided—they *could* be but they are not going to be on this particular occasion. But one of them in fact *is* subdivided in the description which follows, so the use of *could* is misleading here. Hence the emendment to *can*. The first sentence in the second paragraph of the passage maintains the misleading implication of the last sentence of the first paragraph. The reader is further discouraged from predicting any subdivision by the use of the expression *is composed of* which suggests that the epidermis is going to be described as consisting of only one layer—a hard and dry outer one. In fact, the epidermis is represented as consisting of *two* layers. To make this explicit, we can insert a proposition—P6—and alter *The epidermis is composed of a hard and dry outer layer* to P7: *The outer layer of the epidermis is hard and dry.* Just one more example of emendation: the original sentence (*It is*) *this inner layer* (*which*) *possesses* (*the*) *pigment* is reformulated as P16. This change is made because of the possible confusion between the *inner* layer of the epidermis (itself the outside layer of the skin) and the *inside* layer of the skin, the corium.

Discourse decomposition, then, is a write-out of the propositional content that a reader is required to recover from a passage. Such a procedure focuses the teacher's attention on possible areas of difficulty: where the reader's predictions are not given sufficient support, or where they are misled, or where he needs to infer relations between propositions which are presupposed but not explicitly indicated in the discourse. Once the teacher is made aware of possible difficulties in this way, he can present or exploit the passage accordingly. He may choose, for example, to present a simplified version of the passage by textualizing it with reference to the discourse decomposition. If he prefers to present the passage as it is, the decomposition will serve as a guide to the devising of comprehension exercises. For our present purposes, discourse decomposition is the first step towards devising gradual approximation exercises.

The next step is to select from these propositions a certain number which extend the diagram labels and then to present them as incomplete sentences. We might call this a word to sentence exercise. This is what it might look like:

Word to sentence exercise

Put the correct form of the verb in the blanks: *call, have, contain, be.*

D	epidermis	The outside layer of the skin ...... the epidermis.
I	outer layer	The epidermis ...... an outside layer.
A	inner layer	The epidermis ...... an inner layer.
G	corium	The inside layer of the skin ...... the corium.
R	sweat glands	The corium ...... sweat glands.
A	hair follicles	The corium ...... hair follicles.
M	basic layer	There ...... two basic layers in the skin.

Make statements about the following:
sebaceous glands, small blood vessels, and *nerves.*

This is, of course, a straightforward structure exercise of the traditional kind. It draws upon the learner's existing knowledge of English grammar. But notice that he is not just constructing sentences for their own sake in isolation from a relevant context of use: they are reformulations of information expressed in the labelled diagram and as such are meaningful statements.

The next step is to associate the writing of statements not with information in the diagram but with information which the learner already has as part of his knowledge, or which he will need to acquire as part of his specialist studies. We set him problems that he cannot solve simply by reference to his knowledge of English. An example of the kind of exercise I have in mind might be the following:

Sentence and statement exercise

Combine the expressions in column A with the expressions in column B to form correct statements.

A	B
1 The outer layer of the epidermis	a make a complex system.
2 The second layer of the epidermis	b is a mixture of fibrous tissue and elastic fibres.
3 The cells in the second layer of the epidermis	c keep the skin in place.
4 The corium	d is hard and dry.
5 The elastic fibres	e is moist.
6 The sebaceous glands	f produce oil.
7 Small blood vessels and nerves	g are used to replace other cells.

By reference only to his knowledge of English, the learner can produce a number of correct sentences. Thus, he can combine 4 and d and thereby compose the impeccable sentence *The corium is hard and dry.* Similarly, he can combine 5 with f to produce the correct sentence *The elastic fibres produce oil.* But although there is nothing objectionable to the compositions as *sentences,* they are quite unacceptable as *statements.* The exercise, then, requires the learner to produce correct instances of usage which are at the same time acceptable instances of use as statements of fact. We therefore engage both his knowledge of English and his knowledge of his subject.

In the next stage in the operation we want to move the learner from the making of separate statements towards their incorporation in continuous discourse. To do this we can present the sentences he has composed (adding others from our stock of basic propositions if necessary) in three sets corresponding to the three paragraphs of the original passage, but present both the sets and the sentences within them in random order. The learner is required to arrange and combine the sentences in such a way as to ensure cohesive propositional development through the three paragraphs. This will require him to replace lexical material with suitable pro-forms and to use his knowledge of English grammar to produce co-ordinate and subordinate constructions. The exercise is also intended to appeal to his knowledge of how discourse is organized and the assumption is that he will have acquired knowledge of this kind from his experience of how his own language is used. This kind of exercise can (as indeed can the others we have been considering) be controlled for difficulty. For the sake of illustration I will assume that the learner needs to be helped in establishing the propositional content of each paragraph (hence the grouping of sentences into sets), but that he can draw upon his experience of language use in his own language to work out the order of paragraphs and the propositional development within each one. We could, of course, adjust the exercise so that more or less help were provided.

Discourse composition

Put the statements in the following sets in the appropriate order and combine them where necessary to make a paragraph. Then arrange the three paragraphs in the most appropriate order to form a complete passage.

A
1 The corium contains sweat glands.
2 The corium is the inside layer of the skin.
3 The corium contains hair follicles.
4 The corium contains sebaceous glands.
5 The corium is a mixture of fibrous tissue and elastic fibres.
6 The corium contains small blood vessels and nerves.
7 The elastic fibres keep the skin in place.
8 The sebaceous glands produce oil.
9 Small blood vessels and nerves make a complex system.

B
1 The outside layer of the skin is called the epidermis.
2 The inside layer of the skin is called the corium.
3 There are two basic layers in the skin.
4 The layers can be further subdivided.

C
1 The cells in the second layer of the epidermis are used to replace other cells.

2 The second layer of the epidermis is moist.
3 The epidermis has an inner layer.
4 The epidermis has an outer layer.
5 The outer layer of the epidermis is hard and dry.
6 The second layer of the epidermis consists of several layers of cells.
7 Cells are worn away in the outer layer of the epidermis.

Learners will, of course, produce a number of versions and the relative merits of each can be discussed in class. Such a discussion is probably best carried out in the mother tongue, although this, again, will depend on particular circumstances. The learners might also be encouraged to write translation equivalents of the passage, thus overtly making reference to their knowledge of how language generally operates as use. The idea is that they should have their attention drawn to the effectiveness of the different versions as instances of discourse and they can refer to how their own language is used in communication in making their assessments. The following is one possible version:

Derived discourse

There are two basic layers in the skin. The outside layer is called the epidermis and the inside layer is called the corium. These layers can be further subdivided.

The epidermis has an outer layer and an inner layer. The outer layer is hard and dry whereas the second layer is moist. The second layer consists of several layers of cells. These are used to replace other cells which are worn away in the outer layer.

The corium is the inside layer of the skin. It contains a mixture of fibrous tissue and elastic fibres which keep the skin in place. It also contains sweat glands, hair follicles, sebaceous glands which produce oil, and a complex system of small blood vessels and nerves.

In devising this particular set of gradual approximation exercises I have made use of 21 of the original 33 basic propositions that resulted from discourse decomposition (A6 being a combination of propositions 28 and 29). These carry what I judge to be the main information in the passage. But what of the other propositions? We could, if we wished, present them to the learner and require him to insert them at appropriate points in the discourse he has composed. Alternatively, we might at this stage simply present the learner with the original passage in order to demonstrate how his own discourse can be further elaborated. The former course continues gradual approximation through composition, the latter shifts the emphasis to comprehension.

This reference to composition and comprehension brings me to one point I would like to make about the gradual approximation exercises I have suggested here. It might be objected of them that they are only devices for the teaching of writing whereas the kind of student I specified at the beginning was one whose basic requirement was for a reading knowledge of English. My reply to this would be that these exercises involve the learner's participation through writing but that this activity is used to make him aware by experience of how English sentences can be put to relevant communicative use, actually to involve him in the discovery of how discourse is realized through the particular medium of the English language. This awareness, this discovery, is as crucial to comprehension as to composition: both of these activities are aspects of the communicative competence, of the basic process of interpretation which underlies all language use.

Of course (and here I come to a second point about these exercises), as learning proceeds there will be less need for the learners to participate through the overt activity of writing, and the process of approximation can be made less gradual until the point is reached when an instance of discourse is put in direct juxtaposition with the diagram or other non-verbal representation serving as the priming device, the 'pretext'. What I have offered here are only examples of the *kind* of exercise that might be devised.

The gradualness of the approximation process can, then, be adjusted to suit the learner, to accord with his level of attainment. Another dimension of grading is the difficulty of the discourse towards which the approximation is directed. The passage I have used here for demonstration purposes (taken at random from the textbook cited) does not require the addition of too many propositions in the discourse decomposition to provide for presuppositional gaps. At more advanced levels of instruction, however, more assumption is made about shared knowledge: the reader is expected to be able to infer what is meant on the basis of what he knows about the subject and the ways it is communicated. The choice of passages for gradual approximation treatment, and the kind of treatment given to them, will obviously take this development into account.

It will do so in accordance with the basic principle which I adduced as the starting point for the kind of teaching strategy that I have tried to illustrate here. The exercises I have suggested are of a preliminary and tentative nature and I hold no special brief for them as such. What I would defend, however, is the principle from which they derive: that the teaching of a foreign language (and indeed the teaching of anything) should lead the learner to participate in the exploration and extension of his own linguistic and non-linguistic knowledge and experience. Any language teaching procedure which achieves this, no matter how contrived, will involve the learner in the reality of actual communication.

Notes

Paper presented at the Georgetown Round Table, Washington, April 1976.
1 From Peregrine, F. A. W., A. Fox, A. P. Ingram, A. B. Humphries (1968). *Farm Animals: a basic guide to their husbandry*. London: Hutchinson Educational.

SECTION FOUR

Discourse

Here we take up for further elaboration the theme of discourse description introduced in Section Two. The first paper (Paper 7) shows how the distinction between text and discourse emerges from a consideration of different approaches to the description of language in use. In the paper that follows there is a similar examination of different approaches to linguistic description, but this time in reference to the problem of translation equivalence.

Both of these papers refer back to Section Two in that they develop the discourse theme and take up once more the question of the universality of scientific discourse in particular. But they also refer forward to the papers which follow in this section. Paper 7 does so in postulating two types of relationship beyond the sentence: cohesion, defined as the overt structural link between sentences as formal items, and coherence, defined as the link between the communicative acts that sentences are used to perform. Paper 8 prepares for the papers which follow by working out the difference between the surface forms of sentences and their semantic and pragmatic values.

Paper 9 explores these questions further as part of a general survey of approaches to discourse description. The semantic value of sentences is now interpreted as the propositions they are used to express and their pragmatic value as their illocutionary function. Cohesion, it is suggested, is the propositional relation, and coherence the illocutionary relation between parts of a discourse.

As always, of course, such neat equations and clear cut divisions give only the illusion of truth: they impose a convenient clarity on complex matters for the purposes of further investigation. In the case of cohesion and coherence, for example, they serve as points of reference whereby other problems can be put into perspective: how propositional and illocutionary development in discourse interrelate and reinforce each other, how the language user draws on his knowledge of rules to make sense in the actual process of interpretation, and so on. These, and other problems are introduced, but left unresolved, in the last part of Paper 9, which gives some indication of the expanse of terrain that has yet to be explored.

The question of the relationship between rules that people know and the procedures they use is discussed in some detail, but with appropriate tentativeness, in the last paper in this section, which therefore moves the inquiry naturally on to the theme that is central to the section that follows.

7 Directions in the teaching of discourse

The purpose of this paper is to suggest that there is a need to take discourse into account in our teaching of language, and to consider how far the attempts made by linguists and others to analyse discourse might help us to do this. In this paper I shall be concerned exclusively with English and with English teaching, but I believe that what I have to say has a more general application.

I think it is true to say that, in general, language teachers have paid little attention to the way sentences are used in combination to form stretches of connected discourse. They have tended to take their cue from the grammarian and have concentrated on the teaching of sentences as self-contained units. It is true that these are often presented in 'contexts' and strung together in dialogues and reading passages, but these are essentially settings to make the formal properties of the sentences stand out more clearly—properties which are then established in the learner's mind by means of practice drills and exercises. Basically, the language teaching unit is the sentence as a formal linguistic object. The language teacher's view of what constitutes knowledge of a language is essentially the same as Chomsky's: a knowledge of the syntactic structure of sentences, and of the transformational relations which hold between them. Sentences are seen as paradigmatically rather than syntagmatically related. Such a knowledge 'provides the basis for actual use of language by the speaker-hearer' (Chomsky 1965: 9). The assumption that the language teacher appears to make is that once this basis is provided, then the learner will have no difficulty in dealing with the actual use of language: that is to say, that once the competence is acquired, performance will take care of itself.

There is a good deal of evidence to suggest that this assumption is of very doubtful validity indeed. It has been found, for example, that students entering higher education with the experience of six or more years of instruction in English at the secondary school, have considerable difficulty coping with language in its normal communicative use. So long as language is taught in a vacuum, as a set of skills which have no immediate utility, it is possible to believe that one is providing for some future use by developing a stock of grammatical competence which will be immediately converted into adequate performance when the need arises. It is only when language teaching has to be geared to specific communicative purposes that doubts as to the validity of this belief begin to arise. In many parts of the world the teaching of English has assumed the crucial auxiliary role of providing the means for furthering specialist education, and here it has become plain that a knowledge of how the language functions in communication does not automatically follow from a knowledge of sentences. This role for English requires a new orientation to its teaching.

What this orientation amounts to is a change of focus from the sentence as the basic unit in language teaching to the use of sentences in combination. Once we accept the need to teach language as communication, we can obviously no longer think of language in terms only of sentences. We must consider the nature of discourse, and how best to teach it. Language teaching materials have in the past been largely derived from the products of theoretical sentence grammars. We now need materials which derive from a description of discourse; materials which will effect the transfer from grammatical competence, a knowledge of sentences, to what has been called communicative competence (Hymes 1970, Campbell and Wales 1970), a knowledge of how sentences are used in the performance of communicative acts of different kinds. Grammatical competence remains in a perpetual state of potentiality unless it is realized in communication. As Hymes puts it 'There are rules of use without which the rules of grammar would be useless' (Hymes 1970: 14). We might hope, as applied linguists, that theoretical studies of discourse might indicate the nature of such rules, and give us some clues as to how we might approach teaching them.

I have referred to discourse as the use of sentences in combination. This is a vague definition which conveniently straddles two different, if complementary, ways of looking at language beyond the sentence. We might say that one way is to focus attention on the second part of my definition: *sentences in combination*, and the other to focus on the first part: *the use of sentences*. I think it is important, from the applied linguistic point of view, to keep these two approaches distinct, though, as we shall see later, linguists have recently attempted to conflate them.

The study of discourse in terms of the combination or interconnection of sentences is, of course, exemplified in the work of Harris. 'Language', he observes, 'does not occur in stray words or sentences, but in connected discourse' (Harris 1952: 357), and he sets out to discover what the nature of this connection might be by applying his well-tried distributional method. By means of transformational adjustments to surface forms, he is able to establish equivalence classes of morphemes and to show that

in many cases two otherwise different sentences contain the same combination of equivalence classes, even though they may contain different combinations of morphemes.
Harris 1952: 373.

He is thereby able to discover a patterning in the discourse in terms of chains of equivalences. What he does, then, is to reduce different message forms to make them correspond to a common code pattern. The fact that the variation in the message form may have some signifi-cant communicative value is for him irrelevant. His concern is not to characterize discourse as communication, but to use it to exemplify the operation of the language code in stretches of text larger than the sentence. He himself recognizes the limited scope of his analysis:

> All this, however, is still distinct from an *interpretation* of the findings, which must take the meanings of morphemes into con-sideration and ask what the author was about when he produced the text. Such interpretation is obviously quite separate from the formal findings, although it may follow closely in the directions which the formal findings indicate.
> *Harris 1952: 382.*

The notion that an understanding of the nature of discourse as communication may be dependent on a prior formal account is a significant one, pointing as it does towards a fundamental problem in linguistic description which has to do with the distinction I have made between the two approaches to the analysis of discourse. The notion is a common one among linguists of the transformational-generative persuasion. Thus, Chomsky himself states:

> There seems to be little reason to question the view that investigation of performance will proceed only so far as understanding of under-lying competence permits.
> *Chomsky 1965: 10.*

The belief is that a native speaker's knowledge of the sentences of his language can be accounted for in terms of invariant rules of an algebraic kind. It is assumed that once the 'correct' grammar consisting of such rules is written, it will provide a basis for the study of perform-ance as a whole, including the study of language in its social contexts of use. There have been objections to this neat isolation of competence as representing the sole concern of the linguist. Hymes (1970) and Labov (1970), for example, have suggested that it is likely that an adequate description of the formal operation of language is dependent on an investigation into certain aspects of performance, and recent developments in generative grammar in fact give strong support to this suggestion. It is significant in the light of Harris's implication of the primacy of formal analysis that Labov should point to discourse analysis as being the very area of inquiry where such primacy cannot be established:

> There are some areas of linguistic analysis in which even the first steps towards the basic invariant rules cannot be taken unless the social context of the speech event is considered. The most striking examples are in the analysis of discourse.
> *Labov 1970: 206–207.*

Since Harris has taken a considerable number of steps in the description of discourse, the question naturally arises as to how he has managed to do this without considering speech events and social contexts at all. The answer is, of course, that whereas Harris conceives of discourse in purely formal terms as a series of connected sentences, Labov is thinking of the way language forms are used to perform social actions:

> Commands and refusals are actions; declaratives, interrogatives, imperatives are linguistic categories—things that are said, rather than things that are done. The rules we need will show how things are done with words and how one interprets these utterances as actions: in other words, relating what is done to what is said and what is said to what is done. This area of linguistics can be called 'discourse analysis'; but it is not well-known or developed. Linguistic theory is not yet rich enough to write such rules, for one must take into account such sociological, non-linguistic categories as roles, rights and obligations.
> *Labov 1969: 54–55.*

Harris's work, well-known though it is, gets no mention; and it is clear that by this definition it has nothing to do with discourse analysis at all. We are confronted, then, with two quite different kinds of inquiry both contending for the same name. A terminological distinction seems to be called for. I propose that the investigation into the formal properties of a piece of language, such as is carried out by Harris, should be called *text analysis*. Its purpose is to discover how a text exemplifies the operation of the language code beyond the limits of the sentence, text being roughly defined, therefore, as *sentences in combination*. Changing the name of Harris's kind of inquiry is to some degree justified by the fact that he himself seems to use the terms *text* and *discourse* interchangeably, as in the following quotation:

> . . . the formal features of the discourses can be studied by distributional methods within the text.
> *Harris 1952: 357.*

We may now use the label *discourse analysis* to refer to the investigation into the way sentences are put to communicative use in the performing of social actions, discourse being roughly defined, therefore, as *the use of sentences*. Having distinguished these two areas of inquiry, I want now to consider what value their respective findings might have for the teaching of language both as text and as discourse. If we are to teach language in use, we have to shift our attention from sentences in isolation to the manner in which they combine in text on the one hand, and to the manner in which they are used to perform communicative acts in discourse on the other. What help can we get from the theorists?

Text analysis is exemplified most obviously by Harris. It is also exemplified, perhaps less obviously, in the work associated with Halliday, which comes under the headings of 'register analysis' and 'grammatical cohesion'. I will deal with each of these briefly in turn and indicate what relevance I think they have for the teaching of language. Although register analysis is not concerned with the way sentences are connected together in sequence, it falls within text analysis in that its purpose is to define varieties of language solely in terms of the occurrence of formal linguistic elements:

> It is by their formal properties that registers are defined. If two samples of language activity from what, on non-linguistic grounds, could be considered different situation-types show no differences in grammar or lexis, they are assigned to one and the same register . . .
> *Halliday, McIntosh, and Strevens 1964: 89.*

What has to be noted here is the deliberate rejection of the relevance of the 'sociological, non-linguistic categories' which, as we have seen, Labov represents as having a direct bearing on rules of discourse. Registers are, then, types of text, not types of discourse, since they are not defined in terms of what kind of communication they represent. The results of a register analysis of, say, a selection of scientific texts, will be a quantitative account of the frequency of occurrence of whichever formal elements were selected to be counted in the first place (see, for example, Huddleston *et al* 1968). That is to say, it will indicate how the texts concerned exemplify the language code: it will tell us nothing directly (though we may hazard a few guesses) about the communicative acts which are performed in the use of such formal elements. Register analysis has been taken up, and in some extent taken further, by Crystal and Davy (1969) under the name of 'general stylistics', but in spite of the refinements which they introduce into the analysis, it remains the analysis of text, as the following quotation makes clear:

> . . . the procedures for approaching stylistic analysis are no different

from those made use of in any descriptive exercise: the primary task
is to catalogue and classify features within the framework of some
general linguistic theory.
Crystal and Davy 1969: 60.

Register analysis, or general stylistic analysis (in the sense of Crystal
and Davy), is open to a number of rather serious theoretical objections,
of which perhaps the principal one has to do with the difficulty of
establishing when a formal difference is significant or not, when a
certain linguistic feature is or is not stylistically distinctive. No two
pieces of language are alike: but how non-alike do they have to be
before they become stylistically distinct and specimens of different
registers? We are not at present concerned with theoretical issues but
with deciding on what value such an approach to text analysis might
have for language teaching. As I mentioned earlier, this approach does
not seek to establish the way in which sentences are connected. On the
contrary, the analysis is an atomistic one which breaks a piece of
language down into its constituent linguistic elements. This procedure
yields information about the relative frequency of different linguistic
forms in the texts that have been examined. The question is: how can
this information be used in language teaching? It provides some guide
as to which linguistic elements to include in a course designed for
students who are to deal with the kind of texts which provided the
material for analysis, but it gives no indication at all as to how such
elements are to be presented as text. What usually happens is that the
findings of such an analysis are used to produce remedial courses in
which the most frequent linguistic elements are presented within the
framework of sentences. I think that the essential shortcoming of
register/general stylistic analysis, as preached and practised by Halliday
et al and Crystal and Davy, is that it does not provide teachers with any
directions as to how they might move from the sentence to the text.
And yet the very reason for adopting the findings of such analysis is
generally speaking to direct language teaching towards meeting the
special needs of students, and to prepare them for their encounter with
language in use as a medium for their specialist subjects. Register
analysis may have its uses, but it seems to have very little value for the
teaching of text, and none at all, of course, for the teaching of discourse.

The study of grammatical cohesion, on the other hand, does have
direct relevance to the teaching of text, since it aims to discover 'the
characteristics of a text as distinct from a collection of sentences'
(Hasan 1968: 24, now incorporated into Halliday and Hasan 1976).
This aim is not very different from that of Harris, whose analysis
begins with an observation which might easily have served as a rubric
for Hasan's work:

Language does not occur in stray words or sentences, but in connected discourse . . . Arbitrary conglomerations of sentences are
indeed of no interest except as a check on grammatical description.
Harris 1952: 357.

But although the aims of both are alike, their approaches towards
achieving them are quite different. Whereas Harris sets out to establish
patterns of formal equivalence, Hasan is concerned with the cohesive
function of certain linguistic forms. Harris deals with formal elements
like equivalence classes, whereas Hasan deals with such functional
notions as anaphora and cataphora. The relevance of her work for
language teaching lies in the fact that it indicates how language items
take on particular values in context. For example, the lexical item *iron*
stands in a relation of hyponymy to the lexical item *metal* in the semantic
structure of English, but within a text they may have the value of
synonymous expressions:

In engineering it is rare to find *iron* used in its pure form. Generally
the *metal* is alloyed with carbon and other elements to form wrought
iron, steels, and cast irons.

This is a simple instance of what Hasan refers to as 'substitution'. It
is not always so easy to discover the referential value of items in a text.
In the following, for example, the term *process* does not form a synonymous link with any preceding noun, and the term *ingredient* forms a
link with a noun (i.e. *metal*) with which it has no semantic association
in the code of the language at all:

Most alloys are prepared by mixing *metals* in the molten state; then
the mixture is poured into moulds and allowed to solidify. In this
process, the major *ingredient* is usually melted first.

Similarly, items like the demonstrative pronoun *this* cause considerable
difficulty in texts because of the very wide range of values they can have.
As Hasan points out, *this*

may have as referent not merely a nominal but any identifiable
matter in the preceding text. Such matter may extend over a sentence,
an entire paragraph, or even longer passages.
Hasan 1968: 58.

The importance of the work on grammatical cohesion is that it is a
description of the devices which are used to link sentences together to
form text and as such provides the language teacher with an inventory
of points he must incorporate into exercises to develop a knowledge of
this aspect of language use.

Hasan makes a distinction between 'The internal and the external aspects of "textuality" ', the first having to do with cohesion, the second with the way language links meaningfully with the situation in which it is used. She speaks briefly about the external aspect of textuality in terms of register and her point seems to be that a piece of language can be recognized as text if its linguistic features can be plotted along a number of situational dimensions in such a way as to assign it to a specific register, even if cohesive links are missing. Similarly, Halliday defines the 'textual function' of language as having to do with 'making links with itself and with features of that situation in which it is used' (Halliday 1970a: 143), pointing out that cohesion is one aspect of the textual function as a whole (presumably that which relates to language 'making links with itself'). This function, says Halliday, 'enables the speaker or writer to construct "texts", or connected passages of discourse that is situationally relevant' (Halliday 1970a: 143). Here, text and discourse are not kept terminologically distinct but in my terms the external or situational aspects of 'text' or 'textuality' or 'texture', (Halliday 1970) have to do with discourse and are not concerned with *grammatical cohesion* between sentences, but with *rhetorical coherence* of utterances in the performance of acts of communication.

The distinction between *cohesion* and *coherence* brings us to a consideration of discourse. Advances in our understanding of discourse have not come from linguistics as it is generally understood but from the two areas of inquiry which we might call the sociology of language on the one hand and the philosophy of language on the other. I do not propose to attempt a review of this work, but only to indicate briefly where I think these two approaches converge, and what relevance they have for the teaching of language.

We may take the distinction between cohesion and coherence as our starting point. Labov as we have already noted has pointed out that there are certain rules of discourse which cannot be described without reference to social context. That is to say, the description of such rules depends on reference to what Hasan calls 'external aspects of textuality', or what Halliday calls 'features of the situation'. Let us consider two pieces of dialogue:

A Can you go to Edinburgh tomorrow?
B Yes I can.

A Can you go to Edinburgh tomorrow?
B B.E.A. pilots are on strike.

In the first of these exchanges, we have a cohesive text in that B uses an elliptical form of the sentence 'Yes, I can go to Edinburgh tomorrow' (ellipsis being one of Hasan's categories of cohesion). In the second exchange, there is no cohesion between the sentences which are used.

And yet the two utterances in combination make sense: we understand that B is saying that he cannot go to Edinburgh because the strike rules out what he considers to be the only reasonable means of getting there. It seems justifiable to claim, then, that the second exchange is coherent as discourse without being cohesive as text. The question is: can we support this claim by postulating rules of discourse which will account for the rhetorical connections between the two utterances in the second exchange?

Labov takes the view that discourse rules have to do with the sequence of actions which are performed in the issuing of utterances. As he puts it:

> Sequencing rules do not operate between utterances but between the actions performed by these utterances. In fact, there are usually no connections between successive utterances at all.
> *Labov 1970: 208.*

Labov is of course thinking primarily of spoken communication here. Written communication of its nature requires a much higher degree of interdependency between cohesion and coherence. But it remains true for both media that discourse is characterized in terms of communicative actions and not in terms of linguistic forms. How, then, might we characterize the communicative actions performed in the second exchange? What Labov does is to specify a number of preconditions which have to be met for a given utterance to count as a particular communicative act. For an utterance to be seriously intended as an order, or a request for action, for example, the speaker, A, must believe the following:

1 That X, the action he refers to (e.g. going to Edinburgh), should be carried out for some purpose.
2 That the hearer, B, has the ability to do X.
3 That B has the obligation to do X.
4 That A has the right to ask B to do X.

The coherence of our second exchange is accounted for by the fact that each utterance focuses on the second of these preconditions. For A's utterance to be interpreted by B as an order, the other preconditions must be understood as obtaining by virtue of the situation, including, of course, the relationship between the two people. In these circumstances it is only necessary for the speaker to draw the hearer's attention to one precondition for the act of ordering to be performed, and only necessary for the hearer to refer to the same condition to decline to act upon the order.

The key to this approach to the analysis of discourse lies, then, in the understanding of what conditions must obtain for an utterance to count as a particular communicative act. An investigation into these conditions has been a feature of recent work in the philosophy of language. Searle (1969), following the lead of Austin (1962), has specified the conditions attendant upon the acts of promising, advising, warning, greeting, congratulating, and so on. We might expect that as this kind of work proceeds, and as we learn more about the relationship between what is said and what is done, we shall be able to describe a type of discourse in terms of the kinds of communicative acts it represents, and the manner in which they are given linguistic expression. Thus we might hope that we shall be in a position to characterize varieties of language not as registers or types of text, but as different ways of communicating. To take an example, scientific varieties of English are, as I have noted earlier, generally represented as types of text, exemplifying a high incidence of forms like the passive, certain modals, certain types of adverbial clause, and so on. There seems no reason why they should not, in course of time, be represented as types of discourse consisting of certain combinations of such acts as definition, classification, generalization, qualification, and so on, combinations which in many cases constitute larger communicative units like explanations, descriptions, and reports, and which may be said to reflect the actual methodology of scientific inquiry. It should be noted that although it is convenient to consider acts of communication initially as corresponding with sentence-like stretches of language, there is no reason why such a correspondence should be assumed. In the case of acts like describing and reporting, for example, the conditions attendant on their performance in any particular type of discourse are likely to be communicative acts in their own right.

What I have tried to do in this paper is to distinguish two ways of looking at language beyond the limit of the sentence. One way sees it as text, a collection of formal objects held together by patterns of equivalences or frequencies or by cohesive devices. The other way sees language as discourse, a use of sentences to perform acts of communication which cohere into larger communicative units, ultimately establishing a rhetorical pattern which characterizes the piece of language as a whole as a kind of communication. Both approaches to the description of language have their purposes, and if I have sometimes appeared to be recommending the latter at the expense of the former, this is only to restore the balance for language teaching, which should, in my view, be as much concerned with discourse as with text. What is important is that we should recognize the limitations of a particular approach to analysis, and not be too easily persuaded that it provides us with the only valid characterization of language in use. My reason for pointing to the limitations of register analysis and general stylistics (in the sense of Crystal and Davy) was that this approach has too often been represented as the only one to adopt when delimiting the language of a particular area of use. To be fair, and to maintain the balance, one might point to a similar atomistic approach to the description of discourse: the traditional rhetorical one which searches passages of prose for metaphor, litotes, oxymoron, synecdoche, and so on, or to more recent studies in rhetoric which focus on the 'topic sentence' and describe the development of discourse only in terms of its referential function.

I have said that text analysis and discourse analysis are different but complementary ways of looking at language in use. I am aware that recent work in linguistics has attempted to integrate features of discourse into a unitary model of grammar by writing presuppositions, illocutionary act indicators, and so on into the base component of a generative grammar (see, for example, Ross 1970, Lakoff 1970). The result seems to have blurred the distinction between sentence and utterance and between semantics and pragmatics, and to create, in consequence, a good deal of confusion in linguistic description. One might point, for example, to the long discussion on the verb 'Remind' in recent editions of *Linguistic Inquiry*, initiated by Postal (1970), and to the corrective statements by Bar-Hillel (1971) and Bolinger (1971). It is interesting, in this connection to see linguists tending towards the same error as beset linguistic philosophers of an earlier era (see Strawson 1950). Both Postal (1970) and Karttunen (1970, 1971), for example, in their attempts to bring discourse features into grammar seem to me to be confusing what Strawson shows so clearly must be kept distinct: a sentence, and a use of a sentence (Strawson 1950: 6), or, in my terms, text and discourse. Discourse must, of course, ultimately be accounted for in a total linguistic description, as both Hymes and Labov insist, but this does not necessarily involve incorporating it into a prescribed generative model of grammar.

There is, then, a good deal of turmoil in linguistics as a result of its attempts to account for the communicative properties of language. Meanwhile, the language teacher cannot wait for the dust to settle. I believe that it is urgent that he should incorporate text and discourse into his teaching. While linguists are arguing among themselves, there is a great deal that can be done. We can set about devising exercises to develop a knowledge of grammatical cohesion. We can consider how far we can select and grade teaching material in terms of communicative acts rather than simply in terms of linguistic structures. We can, in short, be working out ways in which we can teach our students to use the foreign language to define, classify, generalize, promise, predict, describe, report, and so on; to make them aware of how the language is used for the particular kind of communication they are concerned with. Some ways of how this might be done are suggested in Allen and Widdowson (1974a and b). In time we might hope that linguists will provide us with more specific directions to follow. Meanwhile, the applied linguist, working, as it were, from the pedagogic end, can begin to specify the nature of different communicative acts, the way they are realized, the way they combine in different varieties of language use. These specifications may well develop from attempts to design language teaching materials which focus on the teaching of discourse. The applied linguist does not always have to wait, indeed, he cannot always wait, for the linguist to provide him with something to apply. He may follow his own path towards pedagogic application once the theorist has given a hint of the general direction. He may even, on the way, discover a direction or two which the theoretical linguist might himself explore with profit.

Notes

Paper presented at the first Neuchâtel Colloquium in Applied Linguistics, May 1972, and published in the proceedings: Corder and Roulet 1973.

8 The deep structure of discourse and the use of translation

The purpose of this paper is to explore, in tentative fashion, different ways of looking at the process of translation with a view to discovering their potential utility for the teaching of foreign languages. The use of translation as a teaching technique has long been viewed with suspicion by language teachers and many, of course, proscribe it altogether as a matter of principle. I want to argue that translation, conceived of in a certain way, can be a very useful pedagogic device and indeed in some circumstances, notably those where a foreign language is being learnt for 'special purposes' as a service subject, translation of a kind may provide the most effective means of learning.

As is pointed out in Catford (1965), the central problem in the theory and practice of translation is concerned with specifying the nature of equivalence in respect of two pieces of language. Clearly, what counts as equivalence will be determined by the model of linguistic description which is being used in the translation process. Thus a model which accounts only for the surface structure of sentences will only be able to assign equivalence to two sentences from two languages if they both exemplify overt grammatical features which the model specifies in some way as being common to both language systems: such features might include tense, aspect, voice, and so on.

Let us suppose that English is the source language (SL) and French the target language (TL) and that we wish to make use of a taxonomic structuralist model to establish translation equivalents between the two languages. Such a model will assign different structural descriptions to the following sentences in the SL:

1 The postman opened the door.
2 The door was opened by the postman.

It will also assign different structural descriptions to the following sentences in the TL:

3 Le facteur ouvrit la porte.
4 La porte fut ouverte par le facteur.

Now, with reference to this model, one might say that 1 is equivalent to 3 and 2 to 4 on the grounds that these pairs exemplify common grammatical features: both 1 and 3 expound (to use Halliday's term) active voice and simple past tense whereas 2 and 4 expound the passive voice with the simple past tense. To say this, however, is to make certain assumptions which, on examination, are of very doubtful validity. To establish these equivalences one has to argue in the following way: in the system of English the simple past tense contrasts with the present perfect in the same way as the passé simple contrasts with the passé composé in the system of French, so that in Saussurean terms they have the same value (valeur) in their respective systems. The same argument would apply to the active and passive in the systems of the two languages. But although the terms may *appear* to be comparable, their value derives uniquely from the manner in which they contrast within each system and there is no principled way of establishing their equivalence across systems (for a more detailed discussion, see Van Buren 1974).

One difficulty with the taxonomic structuralist model, then, is that it provides no way of establishing equivalent formal value of a Saussurean kind. Another difficulty is that it cannot account for communicative or functional value. Even if one were able to set up a formal correspondence which established an equivalence relation between 1/3 and 2/4, to do this would be to ignore the fact that the passé simple is used very restrictively in French and does not have the same value in respect of range of use as the simple past in English. If one is thinking of equivalence in terms of communicative value then one would be inclined to reject 3 and 4 as translation equivalents of 1 and 2 in favour of the following:

5 Le facteur a ouvert la porte.
6 La porte a été ouverte par le facteur.

The kind of linguistic model we are considering, however, would be likely to invoke some measure of structural similarity to relate 5 and 6 not to 1 and 2 but to the following sentences in English:

7 The postman has opened the door.
8 The door has been opened by the postman.

Furthermore, of course, in some contexts, 5 and 6 would indeed have the communicative value which would require 7 and 8 as equivalents and not 1 and 2.

If we are using a taxonomic structuralist grammar as a descriptive model, then there would appear to be no principled way in which we can account for the equivalence in terms of either formal or functional value. What such a model does, in effect, is to elevate a number of overt grammatical categories like tense and aspect to the status of universals and to assign formal equivalence by reference to some *ad hoc* measure of similarity in the realizations of these categories. Such a procedure yields the following equivalent pairs:

1 ------ 3
2 ------ 4
5 ------ 7
6 ------ 8

Let us now consider equivalence in relation to a transformational-generative grammar such as is outlined in Chomsky (1965). Such a model of description will represent 1 and 2, 3 and 4 as equivalent in relation to a common deep structure. This will presumably allow us to say that 1 may be equivalent to 4 and 2 to 3. But (as is observed in Kac 1969) a grammar of this kind will also represent a whole range of different surface structures as equivalent and these will include in the present case:

9 It was the postman who opened the door.
10 It was the door that was opened by the postman.

Similarly, one can cite sentences in French which might be said to represent different surface realizations of a common deep structure source. Thus one might regard the following as equivalent to 3 and 4:

11 Ce fut le facteur qui ouvrit la porte.
12 Ce fut la porte qui fut ouverte par le facteur.

We have now, as it were, extended the range of equivalence, and it would be convenient if we could say that the underlying structure of 1–2 and 9–10 is equivalent to that of 3–4 and 11–12, so that any of the English sentences can count as equivalent to any of the French ones. Unfortunately, to do so would be to make the same mistaken assumption as before: that is, that the categories which appear in the deep structure of a Chomsky model (1965) are realized in the same way in both languages.

At the same time, the fact that translation is possible at all suggests that it should be possible to arrive at a semantic base which would generate a proposition of which all of the sentences cited so far are alternative realizations. I do not wish (and in any case I do not feel competent) to discuss what form such a deep structure should take (see Krzeszowski 1975), but in principle it is possible to conceive of a deep structure which would serve as an underlying propositional reference for the sentences that we have been considering. We might call this (without, however, invoking temporal associations) a kind of 'proto-deep structure' and represent it as follows:

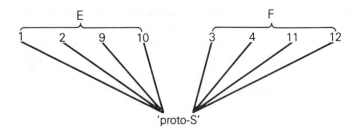

Of course, each of these surface forms can be differentiated from the others by reference to the transformational rules required for its derivation, but they can all be regarded as linguistically equivalent at the deeper level of analysis in that they are all paraphrases of each other (see Katz and Postal 1964: 157). It is, of course, the unique feature of this model of description that it provides for covert equivalence of this kind.

But although it is possible to claim that all of these sentences are equivalent in terms of basic grammatical properties, they clearly have different functional value: they are not in free variation as potential utterances. This difference can be accounted for in a number of ways. One can distinguish between different linguistic functions as Halliday does (Halliday 1967/1968, 1970a, etc.) and say that these sentences are equivalent in respect of ideational function but not in respect of textual function. Alternatively, one might say that they are equivalent in that they all express the same propositional content, but not so in that they differ in topicalization (Fillmore 1968) or in focus (Chomsky 1968). In both cases what one is saying, essentially, is that the different forms are equivalent as sentences in isolation but not as utterances or kinds of message. I shall return to this point presently.

Meanwhile, let me recapitulate. A descriptive model which deals only in surface forms will only assign equivalence between sentences within and between languages if these sentences are held to expound (to use Halliday's terms) common ideational, inter-personal, and textual features. A model which distinguishes between deep and surface levels of analysis will assign equivalence to sentences which exemplify common ideational and interpersonal features irrespective of their textual differences. The two models are alike, however, in that neither will allow equivalence to sentences which differ ideationally or inter-personally. As with the taxonomic model, it is difficult to see how the transformational-generative model can give explicit descriptive sanction to our feeling that 1 has the same general communicative value as 5, or provide us with any principled way of regarding them as translation equivalents. Clearly we cannot say that they derive from the same deep structure because to do so would be to conflate 1 and 7, which have different values, both from the communicative and grammatical points of view. We cannot simply add 5 and 7 as derivatives from our 'proto-S': the relationship between these sentences has to be represented differently:

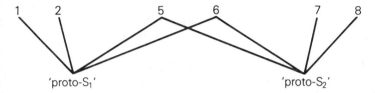

It would seem then that the transformational-generative model of description will assign grammatical equivalence to certain forms which have different communicative value and will deny equivalence to certain forms which have the same communicative value. Thus it will allow us to translate 1 as 4, 9 as 12, and so on, even when the context makes it inappropriate for us to do so, and it will prevent us from translating 1 as 5, 2 as 6, even when the context requires us to do so.

These observations suggest that we should distinguish between three kinds of equivalence. The first of these, which I will call structural equivalence, involves the correlation of the surface forms of sentences by reference to some *ad hoc* measure of formal similarity. The second, which I will call semantic equivalence, involves relating different surface forms to a common deep structure which represents their basic ideational and interpersonal elements. The third kind of equivalence is one which involves relating surface forms to their communicative function as utterances and this I will call pragmatic equivalence. Whereas semantic equivalence has to do with the propositional content of sentences, pragmatic equivalence has to do with the illocutionary effect of utterances. We may now say that 3 is a structural translation of 1 and 4 of 2, that either sentence from the English set 9–10 (and any other sentence relatable to the proto-S) is a semantic translation of either sentence from the French set 11–12, and that 5 can be (but is not invariably) a pragmatic translation of 1 and 6 of 2. We cannot, of course, by definition establish pragmatic equivalence by considering isolated sentences but only by considering what utterances count as in context.

I want now to place the foregoing discussion into broader perspective as a preliminary to relating it to pedagogic issues. When I say that pragmatic equivalence can only be established by considering what utterances count as in context what I mean is that the context, whether linguistic within the discourse or extra-linguistic within the situation, will provide the conditions whereby an utterance can be interpreted as representing a particular message or communicative act. I am not thinking of context in the raw state, as it were. I am not suggesting that the meaning of an utterance is discoverable directly by associating it with features of the context in which it occurs, but that its value as a communicative act derives from its satisfying the kind of conditions specified in Searle (1969), Labov (1969a, 1970), and which certain features of the context (though not all) provide for. Pragmatic meaning is therefore not the same thing as contextual meaning, as neo-Firthians appear to use this term, and by the same token, the communicative teaching of language is not the same thing as contextual language teaching as this notion is generally understood.

The distinction made in the previous paragraph enables us to characterize utterance types by reference to specific sets of conditions which are contextually realized rather than by reference to an unspecific (and unspecifiable) number of 'contexts of situation' *per se*. This allows us to set up communicative acts as utterance types which are defined independently of particular contexts and to provide a list of their most common linguistic realizations, either in relation to general use or in relation to particular universes of discourse. (There is a crucial distinction here which I shall return to presently.) Thus we can say, for example, that the following are pragmatically equivalent (though not equivalent in other respects) in the sense that they can all serve to perform the act of instruction:

13 Press the button twice.
14 The button must be pressed twice.
15 It is necessary to press the button twice.
16 The button is pressed twice.

Now there are differences in 'focus' here, and we may wish to speak of different kinds of instruction. But just as difference of focus does not prevent sentences 9–10 and 11–12 from being equivalent at a deeper grammatical level, so the differences here (which might be associated with Labov's 'modes of mitigation and politeness') need not be inconsistent with establishing pragmatic equivalence at a deeper rhetorical level. Notice that as with the case of 1 and 5 discussed earlier, not all of these potential utterances can be equated semantically. 16, for example, as a sentence can also be (and would usually be) formally linked with a sentence of the form:

17 (Someone) presses the button twice.

It would seem reasonable to say, then, that 16 is semantically equivalent to 17 but pragmatically equivalent to 13, 14, and 15 in so far as these utterances meet the necessary conditions. Other conditions can be specified which would establish 16 and 17 as pragmatically equivalent, as realizations of a different communicative act.

What I am proposing is that we might think in terms of two kinds of deep structure by means of which the two kinds of equivalence—semantic and pragmatic—can be established. Rhetorical deep structure, which accounts for pragmatic equivalence, is most naturally formulated as a set of conditions defining a particular communicative act such as Searle and Labov have made familiar. By reference to such a deep structure (as with the case of grammatical deep structure) we might proceed to set up equivalences across languages. Corresponding to the English set of utterances represented by 13–16 we might cite the following French equivalents:

18 Appuyer deux fois sur le bouton.
19 Appuyez deux fois sur le bouton.
20 Il faut appuyer deux fois sur le bouton.
21 On doit appuyer deux fois sur le bouton.

One might say that these are potential utterances which are representative realizations of the communicative act of instruction and as such are pragmatically equivalent to 13–16 cited above (although, as with the English utterances, this does not preclude the possibility of making more 'delicate' distinctions).

Turning now to pedagogic issues, let us consider what implications can be drawn from the preceding discussion for the use of translation as a technique in language teaching. The objections to the use of translation seem generally to be based on the assumption that it must necessarily involve establishing structural equivalence. It is said, for example, that translation leads the learner to suppose that there is a direct one-to-one correspondence of meaning between the sentences in the TL and those in the SL. Another, and related, objection is that it draws the attention of the learner to the formal properties of the TL sentences and distracts him from the search for contextual meaning—that is to say, meaning which is a function of the relationship between sentences and appropriate situations. But if translation is carried out with reference to grammatical deep structure, as an exercise in establishing semantic equivalence, it is not open to the first of these objections; and if it is carried out with reference to rhetorical deep structure, as an exercise in establishing pragmatic equivalence, it is not open to the second of them.

There would appear to be a case for overtly relating surface forms in two languages to deep structure 'proto-forms' of both the semantic and the pragmatic kinds. What this might involve can be seen from a consideration of the type of syllabus proposed in Wilkins (1972). What Wilkins does, essentially, is to represent the content of a language

teaching course as consisting of categories of what I have called grammatical and rhetorical deep structure. He gives them the subordinate
label 'notional categories'. This label is (I venture to suggest) somewhat
misleading since what he calls 'semantico-grammatical categories' are
elements from grammatical deep structure and are quite distinct from
his 'categories of communicative function' which are pragmatic in
character and are elements of rhetorical deep structure. Wilkins
invokes these notional categories as a principle of selection. The use of
translation would invoke them as a principle of presentation. To do this
would be to provide the learner with a representation of his existing
knowledge and through this representation to link up what he already
knows to what he has yet to learn.

We can think of translation, then, in terms of three alternative
processes, which might be shown diagrammatically as follows:

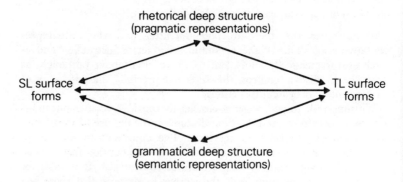

If one follows the path through semantic representations one can
demonstrate how sentences in the SL and TL relate to a common deep
structure such as is, for example, partially realized in the common
propositions of case grammar, deliberately grouping together sentences
in the two languages which are structurally distinct at the superficial
level of analysis. If one follows the path through pragmatic representations, one teaches communicative acts and shows how they may be
realized in formally diverse ways in the SL and TL. Notice that
although I have used the terms SL and TL, semantic and pragmatic
translation (unlike structural translation) mediates neutrally between
the linguistic forms which it relates: there is no 'direction' from one
language to another since the translation is carried out with reference to
conceptual patterns and social acts whose definition is independent of
any particular linguistic structure.

Although such a deep structure approach to translation might seem plausible, there are, however, certain difficulties when it is applied on a large scale to relate two languages. To begin with, there is the assumption that conceptual patterns and social acts which are represented in the grammatical and rhetorical deep structures are invariant across and within speech communities. Now we do not have to embrace a strong form of the Whorfian doctrine to recognize that the fact of language variation itself points to considerable variation in cognition and social behaviour. It would be very odd indeed if language behaviour were the *only* thing that varied and the fact of language variation would be quite inexplicable. Within a single speech community there are groups of language users—scientists, for example—who acquire ways of structuring reality which are not shared by other users of the language, just as there are communicative acts like, for example, scientific explanation or the drawing up of certain legal forms of contractual agreement, which are restricted to specific kinds of social activity. In fact there is likely to be more in common between certain 'varieties' in different languages than between different 'varieties' within the same language. Scientific discourse expressed through one language, for example, is likely to be closer semantically and pragmatically to scientific discourse expressed in another than to other areas of discourse expressed in the same language. Hence translating scientist-to-scientist discourse from an SL to a TL is likely to present far fewer problems than translating it into a different kind of discourse within the same language: that is to say, as far as scientific material is concerned at any rate, translation for peers is easier than simplification for a popular readership.

Let us explore this point a little further. In speaking of semantic and pragmatic equivalence I have made appeal to the notion of universals. This notion is a very tricky one to deal with. On the one hand the possibility of translation would appear to point to the existence of universals of one sort or another. On the other hand, universals have proved extremely elusive of definition. What I should like to suggest is that it may be that we have been looking for them in the wrong place. The grammarian's idealization of data allows him to postulate an abstract system which he represents as underlying the variation of actual language behaviour. Further abstraction leads him to postulate a universal base which he represents as underlying the variation of different language systems. I suggest that universals might be more readily discoverable not as properties of idealized abstractions but as properties of actualized language in certain areas of use, as features, in fact, which distinguish a particular universe of discourse independently of the different language systems which are used to realize it. What I am suggesting, then, is that there are universals of a communicative kind pertaining to certain universes of discourse which are independent not only of particular linguistic systems but also of any general system which underlies them at a deeper level of abstraction.

Let us, for example, consider the universe of discourse which we can, for present purposes, loosely describe as 'scientific'. From the grammarian's point of view, this can be regarded as a variety of the particular language he is concerned with and in consequence is idealized out by a process of standardization (see Lyons 1972). But scientific discourse represents a way of conceptualizing reality and a way of communication which must, if it is to remain scientific, be independent of different languages and different cultures. If one looks at scientific papers written in different languages one notices immediately that a considerable part of the information they convey is communicated by means of symbols, formulae, and diagrams which are a part of the universal metalanguage of science. It seems reasonable to suppose that the verbal component of the discourse with which these non-verbal forms are related (both verbal and non-verbal elements being constituent parts of the discourse as a whole) must also represent concepts and methods which are universally recognized as the defining features of scientific inquiry.

It seems obvious that the learning of science must involve the acquiring of a 'superposed' knowledge of certain universal concepts and methods. The concepts constitute the grammatical deep structure and the methods the rhetorical deep structure of scientific discourse, whether this be superficially realized by Japanese, Russian, French, English, or any other language. Thus, if any language is to serve the needs of scientific discourse it must have the means of expressing such deep structure concepts as, for example, the relationship between solids, liquids, and gases or between acids, bases, and salts which are instances of the universal semantic structure of science. The representations of such a universal semantics would presumably be expressible in terms of symbols, formulae, and conventionalized diagrams which already have the status of an international metalanguage. Such non-verbal devices would, then, serve as the elements of grammatical deep structure of scientific discourse. The pragmatics of rhetorical deep structure would be represented by sets of conditions defining such communicative acts as classification, description, explanation, and so on which constitute the basic methods of scientific investigation and exposition.

What I want to suggest is that semantic and pragmatic translation can be used as a teaching device for learners who need the TL as an additional medium for scientific communication. Its use involves the overt demonstration of how the surface forms in the TL and the SL are alternative realizations of scientific concepts and methods of inquiry which constitute the grammatical and rhetorical deep structure of scientific discourse and which are, by definition, neutral in regard to particular languages and cultures. I have taken science as the most obvious instance of a neutral area of language use, but there are obviously several other domains of what I have called superposed knowledge which extend over cultural and linguistic boundaries and these would include most of the disciplines and technologies of tertiary education, that is to say, most of the special purposes for which a foreign language is learnt as a service subject. Instead of thinking of the language use associated with these domains as being varieties of a particular language it would be more profitable (pedagogically at least) to think of them as universes of discourse which therefore provide universals of a semantic and pragmatic kind by reference to which superficially different realizations in two languages can be related.

In this paper I have been feeling my way, very tentatively, towards some clarification of what might be involved in the process of translation and of how this process might be pressed into pedagogic service. It has been an attempt to discover some rational grounds for two beliefs. The first (expressed in Widdowson 1973) is that the process of learning a foreign language should be presented not as the acquisition of new knowledge and experience, but as an extension or alternative realization of what the learner already knows. The second is one which I have also expressed, not very satisfactorily, elsewhere (Widdowson 1968): that language learning is more likely to be successful when it is associated with particular areas of use, or universes of discourse, which cut across linguistic and cultural boundaries.

Notes

Paper presented at the second Neuchâtel Colloquium in Applied Linguistics, May 1973, and published in the proceedings: Corder and Roulet 1974.

9 Approaches to discourse

What I want to do in this paper is to consider some of the proposals that have been made in recent years concerning the study of the communicative functioning of language in use. These proposals, though all concerned with the description of discourse in one way or another, have come from a number of different disciplines. Linguistics is one, but others, including sociology and philosophy, have laid a legitimate claim to a professional interest in what people do with their language. The proposals of different disciplines naturally embody different theoretical and methodological principles and find expression in different terminology and in consequence the field of discourse study is rather a confused one. It is easy to lose one's way. I have accordingly attempted to discover how differently oriented approaches to the study of discourse might be ordered into a general scheme. My aim is to sketch, in rather rough and ready fashion, a conceptual map of how I see this field of activity so far as it has been explored at present, and to indicate the problems which seem to me to be involved in its further exploration.

But first I want to set the linguistic scene, the background against which these proposals appear.

1 The scope of linguistic description

The orthodox view of the domain of linguistic description, which dates from de Saussure and represents the definition of linguistics as an autonomous discipline, is expressed by Chomsky in the following familiar quotation:

> Linguistic theory is concerned primarily with an ideal speaker-listener, in a completely homogeneous speech-community, who knows its language perfectly and is unaffected by such grammatically irrelevant conditions of memory limitations, distractions, shifts of attention and interest, and errors (random or characteristic) in applying his knowledge of the language in actual performance. This seems to me to have been the position of the founders of modern general linguistics, and no cogent reason for modifying it has been offered.
> *Chomsky 1965: 3 f.*

Since 1965, however, a number of reasons, of varying cogency, have been put forward for modifying this position and, in effect, for re-defining the scope of linguistic description. Even before that date, such a definition of linguistics did not receive universal sanction: a more humanistic tradition of language study has persisted throughout the period of what Chomsky conceives of as 'modern general linguistics' and it finds expression in the following (perhaps less familiar) quotation from Jakobson:

> Linguistics is concerned with language in all its aspects—language in operation, language in drift, language in the nascent state, and language in dissolution.
> *Jakobson and Halle 1956: 55.*

Whereas Chomsky uses the term *language* to refer to the Saussurean *langue*, a well-defined system arrested in time, Jakobson uses the term to refer to the Saussurean *langage*, a complex duality of both system and process operating in a social context and subject to variation and change. Since 1965, a number of reasons have been proposed for modifying the Chomskyan position in the direction of that adopted by Jakobson.

The narrow definition of the domain of linguistic inquiry has been justified by its proponents on the grounds that it isolates the essential aspects of language-as-a-whole upon which all other aspects in some sense depend, or from which they in some sense derive. Thus, de Saussure says that *langue* is a norm underlying 'toutes les autres manifestations du langage' and Chomsky:

> There seems to be little reason to question the traditional view that investigation of performance will proceed only so far as understanding of underlying competence permits.
> *Chomsky 1965: 10.*

But *langue* is conceived of as a static system and competence is con-ceived of as the ideal speaker-listener's knowledge of such a system, so that neither notion can be said to incorporate those aspects of language as a whole which relate to the processes of variation and change which are a natural and essential feature of linguistic behaviour. The postula-tion of an ideal speech-community immediately rules out of court any consideration of these defining features of natural language. As Hockett points out, what the narrow definition in effect does is to reduce natural language to a well-defined derived system, an artificial language. He concludes:

> Since languages are ill-defined, mathematical linguistics in the form of algebraic grammar is mistaken.
> *Hockett 1968: 61.*

Hockett acknowledges that this restriction of the scope of linguistic description may provide a useful approximation for certain purposes, but, he adds:

> ... an approximation is always made possible by leaving some things out of account, and I believe the things left out of account to achieve an approximation of this particular sort *are just the most important properties of human language*, in that they are the source of its openness.
> *Hockett 1968: 62.*

Hockett's objection to Chomsky's approach to linguistic description is reminiscent of Firth's objection to de Saussure's concept of *langue*:

> The multiplicity of social roles we have to play as members of a race, nation, class, family, school, club, as sons, brothers, lovers, fathers, workers, churchgoers, golfers, newspaper readers, public speakers, involves also a certain degree of linguistic specialization. Unity of language is the most fugitive of all unities, whether it be historical, geographical, national, or personal. There is no such thing as *une langue une* and there never has been.
> *Firth 1957: 29.*

Both Firth and Hockett reject the narrow definition of the scope of linguistics on the grounds that it misrepresents the nature of language as an adaptable instrument of human interaction. Language has been removed from a social context and stripped of its significance as a means of communication between people. Such a definition leads to an abstract methodological exercise in formalization which has no ultimate validation by reference to actual behaviour. As Labov puts it:

> It is difficult to avoid the common-sense conclusion that the object of linguistics must ultimately be the instrument of communication used by the speech community; and if we are not talking about *that* language, there is something trivial in our proceedings.
> *Labov 1970: 33.*

That language relates to de Saussure's *langage* rather than to his *langue* and Labov's conception of linguistics approximates more closely to Jakobson's than to Chomsky's. Its concern is not the study of a static and well-defined system assumed to be known, in some rather ill-defined sense, by ideal speaker-listeners in homogeneous speech communities, but the study of the dynamic operation of language in actual, and therefore heterogeneous, speech communities and the way actual, and therefore non-ideal, speaker-listeners use their knowledge in the business of communication. In brief, Labov's linguistics, like Firth's before him, focuses attention on 'the study of language in its social context'.

2 The study of language in its social context

What does the study of language in its social context actually involve and what exactly is its scope of inquiry compared with that of linguistics in a narrow sense as defined by Chomsky and de Saussure? The most straightforward way of drawing the distinction is by consideration of the kinds of idealization procedure which are employed in delimiting the domain of study. In his discussion of idealization, which he sees as the process whereby the sentence is abstracted from primary linguistic data, Lyons (1972) mentions three kinds of procedure of which two, standardization and decontextualization, are of particular relevance to the present discussion.

Standardization is the imposition of unity or homogeneity on language data. de Saussure's postulation of *une langue une* and Chomsky's notion of a completely homogeneous speech community both derive from a concept of language from which all variation has been excluded. This kind of idealization involves the disregarding of dialectal differences and such phenomena as code switching and style shifting—in short, the whole dynamic relationship between linguistic forms and social factors. It assumes that there is no need to inquire into the nature of the speech community since there is a central invariant system to be discovered which underlies all the variation of actual linguistic behaviour. This variation is consequently seen as a relatively trivial phenomenon, a distraction to be removed. One aspect of the study of language in social context is that which concerns itself with language which has not been standardized in this way, with variable *langage*, we might say, rather than invariant *langue*. It concerns itself with the study not of the individual linguist's intuition as in the kind of formal linguistics practised by generative grammarians, but with actually occurring linguistic behaviour. It seeks to establish rules which account for regularity without assuming homogeneity, and which provide a systematic description of language variation. Labov's work (see, for example, Labov 1966, 1972a) has provided the impetus for a considerable and increasing development in this field (see Bailey and Shuy 1973; Fasold and Shuy 1975) which has also resulted in a resurgence of interest in the related question of language change, particularly as exemplified in pidgin and creole languages (see Hymes 1971, De Camp and Hancock 1974).

The investigation of variation and change in language necessarily implies a rejection of standardization as a means of cutting data down to methodological size. Its aim is the scrutiny of actual linguistic behaviour in social contexts in contrast to the narcissistic introspection of intuition which marks recent formal linguistic inquiry. In this respect, this kind of work on non-standardized data might be considered a kind of discourse analysis. But the discourse is being studied as variable linguistic *manifestations*. By this I mean that the central issue is the problem of accounting for different forms of speaking by means of rules which relate them to the same or different systems. The interest is in language *usage* and how its variability can be accounted for, on what codes people use and how these codes are structured. If we now turn to the second idealization procedure mentioned earlier, we can distinguish another aspect of the study of language in its social context, one which looks at discourse from a rather different point of view.

Whereas standardization is the procedure whereby a single and invariant system is abstracted from the complex variability which exists in actual speech communities, decontextualization is the procedure whereby the sentence is abstracted as an isolate from its natural surroundings in discourse. Sentences as abstract linguistic objects can be inferred from discourse but they do not actually occur in language behaviour. Normal language behaviour involves the production of discourse and this derives from the speaker-listener's *realization* of the communicative potential of the rules of his language system. Discourse consists of utterances, with which sentences can be put into correspondence, and these combine in complex ways to relate to extra-linguistic reality to achieve a communicative effect. The decontextualization of language data yields the isolated sentence whose meaning is self-contained. If we reject this idealization, then we are obliged to consider how meanings are conveyed by interrelationship of utterances in contexts of *use*. We are involved in discourse analysis in the more conventional sense of that term: the study of how social interaction is effected by reference not only to rules of usage, which provide for the way the language is manifested, but also to rules or procedures of use, which provide for the way language is realized as a means of communicative activity.

An extension of the scope of linguistics to include non-standardized and contextualized language data, then, yields two areas of inquiry: the study of language variation on the one hand and the study of communicative activity on the other. The first of these looks at linguistic manifestations, investigates different usages, and attempts to set up models of description which will account for the differences in a systematic way. Its focus of attention is on the code or codes available to speakers, on the structure of the instrument of communication. The second of these looks at the communicative properties of language and investigates the uses to which speakers put their knowledge of linguistic codes in order to interact with each other. Its focus of attention is on the functioning of the instrument of communication, on the manner in which it is actually put into operation in the expression of messages. The analysis of variation leads to a revision of the notion of language as a well-defined system of rules, but although it necessarily rejects standardization, it retains decontextualization as a way of idealizing away those aspects of language which are not its direct concern. Its descriptive limit, like that of formal linguistics, is still the sentence. The analysis of communicative activity, however, deals with contextualized language data and takes us beyond the sentence into discourse. Whereas in the study of variation, discourse, actual linguistic behaviour occurring in contexts of normal social interaction, is studied as evidence for underlying regularities which can be incorporated into rules which determine various manifestations, in the study of communicative activity, discourse is studied as an end in itself. It is concerned not with the more exact description of grammatical rules but with their communicative potential and with how language users put their knowledge of such rules to communicative effect, how they negotiate meanings with each other, how they structure an ongoing interaction, and so on. It is with this latter area, the study of discourse as communicative use, that I will concern myself with in this paper.

3 Points of departure

I think it is useful to make a broad distinction between two general methodological approaches to the description of discourse. One takes instances of discourse as the starting point and makes statements about how they are structured as units of communication of one sort or another. The other takes the sentence as its starting point and investigates its potential for generating discourse. The direction of the first approach is from communicative function to linguistic form, and the direction of the second is from linguistic form to communicative function. Both are perfectly legitimate ways of studying language. The difficulty is in knowing how they may be related.

The first of these approaches has a long and honourable history. It is exemplified in literary criticism, in studies of the structure of myth (see, for example, Levi-Strauss 1958) and of folktales (see, for example, Propp 1972). What distinguishes the work done in accordance with this general discourse-based approach is the extent to which the analysis relates its findings to actual linguistic expression: in other words, how close they get to common ground with the sentence-based approach. Sometimes, the gap is very wide. To take an example, Propp (1972) discusses certain thematic constants in fairy stories and isolates the following motif: A sends B on a search and B departs. This underlying theme can be realized in different stories in a variety of different ways, as, for example, in the following variants:

The king sends Ivan to find the princess. Ivan leaves.
The blacksmith sends his apprentice to find the cow. The apprentice leaves.

Propp is essentially interested in the events recorded in different tales and tells how they can be linked to a general theme, but the linguistic expression of these events is not his concern. The analysis in Powlison (1965), on the other hand, moves much closer to common ground with the sentence-based approach. He considers how the theme of a particular folktale is expressed through paragraph organization and how different linguistic forms take on particular value as elements of discourse structure.

One may say that what distinguishes literary stylistics from literary criticism of a conventional kind is that although both are discourse-based, the former attempts to extend the study of literature to a consideration of the specific features of linguistic expression, to move from discourse towards the sentence, whereas the latter tends to use linguistic expression as evidence of something else, character, plot, theme, and so on, and focuses attention on the message which the language is used to convey (for a discussion, see Widdowson 1975). In a similar way, the degree of concern with how elements of discourse structure are linguistically realized distinguishes the work of Sinclair and Coulthard on classroom interaction from that of other investigators, as they themselves make clear (see Sinclair and Coulthard 1975: 8–18).

One general approach to discourse analysis, then, begins with instances of discourse, with actual data, and moves towards linguistic units to the extent that this appears to be necessary for the purpose of the description. The second approach moves outwards, as it were, from the sentence, and deals not with linguistic expressions as realized in discourse but with the abstract potential of linguistic forms. For example, in more recent work in sociolinguistics, there is a close examination of the function in discourse structure of specific constituent utterances (see Sinclair and Coulthard 1975, Labov 1972b, Dundes *et al* 1972, Turner 1974), but these are studied from the point of view of their contextually determined function in the discourse. The second approach, on the other hand, begins with the sentence as an abstracted isolate and represents discourse function as in some sense realizable from a meaning potential within the sentence itself. So whereas in the first approach the focus of attention is on the context in which linguistic forms occur and which provides them with communicative value as utterances, in the second approach the focus of attention is on the meanings of linguistic forms as elements of the language system, having implication of utterance.

To illustrate this difference of approach, we might consider the following instance of language:

Is someone laughing?

If we consider this as a sentence, we will note that it is interrogative in form and suggest that its meaning potential is that it can function in discourse as a question, a request for information. If, on the other hand, we consider this as an utterance in a particular context, then we need to take into account the circumstances under which it was produced in order to interpret its realized meaning as an element of discourse. Thus, Sinclair and Coulthard (from whose data this utterance is taken) point out that in the context of the classroom, there is a procedure for interpretation which can be expressed as follows:

> Any declarative or interrogative is to be interpreted as a *command to stop* if it refers to an action or activity which is proscribed at the time of utterance.
> *Sinclair and Coulthard 1975: 32.*

An application of this procedure has the effect of neutralizing the meaning potential of the interrogative sentence and of realizing the value of this utterance as a command. The utterance would have exactly the same value, according to this interpretative procedure, if it had taken the form:

> Someone is laughing.

The point here is, then, that there is no one-to-one correspondence between the signification of linguistic forms and their communicative value as utterances in context. Discourse meanings are to some degree unpredictable. At the same time they cannot be *entirely* unpredictable: the relationship between form and function is not purely arbitrary, or otherwise there would be no linguistic basis for communication at all. A sentence-based approach to discourse would investigate what it is about this example as a sentence which allows for variable interpretation, and would go beyond the straightforward interrogative-form/ question-function correspondence in search of more subtle features of meaning potential. The fact that context may override the meaning associated with sentences does not mean that one cannot fruitfully explore this meaning, which, though overridden in particular cases, can be said to constitute the essential potential for meaning which is *realizable* in context, even if not actually realized on every occasion.

Whether one looks at discourse from the point of view of the potential value of sentences or of the realized value of utterances, one has to go beyond the superficial appearance of linguistic form. One needs to recognize that linguistic structures are expressive of certain propositions on the one hand and that they count as performances of certain illocutionary acts on the other (see Searle 1969). Let us suppose, for example, that during a conversation A makes the following remark to B:

My son will return the umbrella tomorrow.

B can report this utterance in one of three ways. He may report the occurrence of the actual linguistic form and repeat the sentence that A uses by direct speech:

She said: 'My son will return the umbrella tomorrow.'

Alternatively, he may use indirect speech and report A's proposition and then he has a number of sentences at his disposal. For example:

She said that her son would return the umbrella tomorrow.
She said that the umbrella would be returned by her son tomorrow.

And also, depending on the relative situational settings of the original remark and the report:

She said that her son would take/bring the umbrella back tomorrow/today.

As we shall see in the following section, this by no means exhausts the possibilities. The third way in which B can report A's utterance is by reporting what he understands to be its illocutionary force. In expressing a proposition A also necessarily *does* something with it: promises, undertakes, warns, and so on. Consequently, B may report what A says in one of the following ways:

She promised me that her son would return the umbrella tomorrow.
She warned me that her son would return the umbrella tomorrow.
She predicted that her son would return the umbrella tomorrow.

In these cases, B reports the illocutionary act which he interprets A as performing in expressing this particular proposition.

4 The sentence as the point of departure

I want in this section to look at discourse analysis from the sentence-based point of view and consider a number of proposals that have been made for extending the scope of sentence grammars so as to incorporate information in deep structure about propositional content and illocutionary force.

With certain kinds of sentence, the overtly expressed proposition carries with it an additional covert proposition as a necessary concomitant. This second, covert proposition is said to be presupposed. All wh-interrogative sentences, for example, have this peculiarity. The following sentence:

When did Arthur arrive?

presupposes that Arthur arrived. This fact lends force to the proposal to represent this sentence by an underlying structure like:

Q Arthur arrived at some time.

Here the presupposed proposition is made explicit in the deep structure formulation. The relevance of presuppositions of this kind to discourse analysis is clear when we consider exchanges like the following:

A When did Arthur arrive?
B At ten.

A How did Arthur arrive?
B By car.

The utterances of A and B are cohesive because a formal linguistic link can be established between them by invoking the presupposed proposition *Arthur arrived* in each case:

A When did Arthur arrive?
B (Arthur arrived) at ten.

Presuppositions can be seen as relating also to certain sentence constituents. Kiparsky and Kiparsky (1971), for example, discuss what they call factive and non-factive predicates. Consider the following sentences:

It is significant that he has been found guilty.
It is likely that he has been found guilty.

These would appear on the surface to have exactly the same structure, but in the first there is a covert proposition (which we would presumably wish in some way to indicate in deep structure) that the person referred to has been found guilty. Thus, it is possible to devise a short discourse by representing this single sentence as two sentences:

He has been found guilty. That is significant.

No presupposed proposition of this kind attaches to the second of these sentences, however. We cannot derive from it a discourse of the form:

He has been found guilty. That is likely.

The same sort of observation is made in Fillmore (1971) about what he refers to as verbs of judging. Speaking of the verbs *criticize* and *accuse*, Fillmore makes the following comments:

> Uses of the verb *criticize* presuppose the factuality of the situation;
> but not so for *accuse* . . . Consider the two sentences:
> I accused Harry of writing an obscene letter to my mother.
> I criticized Harry for writing an obscene letter to my mother.
> With *accuse*, there is no presupposition that such a letter was ever
> written; with *criticize* there is.
> *Fillmore 1971: 283.*

In other words, *accuse* is non-factive and *criticize* is factive. If Fillmore
is right, then this again has implications for discourse. The following,
for example, would be adjudged to form a cohesive sequence:

> I criticized Harry for writing an obscene letter to my mother. He sent
> it last week by express delivery.

But if we replace *criticize* with *accuse*, the sequence of sentences would,
according to Fillmore's criteria, be unacceptable as discourse:

> I accused Harry of writing an obscene letter to my mother. He sent it
> last week by express delivery.

In factive sentences the presupposed covert proposition which derives
from the embedded sentence is not effected by the negation of the verb
in the main sentence. Thus, if the sentences we have cited are negated,
the presuppositions remain as before. Karttunen (1971) discusses
presuppositions attaching to a different type of verb—which he calls
'implicative verbs'—in which the assertion of a main statement with one
of these verbs in the predicate commits the speaker to the proposition
expressed in the embedded sentence, so long as this is a positive
assertion. An example of an implicative verb is *condescend* and of a
non-implicative verb *decide*. Thus the sentence:

> Arthur condescended to mow the lawn yesterday.

is said to carry with it the presupposition:

> Arthur mowed the lawn yesterday.

But the sentence:

> Arthur decided to mow the lawn yesterday.

does not, according to Karttunen, carry with it any such implication. If
this is the case, it means that the presupposition attaching to the first
sentence constrains the choice of any sentence which might follow it in
discourse. So we cannot have:

> Arthur condescended to mow the lawn yesterday. But he watched
> television instead.

If we replace *condescended* by *decided*, however, then the discourse becomes quite acceptable.

In the cases we have just considered (and many others could be cited: see Harder and Kock 1976 for a detailed review), the presupposition might be said to attach to the propositional content of the sentence. It remains the same even if an alternative surface form is used. Thus, the following can be said to be 'stylistic' variants of the same underlying structure:

> Arthur condescended to mow the lawn yesterday.
> It was Arthur who condescended to mow the lawn yesterday.

In both cases (assuming for the sake of argument that Karttunen is correct), there is a presupposition that Arthur mowed the lawn yesterday. There are different presuppositions, however, attaching to the different linguistic forms whereby this proposition is expressed. Thus the second but not the first presupposes that someone condescended to mow the lawn and that the someone in question is not Arthur. Whereas the first of these variants could be used to initiate a discourse, therefore, since it presupposes no previous interaction, the second could not since it presupposes that the subject of lawn mowing has already been introduced in some way into the preceding conversation.

Halliday (1967/1968) discusses presuppositions of this kind under the general heading of what he calls 'theme'. He points out that a sentence like:

> The one who discovered the cave was John.

is associated with the covert proposition that somebody discovered the cave, but that a thematic or 'stylistic' variant like:

> What John discovered was the cave.

is associated with the covert proposition that John discovered something. As before, we can see that it is these covert, presupposed, propositions which control whether or not a sequence of sentences makes cohesive discourse. Halliday points out, for example, that the following pair of sentences does not form cohesive links:

> Nobody else had known where the entrance to the cave was situated.
> What John discovered was the cave.

If we select the other variant, however, the two sentences do constitute a cohesive combination:

> No one else had known where the entrance to the cave was situated.
> The one who discovered the cave was John.

It is because these different forms carry different presuppositions of this kind that Halliday rejects the notion, common among grammarians of the transformational-generative persuasion, that the variation in meaning among surface forms is in some sense less 'important' than meaning distinctions that can be accounted for in deep structure. In standard (or 'classical') transformational-generative grammar, such as is exemplified in Chomsky (1965), the two sentences we have been considering would be represented as ultimately relatable (by means of transformational operations) to the same deep structure, roughly paraphrasable as:

John discovered the cave.

In this respect, they would be held to have the same meaning, that meaning being conveyed unchanged from deep structure by different transformational rules. In this view, transformations are devices which can be employed to demonstrate that two structurally different forms are 'really', in the last (or deepest) analysis, expressions of the same meaning and their surface differences are relatively insignificant and superficial (surface and superficial are often used interchangeably in discussions on this matter). If we adopt Halliday's view, however, transformations appear in a different light. They can be seen as devices whereby propositions, expressible in their simplest form as sentences of the kind just cited, can be structurally organized so as to acquire the presuppositions which are appropriate for particular contexts of use. They are conceived of as the means for differentiating rather than preserving meanings, as a way of 'preparing' deep structure propositions for actual communicative operation.

Halliday's discussion of theme relates to those transformations which transpose sentence constituents. But other kinds of transformation can also be considered as ways of preparing sentences to function as elements in discourse. We might briefly consider embedding transformations. The following pair of sentences can be regarded as alternative transformational outputs from the same deep structure source:

Arthur went to the table and picked up the book that was open.
Arthur went to the table and picked up the open·book.

Both of these can be related to a deep structure, the relevant part of which we might roughly show as follows:

Arthur picked up the book the book was open

But although both sentences can therefore be said to express the same proposition, they clearly carry different presuppositions. The first, for example, presupposes that there was more than one book on the table, whereas the second carries no such presupposition. Thus, if the first were to be followed by a sentence which related to the covert proposition, we would be able to infer a cohesive connection:

> Arthur went to the table and picked up the book that was open. He paid no attention to the others.

Here, we are able to provide the expression *the others* with the reading 'the other books'. We cannot do the same, however, with the following:

> Arthur went to the table and picked up the open book. He paid no attention to the others.

In this case, we have no way of realizing the value of the expression *the others* as referring to books. We would most likely assume that it referred to other people who happened to be near the table at the time.

A good deal more could be said about the 'rhetorical' functions of transformational rules (for a detailed discussion see Widdowson 1973) but perhaps enough has been said to justify regarding them as devices for preparing propositions for discourse function by creating appropriate presuppositions.

Both the proposition itself, then, and the manner in which this is fashioned, the different sentential forms which may be used to express it, may carry presuppositions, covert propositions which can serve to project meaning from one sentence to another so as to establish a cohesive relation. As we shall see presently (in Section 5), one of the difficulties about using presuppositions to understand how discourse works is that they are not always reliable: other factors may intervene. Before considering this matter, however, we must turn from the propositional elements of sentences to the question of their possible illocutionary force.

Proposals have been made to extend the modal component of the deep structure of sentences to incorporate an indicator of their illocutionary force. Thus, if we recognize that the sentence:

> Shut the door.

has the illocutionary force of an order, we might wish to postulate a deep structure for it in which the performative verb were made explicit, roughly paraphraseable as:

> I order you you shut the door.

In the same way, Ross (1970) suggests that underlying the surface form:

> Prices slumped.

There is a deep structure paraphraseable as:

> I inform you prices slumped.

This, Ross suggests, may be formalized in something like the following manner:

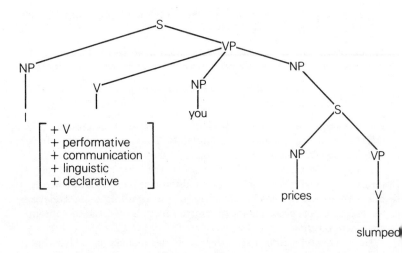

The features specified for the verb could be extended to include the kind of conditions discussed in detail in Searle (1969). That is to say, one might have entries in the lexicon for performative verbs which spelled out the conditions which have to be met for their use. These specifications might take something of the form proposed by Fillmore for his verbs of judging (Fillmore 1971).

As expressed in Searle, these conditions are independent of the linguistic form which the sentence takes. But as Fillmore observes:

> An important fact that is typically omitted from a philosopher's record of the set of happiness conditions of a sentence is that the various conditions are separately related to different specific facts about the grammatical structure of the sentence. For example, from the fact that the form of the sentence is imperative, we infer those conditions that relate to the speaker-addressee relationship; from the presence of the definite article, we infer the understanding that there is some mutually identifiable door, to which the speaker is referring; the others are inferrable from the ways in which we understand the verb *shut*.
>
> *Fillmore 1971: 276.*

From this point of view, illocutionary force is not, as it were, a separate feature of an utterance to be associated with the proposition expressed, but derives from the proposition itself, as the realization of its 'meaning potential'.

The expression 'meaning potential' is taken from Halliday, who has consistently taken the view (which derives ultimately from Firth) that understanding of the social function of language is a prerequisite for an understanding of linguistic structure. In this view, one does not first isolate the abstract system for detached study and then, if one feels inclined, see how it works in a social context for the purposes of communication: rather, one looks to purposes of communication to explain the system. The central question posed by Chomsky and his associates is *how* language is structured: for Halliday, an equally significant question is *why* it is structured in the way that it is. As he puts it:

> But what is the nature and origin of the grammatical system? Grammar is the level of formal organization in language; it is a purely internal level of organization, and is in fact the main defining characteristic of language. But it is not arbitrary. Grammar evolved as 'content form': as a representative of the meaning potential through which language serves its various social functions. The grammar itself has a functional basis.
> *Halliday 1973: 98.*

In Halliday's work we find an attempt to formalize the kind of conditions which Searle talks about into semantic networks which represent sets of options available to the language user. These networks mediate between social situations and sets of linguistic expressions derivable from systems within the grammar. Thus the illocutionary force of a particular utterance is seen to be a functional reflection of its intrinsic linguistic form.

Proceeding towards discourse from the starting point of the sentence, then, involves a consideration of: firstly what is presupposed by the proposition expressed by the sentence, which can be accounted for in the formulation of its deep structure; secondly what is presupposed by the manner in which the proposition is organized as a surface form by different transformational operations; and thirdly what illocutionary act the proposition or a particular manner of expressing it is used to perform, which can be accounted for specifying different conditions or semantic networks and seeing how these are realized by the elements in the proposition, or by the particular form of the sentence that expresses it. A study of these factors, of the 'meaning potential' of sentences, treating these not simply as abstract linguistic forms but as a communicative resource, leads us towards the study of language in its social context from a linguistic base. We have now to consider the second orientation to discourse analysis that was mentioned: that which takes actually attested language use as its starting point.

5 Discourse as the point of departure

The sentence based approach to discourse described in the previous section does not typically deal in actual data: it essentially concerns itself with the potential residing in the language system itself for the realization of discourse, with what might be called the communicative capacity of the system. It extends from the sentence outwards and, to date at least, this extension has not gone much beyond relationships between contiguous sentences. The discourse based approach, on the other hand, confronts the data, actual and not potential instances of communicative behaviour.

To adopt this orientation is immediately to become involved in the problem of what might be called contextual conditioning. By this I mean that although one might associate a particular meaning potential with a particular linguistic form, this potential might not be realized, or the form might take on a different and unpredictable communicative value because of what has preceded in the discourse or because of the circumstances of utterance. An example of such conditioning from the work of Sinclair and Coulthard was briefly discussed in Section 3 in this paper. To illustrate the problem further we can first refer to the so-called implicative verbs which were discussed in Section 2. If we consider the sentence:

Arthur condescended to mow the lawn yesterday.

out of context, we may readily agree that there is a presupposition here that Arthur did in fact mow the lawn. But this presupposition can be neutralized by what follows in the discourse:

Arthur condescended to mow the lawn yesterday. But just as he was about to begin the Browns arrived.

Here the presupposition latent in the first sentence is cancelled out by the second sentence: we take it that Arthur did not mow the lawn after all. In similar fashion, we might agree that the following sentence:

Arthur and Agnes decided to get married.

carries no presupposition, in isolation from a context, that they actually did get married. But this presupposition can be created if the sentence were extended into discourse in the following manner:

Arthur and Agnes decided to get married. They have two children now.

The interpretation of discourse, then, is not simply a matter of recovering the presuppositions attaching to individual sentences as they appear in sequence. The linguistic context in which they occur, and the extra-linguistic context of utterance, create presuppositions of a pragmatic kind or 'implicatures' which can override those which are associated with linguistic forms. As I pointed out earlier (in Section 3), this does not mean that it is not legitimate to investigate the latter: they represent part of the essential knowledge that the language user brings to his understanding of language use. What it does mean, however, is that we cannot assume that meanings, whether explicit or implicit, are carried unchanged into discourse. Discourse is not simply a patchwork of preordained sentential meanings; it is a dynamic process of meaning creation. Misunderstanding of this fact leads to the kind of error made by van Dijk (1972). He cites the following sentences:

We will have guests for lunch. Calderon was a great Spanish writer.

and says that this combination is 'definitely ungrammatical'. He adds:

That is, any native speaker of English will consider this sequence, when presented in one utterance, as nonsense. This, of course, does not prevent the assignment of semantic representations to the individual sentences, but it is impossible to establish any semantic relation between them, that is, one cannot assign a semantic representation to the sequence as a whole.
Van Dijk 1972: 40.

It is true that if we consider these items of language as sentences, there is no way in which we can establish semantic links of cohesion between them. If, however, we consider them as utterances, as actual instances of language use, there is no difficulty at all in conceiving of a context in which they would make perfectly good sense, where they would combine to form a coherent discourse. Imagine a situation, for example, in which a group of people were in the habit of inviting guests for lunch to discuss the work of great writers. A lunch has been set aside to discuss Calderon, but then there is some dispute among the organizers as to whether Calderon merits the title of 'great' and after some debate it is concluded that he does, so the lunch can go forward as arranged. In this context of situation, the sentences cited could be used with complete good sense. In this case, contextual conditioning creates a relationship which is absent from the sequence of sentences considered in detachment from a context.

It would seem, then, that how elements of a discourse relate is only partially dependent on what is stated and presupposed in the individual sentences that comprise it. It is quite possible, as we have seen, for two items of language to be completely unrelated as sentences and therefore to exhibit no cohesion, but to be very closely related as utterances in context and therefore to exhibit coherence as discourse. In Krzeszowski (1975) there is a convincing demonstration of this. He puts forward the hypothesis that

any two sentences representing the same grammatical type, for example any two declarative sentences . . . could be connected by any of the sentence connectives and result in a well-formed sequence. The well-formedness of such a sequence depends on extra-linguistic circumstances attending the uttering of such texts.
Krzeszowski 1975: 41.

He considers two sentences taken at random from a textbook of English:

The men and women eat breakfast together.
The nomads become restless in the big town.

As Krzeszowski points out, these can be quite appropriately related by use of the connective *therefore* under certain extra-linguistic circumstances: for example, we have a socio-cultural situation in which it is offensive to the nomads to have men and women eating together since in their own culture this violates notions of common decency. Other extra-linguistic circumstances can easily be imagined in which the two utterances would be related in the following ways:

The men and women eat breakfast together. Nevertheless, the nomads become restless in the big town.
The men and women eat breakfast together. Moreover, the nomads become restless in the big town.

At the same time, examples could be cited where it would surely be perverse to maintain that *any* two sentences linked with *therefore* constituted a well-formed combination. Consider the following:

John has stopped beating his wife. Therefore he is a brute.

We would be inclined to say here that although one could envisage a world in which beating one's wife were regarded as a kindness and so render this as a well-formed sequence, there is nevertheless something within the language which makes it strange and which would *normally* lead us to see it as deviant. The deviance relates to the presupposition contained in the first sentence and which activates what Ducrot (1972) calls a 'loi d'enchaînement'. In considering this matter, Harder and Kock (1975) made the following comment:

In order to single out the presupposition of a sentence among the components of its meaning, Ducrot formulates the 'loi d'enchaînement' which says, in effect: when one uses the sentence as a step in a chain of reasoning, for example by appending to it a conclusion beginning with *therefore*, then this conclusion cannot base itself on the presupposition of the sentence. If this is attempted, then the

resulting chain of reasoning will appear odd or even invalid. For example, if one has *John has stopped beating his wife*, then the assumption *John once beat his wife* is a presupposition . . . for we can only have *John has stopped beating his wife. Therefore they are getting on better now*, but not *John has stopped beating his wife. Therefore he is a brute*, where the conclusion is based on the presupposition.
Harder and Kock 1975: 33.

A number of other chaining rules, where presuppositions can be said to constrain sentence sequence (and so to be a potential projection of discourse development) were implied in some of the examples discussed in Section 4. It is clear that we have to allow for contextual conditioning, that what is meant on a particular occasion is not simply a function of what is asserted and presupposed by the sentence, but at the same time, meanings do not just spring unheralded from the context. What is conditioned is normal expectation based on the language user's knowledge of what sentences mean by virtue of linguistic rules of one sort or another.

Although I have spoken of the way context may condition meanings, providing a relationship between utterances which is not derivable from the meanings of the individual sentences, it is important to note that the context itself does not create this relationship. It is the language user who makes sense of the language by reference to those features of the circumstances of utterance which he judges to be relevant. He does this by recognizing what it is in the sentence and in the linguistic and extra-linguistic context in which it occurs that realizes the conditions whereby it takes on a particular communicative value. Confronted with an instance of language, we immediately engage certain interpretative procedures which enable us to make sense of it. Some of these procedures like those for ritual insults (Labov 1972b) or classroom interaction (Sinclair and Coulthard 1975) are specific to particular kinds of situation. Some of them, however, are of a quite general kind and fall under the heading of what Grice refers to as 'maxims of conversation', and what Ducrot (1972) refers to as 'laws of exhaustivité, informativité and interêt'.

One of these general procedures takes the form of an assumption that when somebody says something, what he says is meant to be informative and relevant. Thus, when we are presented with two apparently quite disconnected sentences, as in the example about the nomads we have just been considering, we proceed on the assumption that the information expressed in the second sentence must be relevant in some way to the information expressed in the first. This relevance is not signalled by linguistic clues, so we create an extra-linguistic situation which will supply the deficiency.

To consider another example: I am in a room with someone and he says to me:

The door is open.

The fact that I can see quite well for myself that the door is open makes his remark redundant as information. In consequence I seek what relevance it might have in the circumstances in which it was spoken, and I might find that this lies in the fact that the utterance can be understood as realizing one of the conditions attendant upon the act of ordering or requesting. Since the utterance is not informative as a statement, I assume that it must be relevant as another illocutionary act and I investigate whether the situation of utterance provides for the realization of the necessary conditions. If, for example, the conditions for an order are recoverable from the situation, then my likely reaction will be to close the door; if the situation can be seen as realizing the conditions for, let us say, a warning, then my likely reaction will be to lower my voice or stop talking. If I cannot find the relevant conditions, I might say:

So what?

If I see that my interlocutor might regard the conditions for an order obtain in the situation but I do not, then I might respond by deliberately misinterpreting his intent and treating his remark as simply informative:

So I see.

Or by making it clear that I do not accept his reading of the situation:

Close it yourself!

I have already (in Section 4) referred to the kinds of conditions which might be specified in a Searlean type analysis of illocutionary acts. These can be said to represent the language user's knowledge of rules of use in the abstract. What Searle does not concern himself with is the manner in which such rules are put into operation for the production and interpretation of actual discourse by means of the kind of procedure we have been discussing. Labov (1969a, 1972a) specifies conditions of a similar kind but also considers how they are realized in contexts of actual use. He takes an attested instance of discourse as his starting point:

A Well, when do you plan to come home?
B Oh why-y?

As with the cases we have been considering, there is no formally signalled relationship between these two linguistic units as sentences.

To understand what is going on here, we have to know about the extra-linguistic circumstances. These are as follows:

> We must be aware that A is a college student, and that B is her mother; that B has been away for four days helping a married daughter; that A and B both know that A wants B to come home; and that B has said many times in the past that A cannot take care of herself, which A denies.
> *Labov 1972a: 255.*

Our interpretation of this interaction depends on us seeing how this situation realizes the conditions which have to be met for a particular illocutionary act to be performed. Labov formulates these conditions as follows:

> If A requests B to perform an action X at a time T, A's utterance will be heard as a valid command only if the following preconditions hold: B believes that A believes that:
>
> 1 X needs to be done for a purpose Y.
> 2 B has the ability to do X.
> 3 B has the obligation to do X.
> 4 A has the right to tell B to do X.

Given these conditions, our task now is to see whether the situation can be seen as one which can realize them. If so, then A's question is interpretable as a request for action, a kind of mitigated command, which might be alternatively phrased as something like:

A Come home, please.

The question is: does B interpret A's remark in this way? According to Labov, she does, and her question is directed to the first of the conditions specified above: she assumes for the moment that the other conditions hold but wants clarification of the first condition. Her question might be rephrasable as:

B Why do I need to come home?

B's interpretation derives from a procedure whereby she realizes the value of A's utterance in relation to the conditions in the following way:

> If A makes a request for information of B about whether an action X has been performed, or at what time T X will be performed, and the four preconditions hold, then A will be heard as making a request for action with the underlying form *B: do X*.
> *Labov 1972a: 256.*

If this interpretation is correct, then A's next utterance should provide the information that B is covertly requesting: it should also focus on the first of the conditions. In fact, in the data which Labov is considering, this is exactly what happens:

A Well, things are getting just a little too much. (laugh). This is—it's just getting too hard.

What has to be noted is that A is not simply providing information: her utterance is not only informative but relevant in respect to the request she is making. Her remark is both a response to B's request for information and at the same time a repetition of the request by a focusing on one of its defining conditions. She makes use of the following procedure:

If A has made a request, and B responds with a request for information, A reinstates the original request by supplying that information.

What is B's next move? She could, of course, accept that the first condition is now clarified and accede to the request in something like the following manner:

B I'll try and get home tomorrow.

In fact, in the data, B's next remark is:

B Well, why don't you tell Helen that?

We might infer that the suggestion that B is making here is that Helen might more appropriately be asked to help. In other words, she now shifts the focus of attention either to condition 2 or to condition 3: she is questioning her ability or her obligation to assist A in her predicament.

Throughout this exchange we can see a kind of negotiation whereby the two participants employ a variety of procedures to interpret each other's utterances by reference to their common knowledge of the situation and the rule of use associated with making a request for action. The investigation of procedures of this kind has been the particular concern of the ethnomethodologists (for a representative selection of their work, see Sudnow 1972, Turner 1974). Thus, Garfinkel (1972) points out the importance of understanding what he calls the 'practical reasoning' which language users employ in making sense of linguistic activity, the process which 'consists of various methods whereby something that a person says or does is recognized to accord with a rule, (Garfinkel 1972: 315). According to Garfinkel, it is not enough simply to specify rules, one has also to explain how the rules are actually used. As he puts it:

In order to describe how actual investigative procedures are accomplished as recognizedly rational actions *in actual occasions*, it is not satisfactory to say that members invoke some rule with which to

define the coherent or consistent or planful, i.e. rational character of their actual activities.
Garfinkel 1972: 322.

To illustrate the distinction between the linguistic and ethnomethodological perspectives on discourse analysis, and to clarify the discussion in this and the preceding section, we might consider some remarks made in Dressler (1970) concerning what he calls the 'semantic deep structure of discourse grammar'. Dressler begins by presenting an example of his own invented data:

> I walked through a park. The trees were already green. In a beech there was a beautiful woodpecker.

He then comments on it as follows:

> This is well-formed discourse because of semantic coherence or more precisely because of semantic anaphora which holds between the semantic components of the lexical items 'park', 'tree' and 'beech'.
> *Dressler 1970: 205.*

What Dressler is doing here is simply (to use Garfinkel's terms) invoking, in a rather vague way, some rule with which to define the coherent character of this example. The implication is that coherence is a quality of the discourse itself which the reader simply has to recognize by reference to the rules at his disposal. From the ethnomethodologist's point of view, the discourse is well-formed because the reader makes it so by working out the relationships between the parts, by realizing how the semantic links which exist between the lexical items mentioned are relevant to the interpretation of this particular discourse. This can be a very complicated matter and it is interesting to compare Dressler's analysis here with that of Sacks (1972). Sacks also begins with a very short piece of discourse, but it is not invented for illustrative purposes but actually attested data. It is a story told by a child which consists of just two 'sentences'.

> The baby cried. The mommy picked it up.

Dressler would probably make very short work of this by referring to the anaphoric use of the pronoun and the definite article in the second sentence. Sacks, however, in the typical manner of the ethnomethodologists, investigates in detail what kinds of procedures are involved in realizing the value of these linguistic elements in the creative endeavour of making sense. (For a closer comparison between the approaches exemplified by Dressler and Sacks, see Widdowson 1973: Chapter 9).

The difference between the linguistic and ethnomethodological perspectives on the analysis of discourse, the first examining the meaning potential of sentences as a capacity for generating discourse structures and the second examining procedures whereby discourse is actually realized, is expressed by Cicourel in the following way:

> Linguistic and ethnomethodological approaches to the problem of meaning differ markedly. The former has stressed formal properties of language which would be relevant for the development of logical relationships and rules to describe the association between sound patterns and the objects, events or experiences to which they refer. The latter approach has been concerned with the process whereby rules said to cover interactional settings are constructed, as well as with the assessment of claimed measurement of the actual implementation of rules in specific circumstances. Ethnomethodology emphasizes the interpretative work required to recognize that an abstract rule exists which could fit a particular occasion, while linguists minimize the relevance of interactional context-sensitive features when stressing the importance of syntactic rules for semantic analysis. *Cicourel 1973: 100.*

What Cicourel says here can, of course, be referred to the two points of departure for discourse analysis which were outlined in Section 3. But as we have seen, the linguistic, sentence-based approach can be extended so as to be of relevance to 'interactional context-sensitive features' of language in use. It is less evident whether the ethnomethodological approach to analysis can be adapted to take more account of the properties of the language system. A good deal of ethnomethodological work is strongly reminiscent of literary criticism: perceptive and enlightening things are said about how meanings are created but there is little precise statement about the linguistic resources that are brought to bear in the task. In Sacks' analysis of the child's story, which was referred to earlier (Sacks 1972), for example, the knowledge of semantic rules which is applied in the interpretation is transposed from a linguistic to a sociological key, and there is no attempt to relate the analysis to work done in linguistics at all. We may agree with Cicourel that the two approaches 'differ markedly' but advances in the understanding of discourse depend on the two approaches reconciling their differences.

6 Current problems

In this last section I want to try to draw together the threads of what has been a somewhat discursive discussion by considering in outline some of the major problems in discourse analysis that seem to me to emerge from it. These are problems which I think have to be resolved if discourse analysis is to develop from its present rather tentative and unco-ordinated beginnings.

The first of these problems concerns the reconciliation of the different approaches that I have discussed in the preceding sections. From this discussion has emerged a distinction between the rules that people can be said to know in the abstract and the procedures which they employ in applying these rules in the production and interpretation of actual instances of discourse. Broadly speaking, a sentence-based approach will tend towards an account of discourse which focuses on rules to the relative neglect of procedures, whereas a discourse-based approach will tend towards an account which focuses on procedures to the relative neglect of rules. I have argued here that a satisfactory approach will have to take both rules and procedures into account and devise a model which establishes a relationship between them. To consider just one example. In the system of analysis proposed in Sinclair and Coulthard (1975), a number of 'acts' are defined, of which the following are examples:

directive Realized by imperative. Its function is to request a non linguistic response.

clue Realized by statement, question, command, or moodless item . . . It functions by providing additional information which helps the pupil to answer the elicitation or comply with the directive.
Sinclair and Coulthard 1975: 41.

In the case of the directive, there is a correspondence between the meaning potential of the imperative sentence and its realization in discourse as a directive act. Thus the rule specifying meaning potential can be directly drawn upon in the procedure for interpreting an utterance as a directive. In the case of the clue, however, there is no similar linguistic rule that the language user can refer to: he has to make sense of the utterance by relying entirely on the context of its occurrence, to work out whether what is said can be seen as counting as additional information or not. Does this mean that *any* sentence can be used as a clue, that there is in effect no connection between what the sentences mean by virtue of linguistic rules and what its use can be made to mean by virtue of interpretative procedures?

These two definitions of different acts point to another problem. It will be noticed that the directive is said to be realized by a kind of sentence, the imperative, whereas the clue is said to be realized by a number of illocutionary acts, including a command. But how can an act be realized by another act? Do we have to say that on a particular occasion, for example, a clue is realized by a command which is realized in turn by an imperative sentence? If so, then it would appear to be the case that the utterance functions as two acts at the same time. How, then, are these two simultaneous acts, clue and command, to be distinguished?

I think it is necessary to make a distinction between two types of communicative activity. The first relates to the way in which the propositions which are expressed in a discourse are organized and managed, how the interaction is negotiated between participants. This activity is carried out by the performance of what we might call *inter-active acts* (a term coined by my colleague Hugh Trappes-Lomax). Thus, the initiation of an exchange, the prompting of a reply, the introduction of a topic for discussion, and the giving of a clue, are all interactive acts: they create discourse structure by organizing its propositional content, and they are defined internally as it were by reference to their structural function. The acts discussed by Sinclair and Coulthard are, it seems to me, essentially of this type. But illocutionary acts of the kind discussed in Searle (1969) and, from another point of view, in Labov (1972a) are rather different. They are defined independently of their structural function in context, although the context must provide for the realization of the conditions which must be met for them to be effectively performed. Thus, I may perform the interactive act of, let us say, introducing a topic for discussion while at the same time performing the illocutionary act of definition or description. Illocutionary acts are essentially social activities which relate to the world outside the discourse, whereas interactive acts are essentially ways of organizing the discourse itself and are defined by their internal function. To clarify the distinction, we might consider the following short exchange:

A Doorbell!
B I'm in the bath.
A OK.

Now if we consider this from an interactive point of view, we might wish to say (in the manner of Sinclair and Coulthard) that here we have an exchange consisting of three moves, opening, answering, and follow-up respectively, and that the first of these moves is expounded by a single act, let us say a directive, the second by another single act, let us say a reply, and the third by yet another single act, let us say, an accept. In describing the exchange in this way we have given an account of its interactive structure. But this is only a partial account of what is going on here. If we assume that A and B (her husband, let us say) know that the ringing of the doorbell is audible to both of them, then in accordance with general interpretative procedures discussed in Section 5, B will recognize that A's utterance is not informative. He will then proceed to look for its relevance and will note that the situation is such as to lead A to suppose that the conditions obtain for her utterance to count as a request for action. B's utterance can now be interpreted as an indication to A that one of these conditions (condition 2 in Labov's rule, cited in Section 5) does not in fact obtain. The illocutionary force of his utterance, therefore, is that of offering an excuse for not complying with what he understands to be A's request. Now A's next remark can be seen as an acceptance of B's excuse and therefore as a cancellation of the original request but at the same time it is an undertaking to carry out the action herself. The situation is not unlike that between mother and daughter which is discussed by Labov and which was referred to earlier. Thus B's utterance can be interpreted as having both the interactive value of reply and the illocutionary value of excuse, and A's second utterance can be interpreted as having both the interactive value of accept and the illocutionary value of under-taking. What about A's first utterance? Here it would seem that interactive and illocutionary function converge, and that the term *directive* is equally applicable to one type of act as to the other. The question is whether there are other acts which have similar dual function and in general whether we can find some principled way of associating interactive and illocutionary functions and of accommodating them both within the same model of discourse.

One major problem in discourse analysis, then, has to do with the relationship between the meaning potential of sentences and the realized meaning of utterances in context. A second has to do with the relationship between interactive and illocutionary function. I want, now, to mention a third problem: the relationship between procedures which result in what I will call immediate interpretation and those which result in what I will call selective interpretation.

The procedures which have been discussed in this paper have been those concerned with immediate interpretation. That is to say, they have to do with the processing of meaning, utterance by utterance, as it emerges sequentially in the discourse. But interpretation also works on a more selective level. Some of the meanings we take in as we listen or read are almost immediately discarded as not having a longer term relevance: their function is to facilitate communication, to provide a setting for the main information which is to be conveyed. Some are restructured into conceptual patterns which may bear very little relationship with the patterns of discourse structure within which they were originally presented. The procedures which are employed for immediate intake of meanings and which probably relate to the func-tioning of short term memory, are not the same as those employed for the selective organization of meanings whereby they are related to existing conceptual patterns and are, as it were, prepared for storage in long term memory. Let me illustrate what I mean by immediate and selective interpretation by considering the following passage (cited and discussed in Nyyssonen 1977).

> Pliny the Elder in his highly unreliable Natural History gives directions for distinguishing a genuine diamond. It should be put, he says, on a blacksmith's anvil and smitten with a heavy hammer as hard as possible: if it breaks it is not a true diamond. It is likely that a good many valuable stones were destroyed in this way because Pliny was muddling up hardness and toughness. Diamond is the hardest of all substances, but it is quite brittle so that, even if one could get it cheaply in large pieces, it would not be a very useful structural substance.

By using procedures of immediate interpretation we would go through this passage and work out the value of the propositions and their interactive and illocutionary function as they appeared in sequence as elements in the ongoing development of the discourse. But not all of the information here is of equal importance. At a selective level we might recognize that the essential function of the passage as a whole is that it in the first place explains what is meant by a useful material and secondly distinguishes between the concepts of hardness and toughness. All of the business about Pliny and his Natural History is unnecessary at this level: it is only required as a facilitating device to introduce the main topic at the immediate level of interpretation.

The question of the relationship between immediate and selective interpretation procedures leads us to another problem, and one which has particularly exercised the minds of the ethnomethodologists. This has to do with the status of the analyst's description of discourse from the vantage point of the detached third person observer vis-à-vis the participants' actual experience of the interaction as first and second persons. And if we decide to adopt the latter perspective, do we assume the role of the first person producer or the second person receiver? This question raises the difficulty of establishing correspondence between the first person's intention and the second person's interpretation, which is perhaps especially evident in written discourse where there is interactivity without interaction and where, therefore, there is no possibility of arriving at mutually acceptable meanings by open negotiation.

All of these problems raise issues of a complex kind beyond the competence of any single discipline and well beyond the scope of this present paper.

Notes

First published in Gutknecht 1977.

10 Rules and procedures in discourse analysis

It seems to me that the central issue in discourse analysis relates to the old problem of distinguishing between what people know and what people do. It has been generally assumed that the essential facts regarding what people do with their language can be accounted for by rules describing their knowledge, that performance is a projection of competence. The proposing of an extended notion of competence to embrace a knowledge of how linguistic forms are used in the performance of appropriate communicative acts has not essentially altered the basic assumption that knowledge in some sense *determines* behaviour. It is still generally held that communicative activity is rule-*governed*, with the implication that once the rules are specified we automatically account for how people use language.

But in what sense do rules *determine* behaviour, and how do they *govern* our actions? The fact that there is considerable room for manoeuvre in individual behaviour makes it clear that there are no absolute constraints upon us. A good deal of what we do, linguistically and otherwise, seems not to conform exactly to rules but a manipulation of rules to suit particular occasions. Now, is this individual variation, this freedom of speech, so random as to be beyond the scope of systematic inquiry? If not, there would appear to be two possibilities: either the rules for knowledge which have been specified are not (are not yet at least) sufficiently refined to capture these aspects of use, although in principle they can be so refined; or we need to formulate statements about behaviour which are not expressed in the form of rules, or at least not in the form of the same kind of rules as are used to account for knowledge.

I do not think that it is possible to account for how people behave simply by specifying rules for knowledge, whether these relate to linguistic or communicative competence. It seems to me that if one attempts to do so, one gets into all kinds of difficulties. How, for example, do we explain stylistic innovation and our ability to interpret its meaning and appreciate its effect? There has been a tendency among some generative grammarians to dismiss such phenomena as metaphor, for instance, as in some sense aberrant ways of using language and of course it may be convenient to take this view when constructing a sentence grammar. But metaphor surely lies at the heart of our everyday communicative behaviour. What seems to be abnormal is *non*-metaphorical communication, a strict conformity to rule. Indeed, if language users were strict conformists, their language would presumably lose its capacity for adaption and gradually fossilize.

Now of course innovatory uses of language are understood *in relation* to our knowledge of rules. But how do we bring these rules to bear? How do we use them in the production and interpretation of instances of communicative behaviour? It cannot simply be a matter of correlation: we do not just *identify* instances of use as manifesting the rules we already know. We draw upon our knowledge of pre-existing rules, we create discourse and commonly bring new rules into existence by so doing. All competence is transitional in this sense. Knowledge and behaviour are interdependent: what we do is to some degree relatable to what we know, but what we do also extends the scope of our knowledge. This, I take it, is what learning means. It seems to me that the central task in discourse analysis must be the investigation of this interrelationship.

So I want to suggest a distinction between *rules*, which represent what we know and to which we make reference when we use language, and the *procedures* we employ in realizing the communicative import of language in use. I suppose one might call these procedures rules of performance but this term 'performance' is not free of the taint of dogma and its use here might suggest, firstly, that these rules are of less immediate concern than those relating to knowledge—competence rules—and secondly that they are dependent upon them unilaterally, that the competence rules 'underlie' performance rules. But I want to suggest that both kinds of 'rule' have a claim on our concern and that one kind does not have any natural precedence over the other. I also feel that the notion of rule loses precision when it is applied both to a pre-existing principle and to the manner in which we make appeal to it in actual behaviour. So I think we might find it useful to make a terminological distinction between rule and procedure.

Let me follow established tradition at this point by illustrating the distinction I am trying to make by reference to the game of chess. We may claim that we know how to play the game if we know the moves it is permitted to make with different pieces, that is to say, if we know the constitutive rules of the game. But when we are actually engaging an opponent we do not merely move our pieces in accordance with these rules: we *use* the rules to create openings, to develop a plan of campaign, to make a game of it. Although the moves we make, do, of course, manifest rules and can be referred to as evidence that we know how to play (that we know that the different pieces can only be moved in

certain specific preordained ways), what is of interest to the players (and
the observers of the game) is the manner in which these rules are being
manipulated, the procedures whereby each player tries to get into a
favourable position and which demonstrate his skill in using his
knowledge of the rules. At any point in the game each player is faced
with a number of possibilities, created by his own manoeuvres as
limited by the manoeuvres of his opponent, and he chooses one of the
possibilities, anticipating his opponent's move, and of course shifting
the whole pattern of the game at the same time. As I shall suggest
presently, it is very like conversation. Now certain procedures may in
the course of time take on the status of rules. I know nothing about the
history of chess, nor of the conventions that are held to constitute
acceptable chess behaviour in particular groups of players, but I would
suppose that as certain procedures become common practice they
assume the role of rules and are considered to be constitutive of the
game. So I should think it likely that there is change and variation in
chess just as there is change and variation in language and that in both
cases they proceed from particular ways of using the existing rules.

I want now to make a distinction between two kinds of rule. The first
kind, which I will refer to as *rules of usage*, account for linguistic
competence in the Chomskyan sense: they represent the language user's
knowledge of the formal systems of his language. We might say that
they constitute his basic grammatical source of reference. The second,
which I will refer to as *rules of use*, account for the language user's
knowledge of speech acts and can be said to constitute his basic communicative source of reference. The kind of inquiry conducted in
Austin (1962) and Searle (1969), for example, is directed towards a
formulation of rules of use. Such rules relate to our knowledge of what
it is to promise, warn, predict, insult, and so on, of what certain
activities, not necessarily linguistic, conventionally count as.

Both rules of usage and rules of use are subject to variation. Chomsky
and Searle deal in ideal cases: sentences and acts in standardized
abstraction. But just as there are different kinds of usage operating in
dialects, so there are different kinds of use operating in different
universes of discourse. For example, we may know what it is to explain
something and what constitutes agreement within the conventions
accepted in our particular area of social operation, but it does not follow
that we know what counts as a scientific explanation or a legal agreement. Problems arise when we attempt to transfer rules of use from one
universe of discourse to another. I take it that one of the central concerns
of formal education is to resolve this problem and to extend the
repertoire of such rules.

One of the central concerns in linguistic description, on the other
hand, is the specification of the relationship between these two kinds of

rule. Can we, for example, incorporate illocutions into the modality component of sentences as appears to be proposed in Ross (1970)? Can we not simply deal with speech act analysis in terms of the semantic analysis of performative verbs, as is proposed in Fillmore (1971)? What is the relationship between the semantics of performative verbs recorded in a lexicon and accounted for, therefore, as usage, and the pragmatics of actual communication which attempts to account for the acts that these verbs are customarily used to refer to, and which therefore has to do with use? Is the knowledge of what a verb like *promise* means the same as knowing how to promise as a social activity? Questions like these appear against a background of old issues like the relationship between sign and concept, and between language, thought, and behaviour.

And questions like these are sometimes confused with questions of another kind: those which relate to the link between rules and procedures. Questions concerning the relationship between different kinds of rule (whether, for example, illocutions can be accommodated in the base component of a generative grammar) are different from (though, I assume, ultimately related to) questions concerning the manner in which particular acts are realized in particular circumstances.

How the uttering of a certain linguistic form comes to take on the illocutionary force of a promise, request, explanation, or what have you, has to do with the procedure of making sense. Rules of use are one thing, but *procedures* of use are another. Let us consider an example. Labov proposes a number of what he calls 'preconditions' for the performance of the act of ordering or requesting action. The specification of such preconditions is, in effect, like Searle's characterization of different speech acts, a formulation of rules of use. But Labov then goes on to demonstrate how these rules are deployed in actual behaviour, how speakers put their knowledge to work in creating coherent discourse. Thus, having defined the act of ordering in terms of four necessary preconditions, he then describes what I would wish to call a procedure whereby a particular utterance is taken as counting as this particular act. He expresses this procedure as follows:

> If A makes a request for information of B about whether an action X has been performed, or at what time TX will be performed, and the four preconditions hold, then A will be heard as making a request for action.
> *Labov 1972a: 256.*

It will be noted that it is taken for granted that a request for information will be recognized as self-evident here, but of course one will need to describe the procedure whereby *this* act is realized in discourse by reference to *its* rules. In the paper referred to above, Labov leaves one with the impression that he does not see the relationship between rules and procedures as particularly problematic. This is not the impression one gets from the work of the ethnomethodologists.

In a well-known paper, Sacks, for example, investigates what it is that enables us to hear the two utterances 'The baby cried. The mommy picked it up' as a complete and coherent narrative (Sacks 1972). His investigation makes reference to what he calls 'membership categorization devices'. These consist of collections of membership categories and application rules. The former would appear to be semantic constructs and to be, therefore, Sacks' somewhat idiosyncratic expressions of rules of usage. His application rules, on the other hand, refer to the manner in which the language user's knowledge of such devices is used to make sense of the particular instance of discourse he is concerned with.

One of these application rules runs as follows:

> If some population of persons is being categorized, and if a category from some device's collection has been used to categorize a first member of the population, then that category, or other categories of the same collection *may* be used to categorize further members of the population.

A corollary to this 'rule' is what Sacks calls a 'hearer's maxim', which runs as follows:

> If two or more categories are used to categorize two or more members of some population, and those categories can be heard as categories from the same collection, then: hear them that way.
> *Sacks 1972: 333.*

There are a number of features in Sacks' description which I find a little obscure, but it seems to me that what he is trying to capture are the procedures which language users employ when they make communicative sense of language data, the manner in which they *use* their knowledge of semantics, or, as Sacks would have it, membership categorization devices as encoded in their language.

Both Labov and Sacks are concerned with the way a pair of actual utterances are recognized as being meaningfully related. In the case of Labov, the focus of attention is on the relationship between procedures and what I have called rules of use. In the case of Sacks, the focus is on the relationship between procedures and what I have called rules of usage. Following on from this observation, I now want to suggest that in discourse analysis we are concerned with procedures of two sorts: those which relate to rules of usage and which realize propositional development, which I will call *cohesion procedures*, and those which relate to rules of use and which realize the illocutionary development of discourse, which I will call *coherence procedures*.

By cohesion procedures I mean the way the language user traces propositional development in discourse by, for example, realizing the appropriate value of anaphoric elements, the way in which a sequence of units of information encapsulated in linguistic units is provided with a conceptual unity. The devices of thematization (cf. Halliday 1967/1968, 1973) and grammatical cohesion (cf. Hasan 1968, Halliday and Hasan 1976) can be described by rules of usage, just as can Sacks' categorization devices, but how these devices are actually put to use on particular occasions is a matter of procedure. How, for example, do we select the appropriate value for a pronoun when there is more than one grammatically possible referential link? At what point is it necessary to relexicalize a reference? When does a discourse take on a life of its own so that the cumulative effect of what has preceded in some way takes precedence over the individual meanings? When do the expectations created by the propositional development within a particular instance of discourse override the meanings of particular propositions? To put it another way, when does the unity of the whole cease to depend on the separate signification of the parts? Questions like these have to do with the procedures whereby language users draw upon their knowledge of rules to synthesize meaning in discourse.

By coherence procedures I mean the way in which the language user realizes what communicative act is being performed in the expression of particular propositions, and how different acts are related to each other in linear and hierarchical arrangements. Thus the recognition that a particular expression counts as an invitation rather than an order is a matter of realizing that the context provides for the fulfilment of one set of conditions rather than another. Again, the adjustment of interpretation in the light of new evidence is also a matter of coherence procedure. I may, for example, interpret a particular remark as a casual observation and then be obliged to revise this interpretation as the discourse proceeds and as it becomes apparent that the remark was intended as, let us say, an explanation.

But coherence is not, I think, simply a matter of illocutionary connections in dissociation from propositional development. Procedures of cohesion and coherence are not entirely distinct, any more than are rules of usage and use. I think that there are two ways of looking at the communicative activity that goes on in the creation of discourse coherence. We can, on the one hand, consider a particular instance of discourse as a large scale illocutionary act of the Searlean sort and establish which constituent acts there are within it, these acts in effect realizing the set of conditions which define the large scale act. Thus, we might wish to characterize a particular instance of discourse as a report consisting of such constituent acts as definition, hypothesis, description, and so on. This kind of description focuses on the communicative intent of the speaker/writer in so far as it relates to the illocutionary acts he wishes to perform. In this view, propositions are only of interest to the extent that they serve to realize conditions on different acts. A second kind of approach would focus not so much on *what* communication is achieved in a discourse as on *how* the communication is achieved. Attention here is directed at the interaction management aspects of use. In this approach, different communicative acts are defined internally, as it were, with reference to their function as elements of discourse structure. Examples of such 'interactive' acts would be agreement, disagreement, initiation, response, elicitation, and most of the communicative units described in Sinclair and Coulthard (1975). With acts of this kind, the proposition does not simply enter into the picture as a condition but is central to the act itself. We might say, in fact, that in the case of illocutionary acts of the Searlean kind the proposition is ancillary to the act, whereas in the case of these interactive acts the act is ancillary to the proposition.

We might regard interactive acts, then, as instruments of propositional development. In this respect they serve as the link between cohesion and coherence procedures. But now the question might arise: how can interactive procedures operate when there is no interaction, as would appear to be the case in written discourse? This question touches on the relationship between production and interpretation. It seems to me that all discourse is interactive and that the same interpretative procedures are brought into play whether one is involved in the actual production of discourse or not. When a spoken interaction takes place each participant develops his own scheme which he adjusts according to what his interlocutor says. I am sure that it is a mistake to suppose that one participant's responses are simply reactions to what the other has said: they are, rather, readjustments to his own communicative intents. As I have already suggested, verbal interactions resemble games of chess: each participant works out his moves in advance and modifies them tactically as the encounter develops. In a serious game, analogous to academic argument, each player will be trying to project his own pattern on the game and to force his opponent into error, or at least into a move which can be turned to advantage. The producer of written discourse is playing with an unseen, and often, to some degree at least, an unknown player, although he will usually have a fair idea of what skill to allow for and will play the game accordingly. In the case of written discourse, the player/producer anticipates his opponent's moves by writing them into the discourse. In consequence, the game may well proceed in a way which is different from how the writer originally intended it to go because his anticipation modifies his intentions. And the reader too begins to anticipate from the first move onwards, and plays his own game as he reads. When we talk of monologue and dialogue we refer to the overt differences of surface performance, but it seems likely that the same interactive interpretative process underlies both.

Let me now draw a simple sketch map of what I have been trying to work out. We have rules of usage and rules of use and these together constitute what a language user knows. The relationship between them is problematic but a likely link is modality. We have procedures which represent what a language user does with his knowledge in the creation, productively or receptively, of discourse which has propositional cohesion and illocutionary coherence. A possible link between these is interactivity. Interactivity, then, mediates between the procedures of cohesion and coherence in much the same way as modality mediates between the rules of usage and the rules of use. We might express these relationships as follows:

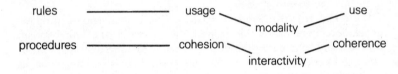

There is a deceptive neatness about this, an enchanting simplicity when viewed from a distance. But there are, of course, all kinds of difficulties. which do not disappear simply by having a frame put around them. A major one has to do with orientation. In what I have said so far, for example, I have assumed that rules and procedures can be inferred from an observation of data; that the methodology of discourse analysis is in this respect straightforward. But it is really not straightforward at all because what the analyst observes is not necessarily what the participant experiences. This is the problem of ethnocentric contamination which social anthropologists have been long aware of, as have researchers into child language acquisition, itself a kind of special branch of social anthropology. It is the same problem which has particularly exercised the minds of scholars working within ethnomethodology. It underlies the conflicts between stylistic analysis and literary criticism.

To put the matter simply, there are two possible methodological perspectives on discourse analysis. One can, on the one hand, deal with instances of discourse from the point of view of the third person analyst: that is to say, one can treat discourse in detachment from its instantiation, after the event, as a product. On the other hand, one can deal with discourse from the point of view of the participants caught, as it were, in the act; that is to say, one can treat discourse as a process. To return once more to our game of chess. At the end of a particular game, one can specify the moves that have been made and thereby give an account of the structure of that particular encounter. But this account does not of course record how the game developed from the players' point of view, it does not reveal the experience of planning moves, modifying them to counter the moves of the opponent, and so on. A product analysis does not capture how the game assumed the structure it did assume, the process of the game's development.

I am not at all sure myself how far process analysis is possible. The ethnomethodologists seem to make claims that they are dealing with process, with the ongoing accomplishment of practical reasoning, but although they make inferences about process, they typically deal with products. There is no evidence, to my knowledge, that they have attempted to conduct experiments which might yield information about how the participants see the discourse at a particular point in its development and what controls their choice of options at this point. A process analysis should presumably take an interest not only in the paths that are taken but in those which are not but could have been.

In fact, I think there is a general and natural tendency for the analyst to withdraw from involvement, to come to terms with his data by putting himself at a distance from it and so reducing it in perspective to methodological size. The analyst is inclined to move from process to product, and then to convert procedures inferred from product into rules of use and then, wherever possible, into rules of usage. There is a comfortable sense of security to be found in the specification of precise invariant rules and we shall perhaps never feel really at our ease until we can express all behaviour as knowledge within a unitary theory of linguistic description; until all the creative procedures of human beings are expressed in terms of exact rules. But one sometimes wonders whether this sense of security is worth the price that one might be paying for it.

Notes

Paper presented at a seminar called 'The development of discourse and conversation', arranged by the Department of Psychology, University of Edinburgh, May 1975, and published in *The Development of Conversation and Discourse*. Edinburgh University Press, 1979.

Procedures of interpretation

In this section, discourse is discussed not as an artefact to be studied objectively but as something achieved by the application of interpretative procedures. The focus of attention shifts from the analyst to the language user. At the same time we move to a more pedagogic position on the applied linguistic spectrum and consider the consequences of this view for the practical teaching of language. There is an implication here that it is the language user's model of language rather than the analyst's that is more relevant for the learner and this prefigures the argument of the papers in Section Seven.

Paper 11 in this section resembles Paper 8 in the preceding one in that it shows how a change of perspective on the nature of language and the purpose in learning it can lead to a reassessment of the value of previously misprized pedagogic activities: translation on the one hand and the teaching of poetry on the other.

Paper 12 deals with the question of authenticity (a question which I return to in the final section). This is, I believe, an important issue because it has been somewhat uncritically assumed in some quarters that a communicative approach calls for the learner's immediate exposure to genuine instances of language use. This assumption is, it seems to me, open to question on two counts. First, it confuses the ends of language learning with the means by which they are achieved. Secondly, it represents language anthropomorphically, as it were: as if it operated with a life of its own without human involvement. Authenticity, I argue, is not inherent in language but is a function of appropriate response and is realized when sender and receiver engage in interaction mediated by the language.

This matter of mediation is taken up in Paper 13, which concentrates on the question of interactivity in written discourse, a notion which appeared in the previous section. In this paper the argument is that there can be no interpretation without inter-action and examples are given of pedagogic activities which will develop an awareness in the learner of the necessarily interactive character of the interpretative process of reading.

11 Interpretative procedures and the importance of poetry

It has long been fashionable to regard poetry as irrelevant to the learning of foreign languages. If it is sometimes reluctantly allowed admittance, it is usually after the main business on the language learning agenda has been completed, as a kind of light entertainment which practical people need not take seriously but which may serve to stimulate interest. In this paper I want to suggest that poetry can be incorporated as an integrative element into a language course and that, properly presented, it can serve as an invaluable aid in the development of communicative competence. I shall argue that although poetry is an abnormal use of language, its interpretation involves the same essentially normal procedures as are required for the understanding of any discourse and that it is precisely because of its abnormality that poetry can be used to direct the learner's attention to these interpretative procedures. The expression 'interpretative procedures' comes from Cicourel (Cicourel 1973) and I shall in the course of my argument draw on (my understanding of) certain ethnomethodological notions regarding the interpretation of discourse. This is because I believe that these notions provide the theoretical perspective which indicates the way poetry can be reinstated as a practical element in a language learning programme.

One can sympathize with the desire of the proponents of structural grading to exclude poetry from their syllabuses. A rationalization of this desire might take the following form. We may say (simplifying somewhat) that there are two main ways in which poetry has traditionally been represented in teaching, and neither of them appears to have much bearing on the practical business of learning a foreign language: in fact they would appear to be contrary to sound language teaching principles. The first represents poems as linguistic puzzles which need to be solved by detailed explanation and the second represents them as aesthetic objects whose essential message can be intuitively perceived by exposure and exhortation. The first way represents poems as complicated texts with little or no reference to their character as discourse and the second way represents poems as a kind of superior discourse conveying special messages without much reference to the way textual features are used in the conveyance. Neither of these representations commends itself to teachers whose concern is to present language in a carefully controlled manner through a structural syllabus so that each element introduced should be thoroughly understood. The first introduces complexities and requires explanations, whereas it is precisely explanation and complexity which the structural syllabus, as a matter of principle, seeks by careful grading to avoid. The second representation draws the learner's attention away from an exact understanding of linguistic elements whereas it is precisely this close attention to detail which characterizes the design of a structural syllabus. In short, poetry can be seen as a potential source of disruption in the step-by-step learning process: something which might be introduced with circumspection to add variety and relieve boredom but not to be regarded as an intrinsic element in the course itself. A kind of side-show.

It must be noted, however, that this rationalization does not provide a case against the inclusion of poetry in a language learning course in principle. It provides a case against including these particular representations of poetry in a language course based on structuralist ideas. But there are other ways of representing poetry and other ways of approaching the teaching of language.

Over the past few years a number of people have recommended a shift of emphasis from a concentration on the teaching of the language system to a concentration on the teaching of the actual social uses to which it is put. It has been suggested that the principles underlying the structural approach should be revised to accommodate the teaching of communicative functions and in some quarters there have been somewhat more extreme counsels which recommend the rejection of the structural approach altogether. As yet, little in the way of actual teaching materials has been produced which embodies these suggestions and exposes them to tests of pedagogic viability, and it is far too early to say to what extent this shift of emphasis can reasonably be adopted as an approach of general relevance to all teaching situations. But whatever difference of opinion there might be regarding the most effective approach to the design of language teaching courses, everyone would agree that their ultimate purpose must be to develop an ability to handle language as an instrument of communication. Although there may be a delimiting of aims which restricts the skills to be acquired, and of the areas of social activity in which communication takes place, it will be generally agreed that there must be no restriction which denies the learner access to an ability to use the language as a means of communication.

Ultimately, then, the aim of language teaching must be to develop a communicative competence in the language being learnt, although there is room for disagreement as to how this aim might be achieved in different circumstances. Now, having said that, it seems to me that the principal difficulty associated with the structural approach as usually practised has always been the problem of how to present linguistic elements in extra-linguistic situations or linguistic contexts in such a way as to make the learners aware of the communicative potential of these elements. If at a certain point in the syllabus, for example, one has to introduce a certain linguistic element (a 'sentence pattern' or 'vocabulary item') one might, following time-honoured practice, contrive a classroom situation or a written passage representing a context in which this element can be made to occur with a fair degree of frequency. This kind of contrivance can be an effective means of indicating what meaning a grammatical feature of a lexical item has as an element of the language system, what I have called elsewhere its signification. But it has two rather serious limitations.

In the first place, since one's purpose is to introduce and establish the form and the signification of the element in focus, one is concerned with the possibility and not the probability of occurrence. That is to say, one is concerned with exemplifying the structure concerned as fully as possible and so one's aim is to produce a pedagogically appropriate text. But if the density of exemplification is achieved at the expense of the probability of such density occurring in any normal and non-contrived use of the language, then one produces language which has little value as discourse. Hence one cannot be demonstrating the communicative function of the structure: one is manifesting its form and signification in a text but one is not showing how it realizes communicative value in a discourse. To do this, one would have to think of a situation or a context in which the recurrence of the linguistic structure in question constituted normal use. Though this is possible, it is difficult; and in practice it is rarely achieved.

The first limitation has to do with the teacher's difficulty in reconciling the need for repetition with a natural communicative use of language. The second limitation has to do with the learner's difficulty in abstracting from particular situations and contexts more general conditions of appropriateness. The point is that the communicative value of a particular linguistic element is not a function of its relationship with the context or situation as a whole, but of its relationship with a set of essential conditions for which the context or situation simply provides the concrete realization. When Firth talked about 'context of situation' he made reference to 'The relevant features of participants' and 'The relevant objects' (Firth 1957: 182). The notion of relevance is crucial. For, confronted with a piece of language in a context or context of situation, how does the learner recognize which features and objects are relevant to the communicative import of the language and which are not? Those which are relevant represent the conditions whereby the piece of language counts as a particular act of communication. If one simply brings together linguistic elements with contexts or situations the learner is left to work out the relevant conditions for himself. Obviously he cannot be said to have acquired communicative competence if he only learns a fixed connection between a particular linguistic form and a particular context or situation. For someone to correctly interpret discourse he needs to be able to recognize relevant conditions in situations he has never encountered before, and the manner in which these give value to structures he may never have specifically associated with these situations in the past. Linguistic ability must be essentially creative. The acquisition of communicative competence involves the learning of interpretative procedures whereby particular situational or contextual factors are recognized as realizations of conditions which determine the communicative function of linguistic elements.

What a language course must ultimately develop in the learner, then, is a technique for deriving the communicative value of linguistic elements as they occur in discourse. The learning of the form and the signification of these linguistic elements, which the structural syllabus promotes, represents a set of facts, a body of knowledge upon which this technique operates to create communication. And communication is created both by receiver and producer. It is common to speak of receptive and productive skills (and even active and passive skills) but these terms refer only to the physiological activity involved. From the cognitive point of view both the initiation and the interpretation of discourse involve creative activity. Learning to comprehend efficiently involves the activation of interpretative techniques or procedures and the same procedures are brought into play in reverse when discourse is composed.

This view of what is involved in realizing the communicative potential of language derives essentially from ideas propounded by the ethnomethodologists. I will not be so imprudent as to lay claim to a complete understanding of what they have to say. Indeed since it is one of their principal contentions that complete understanding is not attainable, they presumably would not want anyone to strive for it. I believe in fact that the very views which they express require that they be expressed obscurely, and that the best way of approaching much of their work is to treat it as if it were a kind of literary writing, a creative rather than an expository form of discourse. Be that as it may, what does emerge fairly clearly from the obscurity is the concept of discourse not as the manifestation of preordained meanings, but as a dynamic process which involves what Garfinkel calls 'practical reasoning' (Garfinkel 1967). Discourse is created as a 'contingent ongoing accomplishment' whereby the participants in an interchange attribute particular value to linguistic elements as they are conditioned by the context and the situation in which they occur. The basic insight that the ethnomethodologists express is that the meanings conveyed in the use of language are not subject to precise specification beforehand in grammars and dictionaries but have to be discovered in the development of the discourse itself. The linguist has led us to think that meanings are fixed in a static well-defined system and subject to variation in 'actual performance', which in some sense is a distortion, whereas the ethnomethodologists suggest that instead of thinking of variation in meaning we might more profitably think of meaning in variation. In this view, variation cannot be idealized out from linguistic data: it is at the very centre of the communicative process. If this is so, then of course a generative grammar which describes linguistic competence in the Chomskyan sense cannot by definition deal with discourse at all.

One form of discourse which has been a source of some embarrassment to generative grammarians for some time is poetry. In poetry we very often find what Katz calls 'semi-sentences' and 'nonsense strings' (Katz 1964). Now if a grammar represents a speaker's knowledge of his language, how does it come about that he knows how to interpret strings which are not well-formed and so cannot be generated by the grammar? This is how Katz puts the problem:

> Though the knowledge a speaker requires to understand well-formed sentences and the knowledge he requires to understand semi-sentences is one and the same, and though a generative grammar can represent all the grammatical knowledge a speaker has and can account for how he is able to understand sentences, yet such a grammar cannot account for how a speaker is able to understand semi-sentences.

This is the somewhat self-contradictory conclusion that he arrives at:

> The task a speaker performs when he understands a semi-sentence involves, in addition to his use of grammatical knowledge, the use of knowledge of another kind.
> *Katz 1964: 402.*

But what is this knowledge of another kind? And how precisely is this knowledge and grammatical knowledge 'used'? Again Katz says that the speaker 'utilizes his knowledge of the structure of the language to find a meaning for something that is not well-formed' (Katz 1964: 414). But of course the speaker must utilize his knowledge of the structure of his language to find meanings in well-formed instances of language use as well. The speaker does not simply require a knowledge of his grammar to interpret discourse: he requires a knowledge of how his grammar is used. And although his grammar can be made manifest as usage by citing isolated sentences contrived by the linguist for the purpose of exemplification, it is not actually realized in use through isolated sentences. Sentences simply serve to manifest grammatical rules but they do not show how these rules are used in the dynamic process of discourse development. A grammar cannot tell us how semi-sentences are understood because if they occur in actual use they are not semi-sentences but elements of a discourse, and a grammar cannot tell us how discourse is understood. It cannot tell us because it does not provide information as to how our grammatical knowledge is actually put to use in communicative behaviour (for further discussion on this and related points see Widdowson 1973).

A number of linguists have pondered on the problem of how to account for what Katz would call semi-sentences and the nonsense strings occurring in poetic discourse, and several suggestions have been made as to how grammatical statements might be framed to make explicit the meaning of deviant strings of this kind and their relationship with well-formed sentences (see Levin 1962, Thorne 1965, Fowler 1969). Interesting though much of this discussion is, it is important to see that it is concerned with a problem of the linguist's own invention. Sentences only exist as the linguist's exemplification of rules within a grammar; and they must by definition be well-formed. Semi-sentences cannot occur in a grammar because they are semi, and they cannot occur anywhere else because they are sentences. They are, in effect, figments of the linguist's imagination.

If we cannot account for the interpretation of discourse, deviant or otherwise, by invoking grammatical knowledge, then how can we account for it? We can account for it, I suggest, by invoking this concept of interpretative procedures. What the ethnomethodologists do when they attempt to explain the nature of these procedures is to focus attention on precisely what is involved in what Katz refers to as the 'use of grammatical knowledge'. There is no 'knowledge of another kind' apart from this and it is these procedures I suggest which are put into operation when we realize the communicative value of linguistic elements in discourse, whether this is poetic or not. In other words, I am suggesting that we interpret poetry in the same way as we interpret other kinds of discourse and that if we did not do so, there would be no way of explaining how poetry is interpreted at all. The difference between the interpretation of poetic and other kinds of discourse is not that we use different procedures, but that in the case of poetic discourse we are more conscious of them. Interpretation is more problematic and so we are inevitably more aware of the process involved. It is this which gives poetry its potential importance in language teaching.

Before going on to develop this last point, let me try to draw together what I have said so far. The kind of structurally graded course which presents grammatical and lexical material so that it appears in a precise step-by-step sequence clearly cannot incorporate poetry as it is commonly represented, that is to say as something linguistically complex which requires explanation, or something vague and aesthetic whose meaning can only be intuitively apprehended. However, a course of this kind, or of any other kind, cannot be said to teach language satisfactorily unless it can also provide learners with the ability to use their linguistic knowledge to create or recreate discourse. The aim of all teaching must be to develop communicative strategies, or cognitive procedures, whereby the language user is able to recognize in a situation or a context just those conditions which operate to provide linguistic elements with their specific value, whether these elements are single lexical items or sentences or combinations of sentences. It is not enough simply to bring bits of language into association with contexts and situations, and leave the learner to work out for himself which contextual or situational features are relevant for the correct interpretation of the language as an instance of communication. A structurally based course, then, must somewhere make provision for the teaching of interpretative procedures, since not otherwise will learners be prepared for their encounter with actual discourse. The structural syllabus is based on the grammarian's orientation to language study and this does not provide a model of description that can deal adequately with discourse. The ethnomethodological orientation, for all the obscurity of its exposition, does provide such a model since it stresses the ongoing creative activity involved in deriving communicative value from linguistic elements as they occur in contexts of use. I suggest that the cognitive procedures that must be brought into operation in the interpretation of discourse containing elements which cannot be put into correspondence with well-formed sentences are the same as those we must employ to make sense of any discourse. The process whereby we interpret poetry is essentially the same process whereby we interpret any other kind of language use, the difference being that in poetic interpretation the process is inevitably more apparent.

Now if it is the case that an understanding of poetry, not as a piece of complex text or as a mysterious message but as a form of discourse, makes us conscious of the procedures we employ in the understanding of any discourse, and if it is the purpose of language courses to develop an awareness of such procedures, then it would seem logical to suppose that poetry can be introduced into such courses to help to develop such an awareness. It should be added that one must, at the same time, take care that the particular poems introduced are graded in terms of textual complexity and abstruseness of message.

Let us consider an example. Let us suppose that the following poem

is judged to be appropriate from these points of view at a particular
stage in a language course:

> *September*
> 1 We sit late, watching the dark slowly unfold:
> No clock counts this.
> When kisses are repeated and the arms hold
> There is no telling where time is.
>
> 5 It is midsummer: the leaves hang big and still:
> Behind the eye a star,
> Under the silk of the wrist a sea, tell
> Time is nowhere.
>
> We stand; leaves have not timed the summer.
> 10 No clock now needs
> Tell we have only what we remember:
> Minutes uproaring with our heads
>
> Like an unfortunate King's and his Queen's
> When the senseless mob rules;
> 15 And quietly the trees casting their crowns
> Into the pools.
> *Ted Hughes*

We will assume that the learner knows the signification of the
grammatical structures and of the lexical items which appear in this
poem, or has access to a dictionary. The question is: knowing these
things, what procedures must be brought to bear to make sense of
expressions like *watching the dark slowly unfold* (line 1), *under the silk
of the wrist* (line 7), and so on. Even if we assume that the learner has
encountered the use of *dark* as a noun, he needs to link its occurrence
here with the expression *We sit late* for him to recognize that here it is
the darkness of night that is being referred to. And this darkness
unfolds. This verb, we will assume, has previously been given a
signification that associates it with object noun phrases which make
reference to tangible substances of a pliant nature: sheets of linen or
paper, for example. But here it is associated with something insubstantial. Clearly for the reader to make sense of this expression, then, he
must recognize that the significations of *dark* and *unfold* are not carried
unmodified into the context: he must realize a kind of mutual conditioning whereby each lexical item draws relevant semantic features from the
other to create a unique concept. The dark is both insubstantial and
substantial, and its unfolding is both perceived (like the unfolding of a
blanket) and imagined (like the unfolding of a story).

Consider now the expression *under the silk of the wrist*. Here the value of *silk* derives from the way it is conditioned by the phrase in which it occurs. The reader is required to select certain semantic features (smoothness and softness, for example) and to disregard others as irrelevant in this instance of use. In other words, he has to employ interpretative procedures to work out in what respect *silk* and *wrist* can be conceptually related as the context requires them to be, bearing in mind that the signification of these items will provide no explicit semantic link.

In the cases we have considered so far, the interpretative procedures are prompted by the syntactic relations which hold between the lexical items concerned. These relations, like bearings drawn on a map, indicate where semantic associations are to be found. It often happens, however (particularly in poetry), that associations are not overtly indicated in this way and the reader then has to discover meanings without the help of an explicit syntactic map. Thus, the syntactic relations between *dark* and *unfold* direct the reader's attention to where his interpretative procedures are to be applied, but there are no such directions to guide the reader to a recognition of the link between this collocation and that of *star-tell* in lines 6–7. An interpretation of this poem requires the reader to free himself from a reliance on syntactic clues and to recognize how a number of collocations (*tell-time, tell-story, clock-time, time-late, time-minutes*, and so on) function in effect like the semantic features of a complex concept which represents the central theme of the poem as a whole.

Mention might also be made of the problem posed by lines 12–14. Here the reader has to realize a verbal value for the noun *uproar*, relate this verb not only with the noun phrase *minutes*, with which it is syntactically linked, but also with the noun phrase *the senseless mob*, with which it is not, thereby establishing a meaning relation between the two noun phrases not indicated by syntactic structure, and not sanctioned by their semantic significations. Apart from this, he has to work out the value of *heads* by recognizing how its meaning here is a function of its association with *uproar, unfortunate*, and *senseless mob*. And so on.

It is not my purpose to conduct a full scale stylistic analysis of this poem (interesting though this would be) but simply to point out the kind of procedure involved in arriving at an interpretation of it as discourse. The obvious lack of correspondence between what words mean as lexical elements of the language code, their signification, and what they are required to mean in the context, their value, obliges the reader to engage in what Garfinkel calls 'practical reasoning'. Furthermore, the problematic nature of the task draws the reader's attention to the procedures he must employ. Let me say again that it seems to me that these procedures can essentially be no different from those we employ in the understanding of any use of language, though in poetry more demands tend to be made of them (hence its importance). To take just one example, the kind of reasoning involved in deriving appropriate value in the case of the lexical items we have just considered would appear to be no different in kind from that required in recognizing the value of the item *commercial* in the following instance of use[1]:

> Pure metals are likely to resist corrosion better than metals containing impurities. Thus pure aluminium resists attack better than a commercial variety.

I believe that if teachers can represent poetry as discourse, along the lines suggested above, they will be able to make learners aware of how they use their linguistic knowledge in the interpretation of poetry, and that this will help to develop in them precisely those cognitive procedures which they need in order to deal with discourse of any kind. Once it is accepted that the ultimate aim of a language teaching course is to develop the ability to create and recreate discourse from the resources of linguistic knowledge, and once it is accepted that poetry can be represented as a kind of discourse in which these processes are particularly open to observation, then I think one can begin to see a way of reinstating poetry as an integrative element in language teaching.

Notes

Paper presented at the third Neuchâtel Colloquium in Applied Linguistics, May 1974, and published in the proceedings: Corder and Roulet 1975.
1 I am indebted to H. J. Nyyssonen for this example.

12 The authenticity of language data

Over recent years we have witnessed an increasing concern on the part of the linguist with the communicative functioning of language. There is a feeling abroad that for a linguistic description to be adequate it must not reduce natural language to an algebraic system but should attempt to account for 'authentic' data, the language user's own experience of language in contexts of use. This movement towards an approximation to authenticity has its dangers: it can lead to a linguistics of anecdote, *ad hoc* observation, and a neglect of methodological principles upon which any systematic account must depend. The shift in perspective within theoretical linguistics has had its influence on language teaching and it is now quite common to find the advocacy of an approach which focuses on communicative activity. The review of what should count as adequacy in linguistic description has led to a reconsideration of the criteria for adequacy in language teaching. But again there are dangers. Too exclusive a concern for 'authentic' language behaviour as communication can lead to a disregard of methodological principles upon which the pedagogy of language teaching must depend. What I want to do in this paper is to point out these dangers by investigating the notion of authenticity with reference to the teaching of English for specific, and particularly academic, purposes.

As I have suggested, applied linguistics has been inspired by recent theoretical explorations of the communicative properties of language to question the effectiveness of a teaching approach which concentrates on the manipulation of structures as an end in itself and to advocate one which takes note of how structures are realized in meaningful communicative behaviour. Both in the theoretical study of language and in the practical teaching of languages communicative competence is in vogue. But although this pedagogic concern for communication derives partly from the influence of a prevailing linguistic fashion, it has been given a particular urgency by changing trends in the English language learning market and the emergence of a new kind of consumer. Previously, the main effort in the teaching of English took place within the context of general primary and secondary education. English was a subject like other subjects and the learner's achievement was measured by examinations designed essentially to validate the syllabus rather than to reflect actual communicative needs. In these circumstances teaching was required to prepare learners for the examination but not (except incidentally) for an encounter with language use. The belief in general was that what was learnt was a kind of investment, audited, as it were, at the examination, which could be realized as something of real communicative value if and when the need arose. Recently, however, English teaching has been called upon to meet the needs of people who have to actually use the language for occupational and academic purposes. In these circumstances, it has to cope with a connection with the real world and provide for immediate communicative needs. The investment is a short term one and its value will be judged on immediate returns. English for special purposes (ESP), whether these be occupational (EOP) or academic (EAP), requires a teaching methodology which will guide learners towards an ability to handle language in use. Its adequacy can only be measured by its success in achieving this aim. In general ELT or EFL, it is desirable to adopt a communicative approach to language teaching, but we are not likely to incur any drastic penalty if we do not do so. But in ESP such an approach is not only desirable but mandatory since if we do not satisfy the communicative requirements of the learners the penalties are likely to be severe: our methodology will be exposed as ineffective and sooner or later we are likely to be out of a job.

Developments in theoretical studies of language and the practical requirements of learners, then, both converge on the need to adopt a communicative perspective in the teaching of ESP, one that will develop communicative competence and prepare the learner for an authentic experience of language. But how do we set about devising procedures which will bring this about? The point of view has been expressed that since our aim is to enable the learner to produce and process actual language use, then we should expose him to authentic language data right away. This view represents an understandable reaction against the kind of contrived language data which is a feature of many textbooks and which is simply cited to demonstrate how the rules of the language system can be manifested in sentences. The following will serve as an example:

> Ali and Bashir are brothers. Every morning they get up at five o'clock and wash their hands and face. They have their breakfast at six o'clock. They have an egg and a banana for their breakfast. They had an egg and a banana for their breakfast yesterday morning. They are having an egg and a banana for their breakfast this morning and they will have an egg and a banana for their breakfast tomorrow morning.

We recognize this as artificial language data which has been contrived for demonstration purposes: it does not carry conviction as actual language behaviour. In this respect it is predominantly an instance of usage rather than of use, and is comparable with the kind of sentences which linguists invent to demonstrate the working of linguistic rules. It is, we might say, linguistic data without being language data.

But although we may recognize and deplore the artificiality of this kind of data as lacking in communicative potential or implication of utterance, does it follow that all contrivance is necessarily to be avoided and that the only data we should expose learners to should be actual, attested instances of use? We can only arrive at a satisfactory answer to such a question by considering what we might mean when we talk about authentic language.

I am not sure that it is meaningful to talk about authentic language as such at all. I think it is probably better to consider authenticity not as a quality residing in instances of language but as a quality which is bestowed upon them, created by the response of the receiver. Authenticity in this view is a function of the interaction between the reader/hearer and the text which incorporates the intentions of the writer/speaker. We do not recognize authenticity as something there waiting to be noticed, we realize it in the act of interpretation. Thus the reason we see the data just cited as artificial is that we cannot easily respond to it as an instance of use: if we read it as an instance of usage, then it satisfies our expectations and becomes authentic as usage. What is objectionable about it, therefore, is not that it is in itself inauthentic but that we make it so by requiring it to satisfy an expectation which it cannot satisfy: it does not allow us to respond authentically to it if we want to regard it as natural language behaviour.

I wish to argue, then, that authenticity has to do with appropriate response. But what does this appropriacy entail? I think we have to take a deep breath at this point and plunge into a consideration of author intentions. Let us suppose that we are confronted with a piece of written discourse. How do we establish an authentic relation with it? We do so, I suggest, by recovering the intentions of the writer. Now it may be objected that it is never possible to know whether or not we have in fact done this, particularly in written discourse where there is no opportunity for the kind of negotiation of meanings which goes on in spoken discourse. But I think the inaccessibility of intentions has been somewhat exaggerated. The writer of a particular instance of discourse may have individual intentions, but he has to convey these through certain conventions which define the kind of discourse he is producing. If conventions did not exist to mediate the communication between writer and reader, then intentions could not be conveyed at all. Some of these conventions are linguistic and relate to the shared knowledge of the language code: others are rhetorical and relate to the shared knowledge of how the code is used in particular kinds of discourse. So when I speak of appropriate response, I mean the reader's interpretation by reference to the conventions associated with a particular discourse type. Authenticity, then, is achieved when the reader realizes the intentions of the writer by reference to a set of shared conventions.

It follows from this definition that a discourse may be written in conformity with a set of conventions, but still lack the quality of authenticity for particular readers. When we have conformity on the part of the writer we may say that the discourse is genuine whether or not it is authentic from the reader's point of view. Thus, for example, I may pick up a genuine novel and read it as a political manifesto, thereby not realizing its authenticity as a work of fiction. In short, I am reading it wrongly. Similarly, if I treat a poem as a sample of language for grammatical analysis, the poem is still a genuine poem but it is not authentic as a poem since I do not treat it like one. One of the difficulties of literary uses of language, of course, is that the conventions are frequently very difficult to recognize and the authenticity of some works of literature is so elusive that people will often deny them any literary status whatever.

Authenticity, then, depends on a congruence of the language producer's intentions and language receiver's interpretation, this congruence being effected through a shared knowledge of conventions. It is clear that if this view is accepted it makes no sense simply to expose learners to genuine language use unless they know the conventions which would enable them to realize it as authentic. Thus, confronted with a class of physics students wanting to learn English so as to read textbooks in their subject, I might be tempted to select passages of discourse which are thematically relevant from a whole range of sources on the assumption that I am thereby furthering the communicative purpose for which the learners need the language. But if I then exploit these passages for the traditional kind of comprehension question, structure exercise, and so on, their authentic potential remains unrealized. I might just as well have selected an extract from the Highway Code or *Winnie the Pooh*. The fact that the data is genuine is irrelevant.

If we are to achieve the kind of communicative goals in teaching that ESP requires of us, then we have to confront the problem of how to develop in the learner that awareness of conventions of communication which alone will ensure the necessary appropriacy of response. We do not begin with authenticity; authenticity is what the learners should ultimately achieve: it represents their terminal behaviour.

The belief that one can reach this end simply by exposing learners to genuine instances of discourse is misleading in two respects. Firstly, it misrepresents the essentially interactive nature of discourse. Meanings are not as it were there, present in the text awaiting collection: they are recovered by negotiation with the aid of shared conventions. Discourse is achieved by active interpretation, and unless the receiver is capable of the activity required of him then he can never realize the discourse as authentic. Secondly, it misrepresents the essentially contrived nature of methodology. The whole point of any pedagogic procedure is to defer the learner's encounter with what he will ultimately have to deal with until he has been prepared to cope with it. The pedagogy of any subject aims at guiding learners towards their terminal behaviour by the contrivance of appropriate intervening stages.

Let us then face up to our responsibilities and consider what might be involved in devising a methodology for the adequate teaching of communicative competence. We will suppose that we are concerned with students of science and that they need English in order to read basic textbooks. How do we proceed? There are, I think, two main stages, the selection of discourse in relation to the assumed terminal behaviour of the learners, and the subjection of this material to a pedagogic processing to ensure the eventual achievement of this behaviour. Selection first. It would seem reasonable to make our selection with reference to the kind of discourse which our learners will be expected to deal with at the end of the course. If this is accepted, it will be obvious that in the case in question we will wish to select written discourse which concerns itself with subject matter related to science (and perhaps more narrowly to particular branches of science). We will be inclined to avoid cooking recipes, economic reviews, and epic poetry. But selection according to scientific subject matter will not automatically yield the kind of discourse that is appropriate to our learners' needs. It is useful, I think, to make a broad distinction between three types of discourse all of which might loosely be referred to as 'scientific'. Firstly we have that which is associated with science as a discipline. This is scientist to scientist communication such as is found in papers published in learned journals. It characteristically trades heavily on an assumption of shared knowledge, not only of the subject matter under discussion but of the rhetorical conventions which control the way it is expressed. These conventions can be ultimately related to the philosophy of science. The discourse of science as a discipline differs rhetorically in a number of crucial ways from the discourse of science as a subject. This is science teacher to science student communication such as is found in textbooks. Whereas the discourse of the discipline is typically referential, ratiocinative, elliptical, that of the subject is typically metalinguistic, didactic, explicit. Its rhetorical conventions derive from the methodology of science teaching. Although they may resemble each other in the sense that they deal with scientific subject matter, these types of discourse may be very different in respect to the rhetorical conventions they conform to (although, as we shall see, these differences are ranged along a continuum which relates the two discourse types). Different from either of these is the discourse of science as a topic of interest. This is journalist to general reader communication such as is found in newspapers and popular journals. Rhetorical conventions vary considerably here depending on the readership aimed at.

Now if we are intent on developing in our learners a knowledge of the conventions which constrain the discourse of science as a subject, then it will not greatly advance our cause if we select our data from other kinds of discourse. We do not very effectively establish the conditions for an authentic relationship between reader and a particular type of discourse by training him in an awareness of conventions associated with a different type. Those who advocate the use of 'authentic' data do not always recognize this: they seem often to be content if the data is thematically scientific. But data which is rhetorically inappropriate is just as 'inauthentic' as that which is thematically irrelevant. A popular newspaper account of a new scientific discovery is no more appropriate to the needs of the learners we are considering at present than is a textbook description of rice cultivation or the principles of the capitalist economy. Indeed it might be less appropriate.

For the kind of students we have in mind then, we would be well advised to make our selection from the discourse of science as a subject. Our range of choice is still very wide, however, and we have to narrow it down even further. We can do this by selecting at the relevant level of instruction, using as source the kind of textbooks that the learner will eventually have to read.

Our next task is to process our material, to prepare it pedagogically in some way so as to bring the learner to the point when he is capable of responding to the genuine discourse we have selected in authentic fashion. This is where the 'doctoring' comes in, the pedagogic tampering with data that the 'authentic data' school complains about. My argument would be that the pedagogic process must necessarily involve some kind of tampering in order to bring learners to the point at which they can realize the authenticity of the language by appropriate response. It is not enough to establish ends which are adequate: we must also establish adequate means for achieving them. The central problem confronting us is how to prepare our material in such a way as to guide the learners to an awareness of the communicative conventions operating in the kind of discourse they will be concerned with.

This problem represents the main challenge of ESP. To meet it, one has to identify the selected discourse in terms of its essential rhetorical conventions and then devise techniques for presenting these conventions in the most effective way. Let us consider the identification aspect of the problem first. I said earlier that the language producer's intentions are accessible to interpretation because they are conveyed by reference to sets of communicative conventions. Some of these are, of course, quite simply linguistic conventions incorporated in a shared language code, and we should not forget that the learning of the code is a necessary, if it is not a sufficient, condition for communication to take place. There is some danger that an over-enthusiastic commitment to communicative language teaching might lead us to ignore this simple and essential fact. Other conventions are rhetorical: they have to do with how the code is used in the expression of propositions and in the performance of illocutionary acts of different kinds. If we are to describe discourse with reference to these we have to study what propositions are expressed in the particular type of discourse we have selected, how the resources of the English code are deployed in their expression, what illocutionary acts they are used to perform and how these acts are organized into larger communicative units as routines or paragraphs.

But our concern is not with how all these things are done in individual samples but how they are done in this type of discourse in general. We need to typify a kind of discourse, not to characterize a particular instance. I said earlier that a writer is constrained by convention in his writing. He is not, however, thereby denied all freedom of manoeuvre. Scientific textbooks do not conform to a fixed formula. They exhibit idiosyncratic stylistic variations within the limits of shared rhetorical conventions. If these limits are breached, of course, then the discourse becomes accordingly less genuine and the communication is impaired to the extent that the reader cannot make reference to the shared conventions which act as the necessary mediation between intention and interpretation. Authenticity is then difficult to achieve. But even if stylistic variation is kept within limits so that the practised interpreter can recover the underlying rhetoric, for the learner whose task is precisely to learn what the rhetoric is this variation creates additional difficulties.

In view of this, I think there is a case for presenting versions of some of the selected samples in which the idiosyncratic stylistic effects have been filtered out. This, of course, reduces the genuineness of these samples of data but I would argue that such a procedure ultimately helps to establish the authentic relation I have been speaking of in that it makes the rhetorical conventions more accessible to learner response. As teaching proceeds, the filter can be adjusted to allow more stylistic features to appear until the learner is eventually confronted with genuine samples. In this way I believe we can, by sound pedagogic practice, achieve the desired aim of making genuineness correspond with authenticity.

The writing of versions of discourse to foreground rhetorical features naturally presupposes a knowledge of what these features are. This is the ESP challenge I spoke of earlier. The language teacher who adopts a structuralist orientation to his task can turn to descriptive and pedagogic grammar as a source of reference. But we appear to have no descriptive or pedagogic rhetoric to which the ESP teacher can refer for guidance as to how to teach communicative competence. This should not occasion too much dismay, however. I pointed out earlier that the rhetorical conventions of science as a subject derive from the methodology of science. Essentially what this methodology is concerned with is the process whereby the learner gradually acquires the concepts and procedures of inquiry which define science as a discipline. It represents, therefore, precisely the basic rhetoric of science as a subject which the ESP teacher needs. Furthermore, this very rhetoric has been devised as a methodological procedure for the presentation of just those conventions of thought and expression which the ESP teacher will wish to present as realized through the English language. Hence the pedagogic methodology of science can serve as the guide to the second aspect of our problem: how to devise techniques for presenting the rhetorical conventions of science as a subject in the most effective way.

I do not wish to suggest that all our problems in designing an English for Science programme will be solved by studying the pedagogy of science. For one thing, we still have to consider how its rhetoric is expressed in the particular medium of the English language. For another, we have to fashion techniques which will reconcile the teaching of these rhetorical conventions with the teaching of the linguistic conventions of the code: we are, let us not forget, still teaching English in a second language situation. What I do wish to suggest, however, is that there is a good deal we can learn from our colleagues who are teaching those academic subjects for which we are teaching English. In fact, I want to suggest something rather more than this: that ESP requires a revision of the language teacher's traditional dependence on linguistic description and a readiness to form new alliances. At this point I return to what I said at the beginning of this paper about adequacy.

My argument has been that in ESP we are concerned with developing a methodology which will ultimately provide for the learner's ability to realize an authentic relationship with genuine discourse of relevance to his purposes in learning. I have emphasized that this methodology, like any other, is contrived. But it does not have to be contrived in a contextual vacuum. It can be designed with reference to another methodology whose purpose is to engage the interest of learners in developing their knowledge of a particular area of inquiry, to ensure that what is presented to them takes on the reality of intellectual experience. In other words, this methodology aims at creating an authentic response, and it is only adequate to the extent that it does so. And I think that a language teaching methodology which relates to it can also achieve adequacy through authenticity in the same way. One of the most important effects of an involvement in ESP is that it leads us to recognize that in language teaching we are as much concerned with teaching as with language, that the way other people devise communicative pedagogies is just as relevant as models of linguistic description. In fact, models of linguistic description have not always had a beneficial effect on language teaching. This again, I think, is because teachers have not always recognized the importance of establishing pedagogic principles.

I have said that an uncritical acceptance of the need to present learners with 'authentic' data can lead to an avoidance of pedagogic responsibility. An uncritical acceptance of the authority of models of linguistic description can have the same effect. Teachers have been inclined to be too deferential to linguists in the past, too ready to follow their lead. I do not wish to deny that theoretical linguistics can provide insights which can be exploited in the practical domain of teaching and indeed I pointed out at the beginning of this paper that the impetus towards a communicative approach to language teaching has been inspired in part by developments in theoretical studies of language. But it is perfectly possible, and I would claim necessary, to construct pedagogically oriented models of description which though deriving from such insights are informed also by methodological principles which (as in the case of ESP we have considered) can be established by reference to the teaching of other subjects. Pedagogic descriptions are just as legitimate as are the alternative derivations which are designed to meet the theoretical requirements of formal models of linguistic description: just as legitimate and more adequate for the purpose for which they are designed.

It is important, it seems to me, for the language teacher to recognize that he is the authority in his own domain. Many of the problems in language teaching have in the past been, as it were, self-inflicted, created by the teacher's over-zealous servility in imitating whatever model of linguistic description happened to be currently in vogue. But the teacher should have his own principles of description, his own criteria for adequacy, and these derive from pedagogic considerations. With authority comes responsibility. The teacher's business is the design of effective pedagogic methodologies: those which will lead the learner towards the required terminal behaviour by the shortest possible route. To suppose that, in the teaching of ESP, this will be achieved automatically by exposing the learner to 'real' language is to shirk this responsibility. There is no such thing as authentic language data. Authenticity is realized by appropriate response and the language teacher is responsible for designing a methodology which will establish the conditions whereby this authenticity can ultimately be achieved.

Notes

Paper presented at the TESOL Convention, New York, March 1976, and published in Fanselow and Crymes 1976.

13 The process and purpose of reading

What I want to do in this paper is to present a view of reading which I find to be consistent with my own intuition and convenient for language teaching purposes. I am not sure that I would want to claim any more for it than that. In this view, reading is seen not as a separate ability which can be investigated and taught in disassociation from other aspects of language behaviour (as it often tends to be), but as the realization of a general interpretative process which underlies all communicative activity. Furthermore, this process is seen as operating at two different levels of mental activity, the first dealing with the immediate apprehension of information and the second with the discrimination of this information into patterns of conceptual significance. I will first try to make clear what I mean by talking about reading as the use of a general interpretative process and then go on to discuss the two levels at which they seem to operate. In reference to my title, the first part of my paper, then, will deal with the process and the second, more briefly, with the purpose of reading.

Recent studies of reading have represented it as a reasoning activity whereby the reader creates meaning on the basis of textual clues. I want to suggest that this kind of creativity is not exclusive to reading but is a necessary condition for the interpretation of any discourse, written or spoken. This suggestion is not in the least original: it is one of the cardinal assumptions made by the ethnomethodologists (see Turner 1974). They argue, among other things, that meanings are derived in discourse by a process of 'practical reasoning'. Thus the interlocutors in an interaction *make* sense of what is said, they do not discover it ready made in each utterance, and the meanings that are created in this way can never be complete and explicit but only adequate to the purposes of the interaction. This view of how meanings are negotiated in discourse is consistent with Goodman's comments on the reading process:

> Reading is a selective process. It involves partial use of available minimal language cues selected from perceptual input on the basis of the reader's expectation. As this partial information is processed,

tentative decisions are made to be confirmed, rejected, or refined as
reading progresses.
Goodman 1967: 128.

All I wish to add is that what Goodman is describing here is a general
discourse processing strategy of which reading is simply a particular
realization. It has no special status in this regard.

Certain implications arise from thus considering reading in the
context of more general interpretative activities. In the first place, one is
led to reconsider the nature of the text and of the reader's relationship
with it. The general tendency seems to be to think of reading as *reaction*:
reaction to meanings which, though explicit in the text, cannot always
be fully recovered. There appears to be an assumption that it is only
because of the peculiarities of the decoding operation that the total
meaning contained in a text is not completely grasped. I believe that
this assumption is false. I want to suggest (still following ethnomethodological line) that the *encoding* process is equally imprecise and approximate and that, therefore, there is no possibility of recovering complete
meaning from a text. It is never there in the first place. The act of
encoding is best thought of, I suggest, not as the formulation of
messages, in principle complete and self-contained, but as the devising
of a set of directions. These directions indicate to the decoder where he
must look in the conceptual world of his knowledge and experience for
the encoder's meaning. The encoder, then, relies on the active participation of the decoder and the decoder is successful in his comprehension
to the extent that he understands the directions and is capable of
carrying them out.

In this view, reading is regarded not as reaction to a text but as
interaction between writer and reader mediated through the text.
Reading is an act of participation in a discourse between interlocutors.
It seems to follow from this that reading efficiency cannot be measured
against the amount of information contained in a text. This is in-
calculable since it depends on how much knowledge the reader brings
to the text and how much he wishes to extract from it. Rather, reading
efficiency is a matter of how effective a discourse the reader can create
from the text, either in terms of rapport with the writer or in terms of
his purpose in engaging in the discourse in the first place. This latter
distinction relates to the two levels of reading I mentioned earlier and
which I will return to shortly.

For the moment, however, let me pursue this notion of interaction
a little further. In spoken conversation, where there is an overt negotiation of meanings through reciprocal exchanges, the interaction is
obvious. It is evident that the interlocutors do not piece their meanings
together with careful precision or submit every utterance to analytic

scrutiny. They rely on what Grice calls the 'co-operative principle' (Grice 1975) and assume that some satisfactory agreement as to what is meant will emerge as the discourse progresses.

Sometimes precious little in the way of information needs to be exchanged for the interlocutors to be satisfied with their interaction. This is the case with 'phatic communion', where the participants in a discourse are simply concerned with maintaining their interaction without much regard to what is actually being said. But even when the exchange has a more informative purpose and where the interlocutors' interest and conceptual worlds are more seriously engaged, what is actually expressed is quite commonly vague, imprecise and insignificant; satisfactory only because it provides the interlocutors with a set of directions to where they can find and create meanings for themselves. Whether or not the meanings of encoder and decoder ever entirely coincide is something we shall never know: I would imagine it is very unlikely since such a coincidence would depend on an identity of conceptual worlds. But fortunately these do not have to coincide for communication to take place: a rough correspondence is all that is necessary. The notion that we understand other people must always be to some degree an illusion. All that we share is that highest common factor of personal meanings which is communicable by the social means of language.

I believe that written discourse, no less than spoken, must, by definition, operate in accordance with the co-operative principle. Reader and writer are engaged in an interaction in which language is used as a clue to correspondence of conceptual worlds. Unlike spoken discourse, however, written discourse is non-reciprocal and this has certain important consequences for how the interaction is realized. I suggested earlier that encoding is a matter of providing directions and decoding a matter of following them. In spoken discourse of a reciprocal kind such directions do not need to be very precisely specified by each interlocutor: they can be worked out co-operatively between them as the interaction proceeds. Consider, for example, the following exchange:

A I think there are really three creative ideas that have been central in science.
B Which are they then?
A The ideas of order, causes, and chance.
B But surely these ideas are not peculiar to science.
A That's true, but . . .
B The idea of order least of all . . .
A They have applications to science but of course they are all older than these applications.
B Right. And they are wider and deeper than the techniques of science that express them.

A Yes. They are common sense ideas.
B How do you mean?
A Well, they are all generalizations which we all make from our daily lives.
B O.K. And which we go on using to help us to run our lives.

Here the interlocutors establish between them that the expression 'central to science' does not imply 'peculiar to science' and so a particular direction is clarified. Similarly, they negotiate agreement on the expression 'common sense'. In the case of other expressions, however, there is an assumption that they indicate points of correspondence in the conceptual worlds of A and B: thus, no further specification is thought to be required for expressions like 'creative' or 'central' or 'wider and deeper'. This does not mean that A and B would necessarily agree on the meaning of these expressions if they were to be singled out for discussion but only that the two interlocutors assume agreement for the purposes of the present interaction. Later developments may prove them wrong. They might suddenly realize that their assumptions are mistaken, that they have been talking at cross-purposes because of a lack of correspondence. B might come out with a remark like:

B But I am not sure that your example shows this idea to be *creative*.
A Well, what do you mean by creative then?

But how does this co-operative principle work in written, non-reciprocal discourse? In the very act of asking a question like this I have indicated the answer. Because in putting such a question and providing it immediately with a reply, I assume the roles of both addresser and addressee. I incorporate the interaction within the encoding process itself. As I write, I make judgements about the reader's possible reactions, anticipate any difficulties that I think he might have in understanding and following my directions, conduct, in short, a covert dialogue with my supposed interlocutor. The example of spoken interaction which we have just been considering was, in fact, simply a reciprocal version of a short passage from J. Bronowski's book *The Common Sense of Science*. The non-reciprocal, written version runs as follows:

> There are three creative ideas which, each in its turn, have been central to science. They are the idea of order, the idea of causes, and the idea of chance ... None of these ideas is peculiar to science; but all three are, of course, older least of all. They have applications to science; but all three are, of course, older than these applications. All are wider and deeper than the techniques in which science expresses. They are common sense ideas: by which I mean that they are generalizations which we all make from our daily lives, and which we go on using to help us to run our lives.
> *Bronowski 1960: 18.*

From the decoding point of view, the reader also assumes the dual role of addresser and addressee, and reconstitutes the dialogue. Rapport between writer and reader is established to the extent that the latter's possible reactions have been anticipated.

Written discourse is produced and received in detachment from an immediate context of utterance and this can easily mislead us into regarding it as a radically different mode of communication from conversation. I have represented it here as having the same underlying character. It is, in my view, a derived mode: one in which interaction, overtly reciprocal in face-to-face exchanges, is idealized into a covert cognitive process, one in which social actions, as it were, are internalized as psychological activity. The difficulties that one has in dealing with it arise from the fact that one has to abstract interaction from its concrete realization in non-reciprocal discourse, and enact a dialogue by assuming the roles of both interlocutors.

In the teaching of reading (and writing) one must, I believe, make the learner aware first of the essentially imprecise character of communication through natural language. Most of our teaching encourages learners to believe that exact meanings can, in principle, be fully recoverable from texts, that texts will yield their total content if they are scrutinized in sufficient detail. We thus discourage a normal use of natural language and deny learners access to their own conceptual world which alone ensures that reading will, in any really significant sense, be meaningful. And then, I think we should make it clear that the independence of written discourse from an immediate context does not make it any less interactive as a mode of communicating. My two versions of Bronowski suggest one way in which this might be done. Thus one might decompose a written passage into its constituent utterances and require learners to ask pertinent questions at possible points of interaction, building up dialogue sequences for later conversion into paragraphs of written language. In this way one can easily show how different paragraphs can develop from the same opening statement depending on what kind of directions are required by different interlocutors. Consider the following sequence, derived from another passage from Bronowski's book:

A The whole structure of thought in the Middle Ages is one which we find hard to grasp today.
B Why should this be so?
A The principles by which this structure was ordered seem to us now outlandish and meaningless.
B Can you give an example?
A Yes. Take the simple question: Why does an apple when it leaves the tree fall down to the ground?

B Why do you take that question in particular?
A The question had been asked often since the fourteenth century.
B Why at that time particularly?
A Because at that time the active and inquiring men of the Italian Renaissance began to take an interest in the mechanical world.
B Well, how did they answer the question?
A For answer, they went back to the works of the Greek philosophers.
B And what answer did they find?
A Well, to us, the answer smacks of the most pompous tradition of philosophy, and does less to explain the world than to shuffle it in a set of tautologies.
B Why do you say that? Come on, don't keep me in suspense!
A The Middle Ages answered the question about the apple in the tradition of Aristotle: the apple falls down and not up because it is its nature to fall down.
B Well, that does not tell us very much.
A Exactly, the answer seems quite meaningless to us these days.

This interaction can be said to underlie the actual paragraph in Bronowski, which runs as follows:

> The whole structure of thought in the Middle Ages is one which we find hard to grasp today. It was orderly structure, but the principles by which it was ordered seem to us now outlandish and meaningless. Take such a simple question as that which is said to have turned Newton's mind to the problem of gravitation: Why does an apple when it leaves the tree fall to the ground? The question had been asked often since the fourteenth century, when the active and inquiring men of the Italian Renaissance began to take an interest in the mechanical world. For answer, they went back to one of the great re-discoveries of the Arabs and the Renaissance, the works of the Greek philosophers. To us, this answer smacks of the most pompous tradition of philosophy, and does less to explain the world than to shuffle it in a set of tautologies. For the Middle Ages answered the question in the tradition of Aristotle: the apple falls down and not up because it is its nature to fall down.
> *Bronowski 1960: 26.*

This, however, is not the only possible interaction that might develop from Bronowski's opening statement. Consider the following alternative:

A The whole structure of thought in the Middle Ages is one which is hard to grasp today.
B What do you mean exactly by 'structure of thought'?
A Well, I mean the medieval way of thinking about things. It seems very strange to us in the present age.

B Can you give me an example?
A Yes, take a simple question like: Why does an apple fall to the ground when it leaves the tree?
B Because of gravitation.
A Right. That's the obvious answer for us because of Newton. But in the Middle Ages they had to look elsewhere for an answer.
B Where?
A They looked to Aristotle.
B But what did they find?
A They found the answer: The apple falls down and not up because it is its nature to fall down.

This exchange can be converted into a written discourse to yield the following paragraph:

> The whole structure of thought in the Middle Ages is one which we find hard to grasp today. The medieval way of thinking about things seems very strange to us in the present age. Consider, for example, the simple question: Why does an apple fall to the ground when it leaves the tree? Because of Newton, the answer to us is obvious: gravitation. But the Middle Ages had to look elsewhere for an answer. They turned to Aristotle, and the answer they found was: The apple falls down and not up because it is its nature to fall down.

Sufficient indication has perhaps been given of how one might approach the presentation of reading as an interactive process. I want now to turn to the question of purpose. Why, after all, do we engage in this process? What is reading *for*?

The interactive process that I have discussed so far works towards a clarification of what I have called directions for discovering where meaning is to be found. In the case we have just been considering, for example, the development of the paragraph can be seen as a means of ensuring that the reader will accept the truth of the opening statement and incorporate it within his conceptual world. The additional information that Bronowski provides to clarify and illustrate (adopting the dual role of addresser and addressee) has an essentially *facilitating* function. In reading we apprehend this information in the process of immediate interaction but then, once its function has been fulfilled, we allow it to recede into the background. At one level, then, reading is a matter of immediate apprehension through interaction, but this procedure serves only to provide a more accurate specification of directions to meaning. At a more discriminating level, the reader sorts out what is merely facilitating from what he wishes to accept as a permanent addition to his world of knowledge and experience. This, I suggest, is his real purpose in reading: not simply to engage in an interaction but to derive from this interaction something which sustains or extends his conceptual world. At the immediate apprehending level reading, we may say, is a heuristic procedure. At the discriminating level it is an epistemological one.

Which information is simply apprehended for temporary use and which is singled out as significant at a more discriminating level will, of course, depend to a considerable degree on what the reader already knows and what he wants to find out in his reading. If the interaction is successful, so that there is close rapport between writer and reader, then there will be agreement on relative significance. But it is always possible for the reader to impose his own weighting on the information he receives. He may then be accused of missing the point or taking remarks out of context. As I pointed out earlier, since conceptual worlds do not coincide, there can never be an exact congruence of encoder's and decoder's meanings. Communication can of its nature only be approximate.

At the same time, of course, communication could not take place at all if text could not be realized as discourse which set conceptual worlds in correspondence. And description of discourse structure would be impossible.

Conclusions that rhetoricians (both ancient and modern) and common readers arrive at about the way discourse is structured are based on an assumption that encoder and decoder can agree on relative significance, on which items of information are to be epistemologically salient, and which are intended to provide heuristic support.

Turning now to pedagogic matters, it seems to me that the distinction that I have been trying to make here is rarely taken into account in the design of reading materials. Comprehension questions, for example, commonly require the learner to rummage around in the text for information in a totally indiscriminate way, without regard to what purpose might be served in so doing. Learners are seldom required to use the information they acquire, either within an interaction process to facilitate access to the most salient directions towards meaning or to follow these directions into their own conceptual worlds. Reading is thus represented as an end in itself, an activity that has no relevance to real knowledge and experience and therefore no real meaning.

The situation could be improved, I suggest, by making the learners aware, through participation in the kind of interactive exercises I proposed earlier, of how much written discourse serves an essentially facilitating function, of how much of it therefore, once this function has been discharged, can then be ignored. We should try to encourage learners to relate what they read to their own world of knowledge and experience. We can do this, in part, by selecting reading material that is likely to appeal to their interests, but there is no point in doing this unless we also ensure that their interests are actually engaged by allowing them the same latitude of interpretation that we as practised readers permit ourselves. The texts have to be converted into discourse and the language put to creative use.

I have tried, on the odd occasion, to answer comprehension questions of the kind that are current in language teaching textbooks (and that I have been responsible for producing myself from time to time) and have found the experience a chastening one. I perform very badly indeed. This must be either because I do not know how to read properly, which I am reluctant to admit, or because the questions are just not relevant to proper reading, because they do not involve the learner in the necessary process of interaction which provides the heuristic means to an epistemological purpose. The second is, I think, the more likely explanation.

Notes

Paper presented at the TESOL Convention, Miami, April 1977.

Simplification

The notion of simplification is interpreted in this section in two complementary ways: as a pedagogic technique and as a learning strategy. The first paper (Paper 14) adopts the first interpretation and distinguishes between different ways in which a written passage might be simplified so as to make this meaning more accessible to learners of limited competence. The essential argument is that a modification of lexis and syntax does not necessarily make a passage simpler to interpret as discourse but may indeed make it more difficult. Another point implied rather than openly argued here, is that a technique for simplification should not simply make a particular piece of writing more accessible but should also allow for the development of abilities in the learner which he can bring to bear on other reading material. This brings us to the second paper in this section.

This deals with simplification as a learning strategy. It reviews certain ideas current in the literature on error analysis and suggests that a distinction needs to be made between code rules, which define what the learner knows and context rules, which represent strategies for communication acquired in learning the mother tongue. This distinction is related to that between rules and procedures suggested in Paper 10. When the learner produces forms which are simplified in reference to code rules of the language, the teacher sees them as errors and therefore as signs of failure in learning. But these forms can also, and more satisfactorily, be seen as the learner's assertion of his own communicative strategies and therefore as signs of success in developing context rules in the foreign language.

Both Papers 14 and 15 end with the suggestion, made elsewhere in this book, that in the presentation of language we might with profit make reference to the educational principles embodied in the pedagogies of other subjects, and that language teaching might be integrated with other parts of the curriculum rather than be conducted in isolation as a subject in its own right. It may well be, paradoxically enough, that this isolation creates the very difficulties which language teaching pedagogy is devised to solve.

The last paper in this section compares two types of abnormality in language use: pidgin, in which the referential force is dominant at the expense of the expressive; and babu, in which the reverse is the case. To give an example the following revision of Wordsworth's lines in *The Highland Boy* illustrates a yielding to the expressive force and a corresponding shift in a babu direction:

> A household tub, like one of those,
> Which women use to wash their clothes. (original version)

> A shell of ample size, and light
> As the pearly car of Amphritite,
> That sportive dolphins drew. (revised version)

The pedagogic point that I make in the paper is that much of what is taught in the foreign language classroom is babu in that it amounts to a manipulation of linguistic forms of increasing complexity without meaningful content or communicative import. This, I argue, in terms of developing a genuine ability to use language, is just as abnormal as are the pidginized forms that learners produce and which are penalized as errors—even though these forms arise as a natural consequence of the contact situation represented by the classroom.

A footnote on terminology. In the original version of Paper 15 I used the terms *reference* and *expression* instead of *code* and *context* to label the different types of rule. The latter pair of terms is preferred here to avoid confusion with the use of the former pair in Paper 16, where they are given a different sense. There are no doubt other examples of terminological inconsistency in this book, but in this case it would have been too blatant to escape notice.

14   The simplification of use

In language teaching, simplification usually refers to a kind of intralingual translation whereby a piece of discourse is reduced to a version written in the supposed interlanguage of the learner. In this paper I want to consider what is involved in this process and what purpose it serves. And I want to make a few provocative suggestions about how we might give the notion of simplification a broader significance.

Like translation, simplification can be carried out at different levels. I want to suggest two here. On the one hand, the simplifier can concentrate on replacing words and structures with approximate semantic equivalents in the learner's interlanguage omitting whichever items prove intractable, thereby bringing the language of the original within the scope of the learner's transitional linguistic competence. This kind of simplification focuses on the way in which the language system is manifested: it is an operation on usage. On the other hand, the simplifier can concentrate on making explicit in different terms the propositional content of the original and the ways in which it is presented in order to bring what is communicated in the original within the scope of the learner's transitional communicative competence. In this case, simplification focuses on the way in which the language system is realized for the expression of propositions and the performance of illocutionary acts: it is an operation on use. Let us consider an example. We will suppose that we wish to simplify the following:

1 The majority of alloys are prepared by mixing metals in the molten state; then the mixture is poured into metal or sand moulds and allowed to solidify.
2 Generally the major ingredient is melted first; then the others are added to it and should completely dissolve.
3 If a plumber makes solder he may melt his lead, add tin, stir, and cast the alloy into stick form.
4 Some pairs of metals do not dissolve in this way and when this is so it is unlikely that a useful alloy will be formed.
5 If the plumber were to add aluminium, instead of tin, to the lead, the two metals would not dissolve—they would behave like oil and water;

when cast, the metals would separate into two layers, the heavy lead below and aluminium above[1].

If we were to simplify this passage as an instance of usage, we would scan each sentence and note those structures and lexical items which did not occur in the learner's interlanguage (which might be represented by a checklist of items) and replace them as far as possible with those which did occur. Thus in Sentence 1, for example, we might replace *The majority of alloys* with *most alloys*, *prepared* with *made*, *metals in the molten state* with *melted metals*, *solidify* with *become solid* and *by mixing metals* with *by a mixture of metals*. And so on to the next sentence. We should note that two of the lexical items appearing in the first sentence do not easily lend themselves to this kind of procedure: *alloy* and *mould*. Here we would find it difficult to incorporate an equivalent within the passage itself and we would probably be obliged to provide a footnote gloss of a periphrastic kind.

Now although this process brings individual lexical items and structures within the scope of the learner's linguistic competence, it does not necessarily make it easier for him to understand the passage as a whole. There are certain features of use which this process cannot of its nature account for. For example, it may be that the word *ingredient* (Sentence 2) occurs in the learner's interlanguage and so is not replaced. But to understand the value that this word assumes in this context, the learner has to relate it anaphorically to the mixture of metals referred to in the first sentence. Similarly, although he may 'know' the word *others* (Sentence 2) and the word *this* (Sentence 4)—the latter, after all, commonly appears in the first lesson of structurally graded courses—it does not follow that he will be able to associate these items with what they refer to in the passage: it does not follow that he will be able to realize their value in this particular instance of use. In order to understand this passage, then, the learner has to recognize how the different lexical and structural items are being used in the expression of propositional content, and the way in which this content is developed throughout the passage. This is one aspect of what I have referred to as use: the way in which the propositions expressed in sentences are related to form a cohesive sequence.

If we were to simplify this passage so as to clarify propositional development, it might well involve restructuring it in order to make this development explicit. For example, it will be noted that the sequences of propositions expressed in the first two sentences does not correspond with the sequence of events in the actual process of making and casting alloys. Sentence 2 refers to events which are referred to in the first half of Sentence 1 and which precede the events referred to in the second half of Sentence 1. If we wished to make the propositional

relationships clear, we could simplify this part of the passage by rearranging the sentences, providing referential value for anaphoric
elements where necessary, so that they corresponded to this sequence of
events at the same time. Thus we might represent Sentences 1 and 2
as follows:

> The majority of alloys are prepared by first melting metals and then
> mixing them. The metal which is the major ingredient is melted first;
> then the other metals are added to it and they should completely
> dissolve. Then the mixture is poured into metal or sand moulds and
> allowed to solidify.

This process simplifies one aspect of use in that it clarifies propositional development and strengthens cohesion. But this does not
necessarily simplify another aspect of use; it does not clarify the
coherence relationships between the illocutionary acts which the
propositions are used to perform. On the contrary, the particular version
we have produced complicates the discourse. To see why this should be
so we have to consider the illocutionary function of Sentences 3 and 4.
In Sentence 3, the expressions *melt his lead* and *add tin* relate to the
expressions *the major ingredient is melted first* and *the others are added to
it* in Sentence 2. The recognition of this relationship enables us to link
the propositions expressed in the two sentences and so to establish a
cohesive link between them. But at the same time it helps us to see that
in expressing the proposition in Sentence 3 the writer is providing us
with a particular instance of the general process expressed in Sentence 2.
It helps us to see, in other words, that the illocutionary relationship
between the propositions expressed in these sentences is one of *general
statement + illustration.* The illocutionary function of Sentence 3 is
further signalled by the *if* clause.

But now if we have Sentence 3 follow immediately on from the
propositionally simplified version we have produced, its illocutionary
value is less easy to recognize. We have to interpret the last sentence of
our derived version as a parenthetical comment and not as an element
in the main propositional development. If this is so, however, then it is
misleading to give it independent sentential status, since this necessarily
gives prominence to the proposition expressed. As it stands, the reader
is led to suppose that the next sentence will directly relate to it. But if
Sentence 3 now follows, the relationship is not with *Then the mixture is
poured into metal or sand moulds* but with the sentence which precedes:
*The metal which is the major ingredient is melted first; then the other
metals are added to it and they should completely dissolve.* It is this, the
mixing of the metals, that is being illustrated in Sentence 3 and not
the process of casting.

Or is it? Sentence 3 does after all refer to casting and we recognize that this term *cast* has the same value as the expression *poured into metal or sand moulds and allowed to solidify* occurring in Sentence 1, just as we recognize *solder* as a hyponym of *alloy*. So what prevents us from interpreting Sentence 3 as an illustrative statement referring to the casting process rather than the mixing process? The answer is Sentence 4. This sentence relates to Sentence 2 through the key term *dissolve*: it is this relationship which enables us to associate the term *formed* with its appropriate value. This term is after all potentially ambiguous: it could refer to the composition of the mixture or to the shape it assumes when it is cast and the occurrence of the noun *form* in Sentence 3 might easily lead us to suppose that it is the second sense that is intended rather than the first. Reference to the dissolving of the mixture is taken up again in Sentence 5 and it is clear that the main propositional development in the passage relates to how metals mix to form alloys and not to how they are cast.

If we adopt the simplified version which has been proposed, then, we not only obscure the propositional development of the passage as a whole but we also obscure the illocutionary value of the sentences which follow. Sentence 3 functions as an illustration and we could simplify the passage as discourse by inserting the illocutionary marker *for example*. Sentence 4 functions as a qualification and we could make this clear by inserting the illocutionary marker *however*. But the functions of these sentences only become clear through establishing the cohesion and coherence of the passage as a whole.

Consider the first part of Sentence 4, for example: *Some pairs of metals do not dissolve in this way* . . . In what way? There is no explicit mention of anything dissolving in the immediately preceding sentence (Sentence 3). There *is* such a mention, however, in Sentence 2. We can therefore establish a direct cohesion link between the propositions expressed in Sentences 2 and 4. One way of simplifying the propositional development here, therefore, would be to remove Sentence 3 and allow Sentence 4 to follow directly on from Sentence 2. If we do this, then the illocutionary link between these sentences becomes more apparent: the second is recognized more readily as a qualification of the first and we can mark this overtly by inserting the expression *however*.

But what happens now to the displaced Sentence 3? As we have seen the reorganization of a discourse may simplify it in certain respects but complicate it in others. What is the consequence here, then, of shifting Sentence 3? The fact that propositional development is not explicitly carried through Sentence 3 suggests its subsidiary status as an example relating to Sentence 2. But it also connects up with Sentence 5: cohesive links are made, for example, between '*a* plumber' and '*his* lead' in Sentence 3 and '*the* plumber' and '*the* lead' in Sentence 5. In this case, it is Sentence 4 which intrudes into the propositional development. By shifting Sentence 3, therefore, we strengthen the cohesion of the discourse. The result of the reorganization is as follows:

> The majority of alloys are prepared by mixing metals in the molten state; then the mixture is poured into metal or sand moulds and allowed to solidify. Generally, the major ingredient is melted first, then the others are added to it and should completely dissolve. Some pairs of metals do not dissolve in this way and when this happens it is unlikely that a useful alloy will be formed. If a plumber makes solder, for example, he may melt his lead, add tin, stir, and cast the alloy into stick form. If the plumber were to add aluminium, however, instead of tin, to the lead, the two metals would not dissolve—they would behave like oil and water; when cast, the metals would separate into two layers, the heavy lead below and aluminium above.

What we should note is that if the sentences are reorganized in this way that which functions as the second example, divided as it is from what it is an example of, needs to be marked so that its relationship with the first example is seen to be the same as the relationship between the proposition expressed in Sentence 2 and that expressed in Sentence 4. To ensure that the discourse is coherent we need to insert the marker *however*.

So the shifting of Sentence 3 has consequences for the illocutionary structure of the paragraph as a whole. We might characterize the two versions in general terms by saying that in the original a general statement (Sentence 1) is followed by what we might call a specification (Sentence 2) which is clarified by means of an illustrative statement, or example (Sentence 3), which is parenthetical to the main theme. This theme is resumed in Sentence 4 in the form of a qualifying statement which is in turn illustrated (Sentence 5). The main thematic development, then, is arrested by the inclusion of a clarificatory statement. In the derived version, on the other hand, the main theme is developed first without interruption and the examples are then appended. We might say that in this case the discourse structure reflects the relative centrality of the propositions expressed: the last two sentences have the value of optional illustrative elements which contribute nothing to the basic points that are made but only serve to clarify them. They would not find a place in a summary of the paragraph.

Now it might be objected that far from simplifying this passage I have made it a good deal more complex. The point is that in order to simplify language as use one has to interpret its communicative import. To do this one has to take into account how propositional content is developed, that is to say how cohesion is achieved, and also what the expression of propositions counts as in terms of illocutionary value, that is to say how coherence is achieved. I make no claims for the validity of the labels I have attached to the illocutionary acts in this particular instance of use, but they serve to indicate that in the interpretation of discourse we associate the expression of propositions with some illocutionary value or other, and we make use of labels of the sort I have suggested in reporting it. Thus we would say that in this passage, the author gives a general description of what is involved in the preparation of alloys and then specifies what he means more exactly by in effect providing a gloss on the word *mix*, that he then gives a particular illustration of the general process, and so on.

Once we have interpreted an instance of use, we can then proceed to restate it in a way which will make such an interpretation more accessible. This may incidentally involve simplifying usage, of course, but as a means to an alternative instance of use and not as an end in itself. Our purpose, then, is to bring the language within the scope of what we suppose to be the learner's capacity for applying interpretative procedures on foreign language data.

But if our purpose is to produce discourse in which propositions and illocutions are adjusted to conform to the learner's capacity for processing them, then how, we might ask, does our activity differ from that of teachers of other subjects? All pedagogy involves simplification in that it aims at expressing concepts, beliefs, attitudes, and so on in a way which is judged to be in accord with the knowledge and experience of learners. One of the differences is that other teachers do not normally derive their instructional discourse from specific linguistic sources but draw upon their knowledge of the subject directly. They produce, we might say, *simple accounts* rather than *simplified versions*, and thereby avoid the kind of problem that arises from an over-concentration on usage. For them usage is adjusted only to the extent that it needs to be to achieve the simple account they are aiming for. In their approach, usage is controlled by use.

There does not seem to be any very cogent reason why the language teacher should not proceed in the same way. He can do this by associating the teaching of language with the pedagogic methodologies of other subjects. These methodologies are engaged in the production of simple discourse and its gradual elaboration into more sophisticated kinds of communicative use. This is what the language teacher is engaged in also. It would seem that he might be more effective in achieving his ends by devising ways of exploiting the simple accounts of his fellow teachers rather than by getting involved in the highly complex task of producing simplified versions which require him to recreate from an interpretation of an original discourse which he may not be competent to interpret in the first place. The language teacher has, by training, a considerable knowledge of the usage of the language he is teaching. The danger is that he should assume that this is the only kind of knowledge that the learners need to acquire.

Notes

Paper presented at the AILA Congress, Stuttgart, August 1975.
1 Adapted from W. A. Alexander and A. Street (1969). *Metals in the Service of Man.* Penguin.

15 The significance of simplification

The notion of simplification has been a familiar one in language teaching for a long time. It underlies not only the production of 'simplified readers' but also the whole process of syllabus design. Essentially, it is the pedagogic analogue of the linguist's idealization of data, from which it ultimately derives: the teacher simplifies by selecting and ordering the linguistic phenomena he is to deal with so as to ease the task of learning, and the linguist idealizes by selecting and ordering the linguistic phenomena he is to deal with to ease the task of analysis. In both cases the purpose of the operation is essentially a methodological one. And in both cases there is a danger that something crucial may be left out of account for the sake of methodological convenience. In this paper I want to suggest that something crucial *is* generally left out of account and that the notion of simplification can be given a more general, and significant, definition. In the first part of the paper I shall try to work my way towards this definition, and in the second part I shall try to draw out a number of implications for language teaching pedagogy that seem to arise from it.

In the L2 situation, the simplification process typically takes place in two consecutive stages, the first constituting the teaching input and the second the learning intake (the terms come from Corder 1967), the first being an overt pedagogic contrivance and the second being the consequence of all kinds of psychological processes in the learner. Ideally, of course, the two stages should converge to form one and the simplification of the input correspond to the simplification of the intake. If this were so, the grading would reflect stages in language acquisition and there would be no errors. But errors do occur in plenty and over recent years the area of applied linguistics known as error analysis has arisen to study them and to specify their causes. It would seem reasonable to suppose that error analysis, therefore, should provide us with some clear and adequate definition of the process of simplification and thereby serve as a reliable reference for the design of syllabuses which might in consequence approximate more closely to the learner's own syllabus (see Corder 1967). Let us then consider how reasonable such a supposition is.

Let me first briefly, but I hope not misleadingly, summarize some of the key assumptions underlying recent work in error analysis. Errors occur systematically in learners' language behaviour and are therefore to be regarded as manifestations of a system. They are to be distinguished from lapses in performance, or mistakes, which reflect only the temporary malfunctioning of the production or perception processes and are not systematic (see Corder 1967). The system which errors manifest represents an *état de langue* which the learner has developed for himself, an interlanguage (IL) (Selinker 1972) which is to be conceived as existing at some point between the learner's native language (NL) and the target language (TL) he is in the process of learning. This IL is an 'approximative system' (Nemser 1971), one of a series of states through which the learner moves in his acquisition of the TL, and a knowledge of which constitutes his 'transitional competence' (Corder 1967). The form which this interlanguage takes can be accounted for by reference to a number of processes, five of which Selinker isolates as being of central importance. These are 'language transfer', 'transfer of training', 'strategies of second language learning', 'strategies of second language communication', and 'overgeneralization of TL linguistic material' (Selinker 1972). These processes, and others, can be activated by a variety of 'factors' in the learning situation, of which seven are singled out by Richards and Sampson. The first two of these seem to be indistinguishable from Selinker's first two 'processes', but the others, like 'sociolinguistic situation' and 'age', seem to be more in the nature of settings in which such processes take place (Richards and Sampson 1974).

Now I want to suggest that all of the processes which Selinker refers to are tactical variations of the same underlying simplification strategy and that in general error analysis is a partial account of basic simplifying procedures which lie at the heart of communicative competence and which are not restricted to people engaged in the learning of a second language system. The reasoning behind this suggestion derives from a consideration of the two key notions—error and interlanguage.

The basic distinguishing features of errors are firstly that they are linguistic lapses of regular occurrence and are therefore reducible to rule whereas mistakes are lapses which are random and irregular; and secondly that errors are not correctable by reference to the learner's own knowledge, whereas mistakes are. The distinction is clear enough in principle, but in practice certain confusions arise. They arise, I think, because the rules which control the regularity of lapses are assumed to relate to linguistic competence in the Chomskyan sense. Indeed, the notions of transitional competence and approximative system are represented as a corollary to this regularity. But how is one to characterize those lapses which are persistently regular but which the learner knows are lapses once his attention is drawn to them? By reference to the first criterion these are errors: they are frequently indeed highly fossilized and so should indicate a stable interlanguage system (see Selinker 1972). By reference to the second criterion, however, they are mistakes since the learner knows, if he cannot effectively operate, the target language system. In these cases, then, the learner appears to be competent in the target language system but to perform in the interlanguage. Do we say that his lapses are errors or mistakes? Again, it is not uncommon to find lapses which occur regularly in speech but not at all, or not regularly, in writing. We cannot call these errors with reference to a Chomskyan concept of competence since they only occur when the learner is performing in one mode and not in the other. And yet they are systematic. It would appear to be the case then that the learner's overt behaviour may be controlled by a set of rules which need not correspond with the set of rules which he recognizes as constituting the correct norm and to which he can make reference when required. These two kinds of rule are coexistent. I will refer to the first (those *in praesentia* which characterize what the learner does) as *context* rules and the second (those *in absentia* which characterize what the learner knows) as *code* rules.

Now when the learner is placed in a situation in which his attention is expressly drawn to his knowledge of code rules, as, for example, when he is doing structural drills, his performance is likely to be very different from the one he gives when he is in a situation in which he is required to use his knowledge to some sort of communicative effect. But in which situation does one establish error? If one seeks evidence of his interlanguage in the controlled language exercise, then one will have to accept the likelihood that the description of the interlanguage is not predictive of actual language behaviour. It will account for code rules but not for context rules. If, on the other hand, one seeks evidence of the learner's interlanguage in communicative situations in which learners have less leisure to draw on code rules they know, then one will have to accept the likelihood that the description of the interlanguages does not reflect the learner's transitional competence or approximative system. In this case, the description will account for context rules but not for code rules.

The notions of error and interlanguage seem to depend on an acceptance of a narrowly conceived Chomskyan concept of competence. But once one extends this concept to include 'performance phenomena' like contextual variation, as I have done, then their validity is called into question. It is not only that they are difficult to define in relation to the broader notion of communicative competence but they also lose their status as cardinal concepts. Because if we shift our focus of attention from an exclusive study of linguistic competence to a study of communicative processes in which linguistic competence is included, then what is of interest to us is not simply the learner's interlanguage and how he acquired it, but more crucially what he does with it and why it varies in a regular way under different contextual conditions. Error analysts have dealt with interlanguage change in the direction of closer approximation to the TL. But change is only the temporal consequence of current variation. What needs to be explained is why there is variation, why what I have called code rules do not match context rules, why learners do not act on their knowledge.

The general answer to this question is, I think, that learners do not match what they do with what they know because normal communicative activity does not require them to do so. No language user simply manifests a linguistic system: a linguistic system is realized as communicative behaviour and this realization requires a simplification of the system in a sense which I shall explain presently. In normal language use we are constrained by the requirements of communicative effectiveness and we therefore develop context rules which relate to but are not a direct reflection of the code rules which constitute our linguistic competence.

To illustrate what I mean by this, I want to refer back to the observation I made earlier that lapses occurring in speech might not necessarily occur in writing, and that lapses occurring in communicative settings of one sort or another might not necessarily occur in language exercises. It would seem to be the case that if language behaviour is required to take place in contexts of interaction, it is more likely that code rules will be displaced in favour of context rules. Now it seems to me that this is exactly the phenomenon that Labov describes in his discussion of stylistic variation. He points out that the occurrence of different linguistic forms varies in a regular way in accordance with contextual constraints, and he makes the generalization:

> Styles can be ranged along a single dimension, measured by the amount of attention paid to speech.
> *Labov 1972: 204.*

Thus the speech of, let us say, a member of the working class will approximate to standard usage in those situations where his attention is directed to the way he is speaking, as when he is producing minimal pairs or reading aloud, but will deviate from standard usage in those situations where he is using the language in a normal communicative fashion. We may say that his behaviour approximates more closely to code rules in the former type of situation than in the latter, that in the former situation he is paying attention to usage and in the latter he is paying attention to use. It seems to me that we have an exactly comparable situation with the learner: when his attention is directed to usage, as it is when he is doing structural drills and other linguistic exercises, then he will move in the direction of the standard forms he has been taught, and perform in accordance with the code rules of his interlanguage. But when he is involved in any kind of communicative activity, his attention will be directed to effective use and his performance will accord with context rules. In both cases, then, the language user's attention shifts from usage and the code rules which determine its correctness, to use and the context rules which determine its effectiveness. In both cases, the shift can only be satisfactorily formalized by postulating variable rules.

It would seem to follow from this essential similarity between what a learner does and what a native speaker does that what error analysis might reasonably be expected to concern itself with is the way in which the learner's transitional communicative competence can be accounted as an aspect of general human behaviour (and after all, the communicative competence of all language users is, of its nature, transitional), how the learner's strategies are in effect realizations of universal tendencies. There has in fact already been some attempt to place learners' errors in a wider theoretical and descriptive context and in particular Richards has pointed out the relevance of studies of pidginization and creolization (Richards 1972). But I believe the matter can be taken further.

Creolists have pointed to a number of remarkable resemblances between pidgins and creoles spoken among groups of people between whom there could have been no communicative contact (Hymes 1971, Todd 1974) and this has led to the suggestion that such resemblances are the embodiment in particularly transparent forms of linguistic universals. Similarly, error analysts have pointed to the existence of common errors and have suggested that these are evidence of universal learning strategies (Richards 1974). Clearly, the creolists' recognition of resemblance without contact and the error analysts' recognition of resemblance without interference amount to the same thing and in Ferguson (1971) this is made quite explicit. Ferguson suggests that there are certain basic simplification processes at work which account for a number of similarities between baby talk, foreigner talk, and pidgins, and in particular he deals with the deletion of the copula. I believe that the notion of simplification is the key to an understanding of these resemblances and of the universal features of deviant forms of speaking which Ferguson refers to. So on the cue provided by Ferguson I will now turn to consider this notion.

I want to define simplification as the process whereby a language user adjusts his language behaviour in the interests of communicative effectiveness. This adjustment may involve a movement away from the reference norm of the standard language so as to arrive at forms of speaking judged to be dialectically appropriate in certain contexts of use. This is the kind of simplification that Labov describes. The adjustment may involve either the increase or decrease in complexity of usage. This might appear to be perversely paradoxical. How can one talk of simplification which involves linguistic complexity? One can do so, I suggest, because effectiveness of use in a particular communicative situation might well require explicitness or a conformity to accepted convention which calls for linguistic elaboration. This is a point which is frequently ignored by the authors of simplified readers and language teaching textbooks: the simplifying of usage does not necessarily result in the simplification of use, that is to say, it does not necessarily facilitate communication. On the contrary it very often makes communication less effective. It should be noted that all language use exemplifies simplification in the sense that all language users develop context rules for effective communication, rules which represent a strategic deployment of the code rules which constitute their linguistic competence.

Now when we come to consider learners' errors, it seems reasonable to regard them as efforts to derive context rules from the code rules imposed upon them by the teacher. All of the factors which Selinker refers to can be regarded as aspects of simplification, of attempts to arrive at effective communication. All of them are evidence of transfer, not necessarily marked by the formal transfer of aspects of one language system into another, but of communicative strategies associated with the use of the system already known. This transfer of simplification procedures may result in errors which can be traced to linguistic interference, or to oversimplification, or to any of the other processes which Selinker mentions. What happens, I suggest, is that the learner is provided with a set of code rules which he will act upon with a fair degree of success in those teaching situations which require simple conformity to them. The more he is required to use these rules for a communicative purpose, however, the more likely he is to adopt the normal communicative strategy of simplification; the more likely he is, in other words, to behave like a normal human being and develop context rules to facilitate communication. To say that errors occur as a result of certain psychological processes like language transfer, transfer of training, strategies of second language learning, and so on does not seem to me to go far enough. We need some sort of explanation as to *why* these processes take place. What I am suggesting is that they take place because the learner attempts to adjust the language he is learning to make it an effective instrument of communication and he does so by calling upon those strategies which he employs in the use of his own language. Errors are the result of the learner's attempt to convert linguistic usage into communicative use.

It follows from this view that a learner's errors are evidence of success and not of failure, that the failure to conform to given code rules is the consequence of success in developing context rules. To put it another way, the learner focuses on strategies of use, rather than on norms of usage. In this way, he is in effect providing the language he is learning with a communicative significance which the actual teaching very often does not allow for. Errors can be said to indicate that the learner's instinctive concept of the communicative nature of language, derived from the experience of using his own mother tongue, is proof against the teacher's concept of language as a formal system. It would seem to follow from this that errors should be exploited rather than corrected. Correction will tend to force the learner back from use to usage and to thereby reverse the natural process.

I think that the (relative) failure of a good deal of language teaching endeavour is the result of an attempt to make the language learner conceive of language in a way which is contrary to his own experience. In a sense his errors represent an instinctive protest. He simplifies the system he is presented with by devising context rules to achieve an approximation to communicative effect because the teacher's simplification of linguistic data in terms of code rules does not adequately provide for communicative activity. Although it is perfectly proper to establish a model of the learner's transitional competence or interlanguage by adopting the grammarian's idealization of data, it seems to me that such an exercise does not probe deep enough into underlying causes. It is inadequate in the same way as the generative grammar to which it relates: the communicative dimension is not taken into account. The learner's interlanguage or approximative system takes the form it does, I would argue, because it reflects his communicative competence. And this fact explains also why his lapses cannot be adequately described in terms of invariant rules, but only in terms of variable rules of the kind that Labov has made familiar.

I want to turn now to a brief consideration of the implications that this perspective on learner behaviour has for language teaching. The first point to make is the obvious one—that the language teacher's simplification of language data in the form of the conventional structural syllabus does not correspond with the learner's simplification. The solution to this state of affairs has generally been to devise exercises to draw the learner away from his own simplification towards that of the teacher. But if it is the case that the learner's simplification represents his attempt at developing a communicative strategy, as I have suggested, and if it is the purpose of language teaching to develop such a strategy in the use of the language being learnt, then such exercises are likely to be counter-productive. They establish code rules for their own sake and tend to suppress the learner's natural inclination to develop context rules. Hence, the language being learnt is represented as something which should not be related to the experience of language use which the learner has acquired through a knowledge of his mother tongue. An alternative procedure would be to have the teacher's simplification approximate to that of the learner.

One way in which this might be done is to use the findings of error analysis not for remedial teaching through which the errors are eradicated, but for initial teaching through which errors are exploited. That is to say, one might devise syllabuses which actually presented the erroneous forms which particular groups of learners were prone to produce, gradually bringing 'correct' standard forms into focus as the course progressed. Such a syllabus would seem, on the face of it, to be feasible and would be in line with current approaches to the teaching of communicative competence. But we must be careful not to minimize the difficulties. To begin with, such a syllabus would require considerable reorientation in the attitude of language teachers. The impression is sometimes given that teachers are perversely tradition-bound and that advances in language teaching pedagogy are blocked by their obscurantism. It is important to recognize, however, that the view that language teaching is a matter of acquiring correct usage is deeply ingrained in all language users and not only in those who are professionally concerned with the teaching of language. As is clear from the findings of Labov referred to earlier, there is a general tendency for language users to make reference to norms of correctness in formal situations. Why should this be so? It can only be explained, surely, by exploring a general hypothesis of the kind favoured by apocalyptic scholars like Whorf and Steiner about the nature of language and of habitual human behaviour: for example, that language users need the stability of language norms to provide them with a definition of their universe and so to give them an underlying sense of security. Indeed I think it possible that the Sapir/Whorf hypothesis is tenable in relation to code rules, and that it is only when one attempts to apply it to context rules that difficulties occur.

I would wish to argue, then, that a teaching syllabus which represented the learner's simplification would also run the risk of distorting the learner's concept of language. The conventional syllabus runs counter to the learner's experience by presenting language in terms of code rules and by denying the development of context rules. The syllabus that is based on learner's errors would run counter to the learner's experience to the extent that it would present language in terms of context rules, but would not provide adequately for the development of code rules. To operate efficiently in a language, the learner needs to have both at his disposal, and to realize the relationship between them. This, I take it, is what communicative competence means.

In view of all this, what approach can we take that ensures that what we teach conforms to the learner's experience of language? One possibility is that which is being currently explored under the general rubric of notional or communicative syllabuses. Another is one which I keep on suggesting with irritating persistence (Widdowson 1968, 1973, etc.) and which I shall suggest again now. It is that the language being taught should be directly associated with other subjects in the school curriculum. In the last paragraph or two of this paper I want to try to give some weight to this suggestion by invoking once more the notion of simplification.

All teaching involves simplification. Pedagogic methodology is the process whereby the concepts and procedures of different areas of inquiry are organized and expressed so as to make them congruent with the learner's experience. We might say that the teacher adjusts his language behaviour in the interests of communicative effectiveness. Now if it is the case that this is what the language learner does as well, as I have argued, then it would seem that the simplification as realized in the syllabuses of subjects like general science, geography, history, and so on represents the same basic communicative strategy that the language learner reveals in his linguistic lapses. The difference is, of course, that the former does not find expression in deviant forms: communicative effectiveness is achieved without doing violence to code rules. The language in subject textbooks is controlled by a recognizable communicative need and the correctness of usage does not compromise the appropriateness of use.

I should like to suggest that there is no need to work out a syllabus for the teaching of a foreign language as a separate operation; that indeed it might well be counter-productive to do so. Language syllabuses can be derived from the syllabuses of other subjects, and represent alternative versions of them, allowing for certain relatively minor adjustments, if necessary. Such a proposal means, in effect, that language would cease to be taught as a subject in its own right. I would argue that the methodology of language teaching has, to a large extent, been, as it were, self-inflicted: the consequence of the mistaken initial assumption that languages can be considered as subjects. In fact, language is only a subject in linguistics, not in language learning. Thus, if one wishes to teach usage, it is possible to treat it as a separate subject; but if one wishes to teach use (as I assume as language teachers we do) I do not see how it can be considered otherwise than as an aspect of some other subject, whose methodology must be established beforehand.

There is a final point I should like to make. I have suggested that the language teacher should allow himself to be guided by the pedagogic practice of his colleagues teaching other subjects. I do not wish to imply by this that this practice is perfect. I feel sure that there is plenty of room for improvement in the communicative rapport which constitutes effective teaching method. And this is where the enlightened language teacher can offer reciprocal guidance. For if he can widen the scope of his interest to include considerations of language use, then he will be in a position to indicate to other teachers the way language functions to communicative effect, and, indeed, to demonstrate to them the significance of simplification.

Notes

Paper presented at the fourth Neuchâtel Colloquium in Applied Linguistics, May 1975, and published in the proceedings: *Studies in Second Language Acquisition.* University of Indiana Linguistics Club, Volume 1 No 1.

16 Pidgin and babu

I want to argue in this paper from the proposition that there are two forces in natural language which act in opposite directions and which the language user has constantly to keep in equilibrium. One force acts in the direction of content: this is the referential force. The other acts in the direction of expression: this is the poetic force. de Saussure, of course, regarded these as in a steady state synthesized within the linguistic sign (*signifié*/*signifiant*). I want to suggest that once one looks beyond the convenient fiction of a static system, the relationship between them becomes problematic. The linguistic analyst dealing with abstractions may wish to consider these forces as arrested in suspended animation, but for language users they are, in actuality, frequently in conflict. When the conflict is resolved in favour of the referential force, the result is a movement in the direction of a pidgin. When it is resolved in favour of the poetic force, the result is a movement in the direction of a babu.

The principal characteristics of pidgin are well known. De Camp summarizes them as follows:

> It is characterized by a limited vocabulary, an elimination of many grammatical devices such as number and gender, and a drastic reduction of redundant features.
> *De Camp 1971: 15.*

This stripping down of language to its bare essentials is done in the interest of communicative economy in restricted contact situations. It reduces scope for stylistic option and the range of alternative expression is in consequence severely limited. The emphasis is on content and it is the referential force which is dominant. The development from pidgin to creole and into the post-creole continuum comes as a consequence of the expression force exerting its influence in response to more subtle social needs. How you say something becomes as important as what you say.

In babu, it is the expression that receives primary emphasis. Here how you say something is more important than what you say. The term 'babu' refers to the junior Indian clerk whose knowledge of English helped to sustain the vast bureaucracy of the British Raj. His use of English was characterized by self-conscious elaboration of phrase which, before the days of the typewriter, was often conveyed in written form by means of a careful copper-plate handwriting.

Hancock confusingly includes babu in his list of pidgin and creole languages, equating it with Hobson-Jobson and Chhi-Chhi (or Cheechee). The relevant entry reads as follows:

> Hobson-Jobson, 'Babu English' or 'Chhi-Chhi'. A rudimentary pidgin employed during the period of British rule in India. *Hancock 1971: 520.*

I think this must be wrong. I do not know what Hancock can mean by a 'rudimentary' pidgin but Hobson-Jobson refers only to the *lexical* characteristics of Anglo-Indian English. The book title which provides the name indicates this quite clearly:

> Hobson-Jobson: being a glossary of Anglo-Indian colloquial words and phrases and of kindred terms—etymological, historical, geographical, and discursive.

Chhi-Chhi, on the other hand, refers to an Anglo-Indian *accent*. The term is glossed in 'Hobson-Jobson' as follows:

> CHEECHEE Adj. A disparaging term applied to half-castes or *Eurasians* (qv) (corresponding to the *lip lap* of the Dutch in Java), and also to their manner of speech. The word is said to be taken from *chi* (Fie!), a common native (S. Indian) interjection of remonstrance or reproof supposed to be much used by the class in question. The term is, however, perhaps also a kind of onomatopoeia, indicating the mincing pronunciation which often characterizes them. It should, however, be added that there are many well-educated East Indians who are quite free from this mincing accent.

For further details, see Spencer (1966).

Hobson-Jobson and Cheechee, then, are not at all the same thing and neither can be appropriately described as a pidgin. Babu English is different again, being essentially 'expansive' rather than 'reductive'.

This mode of language use is not confined to Indian clerks. Just as we recognize that pidgin characteristics appear in 'normal' kinds of communication like telegrams and newspaper headlines (see Ferguson 1971: 146), where the referential force is dominant, so we can recognize kinds of language use which have some of the characteristics of babu, where the poetic force is dominant. Examples abound in political speeches, sales patter, and the kind of prepared commentary given by guides showing people round places of historic interest. They also occur in the language learner's language. I shall return to this presently. Meanwhile, there are one or two points I should like to make clear.

Firstly, when I say that in babu language the poetic force is dominant I do not mean that babu language is like poetry. I am using the term 'poetic' in the technical sense defined in Jakobson (1960): it refers to the focusing of the act of speech on the actual form of the message rather than on its content. There *is* poetry (of a kind) that is poetic in this sense, in particular English poetry which was written in accordance with conventions of eighteenth-century poetic diction. Expressions like 'finny brood' and 'feathered tribe' are babu terms for 'fish' and 'birds' respectively. One of Pope's collaborators in the translating of Homer's *Odyssey* (Elijah Fenton by name) provides a striking example of the poetic force at work. He comes across a passage in Homer which (as translated by Loeb) runs as follows:

> So saying, he hurled with strong hand the hoof of an ox, taking it up from the basket where it lay.

This he renders into babu as follows:

> He said; and of the steer before him plac'd,
> That sinewy fragment at Ulysses cast,
> Where to the pastern-bone, by nerves combin'd,
> The well-horn'd foot indissolubly join'd
> (for further discussion see Sutherland 1948).

Fenton's verses are babu in that they are a complete submission to the poetic force.

Poetry is successful to the extent that it achieves a tension between the opposing forces I have mentioned and holds them in precarious equilibrium. What is unique about successful poetry, in fact, is precisely that it resolves the conflict between these opposing forces, and the distinction between content and expression disappears: what is said and how it is said become one. As T. S. Eliot puts it:

> . . . where every word is at home
> Taking its place to support the others,
> The word neither diffident nor ostentatious,
> An easy commerce of the old and the new,
> The common word exact without vulgarity,
> The formal word precise but not pedantic,
> The complete consort dancing together . . .
> *Little Gidding*

A major theme in *Four Quartets* is the difficulty of reconciling the opposing referential and poetic forces. It is a difficulty which confronts all language users, not only poets, and effective communication depends on its resolution.

These forces I have been referring to and the different kinds of 'abnormality' they can give rise to may be expressed diagrammatically in something like the following form:

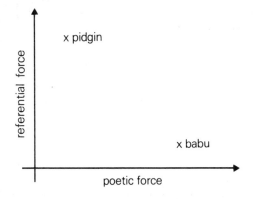

Now there are occasions, of course, when it is appropriate that the poetic force should be allowed to exert itself so that performance moves towards babu on the horizontal axis of language use. In such language, expression is a means of concealing content rather than conveying it directly: it is a device for distracting attention away from what is actually said. This may be done to deceive, as with a good deal of political discourse, where content may be slight or even non-existent. It might be noted, however, that political discourse which inclines towards the babu end of the functional continuum need not necessarily be intended to deceive. It may be used to suggest the special significance of a message and to lend it an appropriate air of portentousness. Winburne (1962) shows, for example, that the basic message of Abraham Lincoln's Gettysburg address can be reduced to the simple proposition 'We dedicate a battlefield'. The poetic force may be allowed leeway to mitigate the effect of an intended illocutionary force, or of the propositional content of an utterance (see the remarks on modes of mitigation and politeness in Labov 1970). In this latter case, we have the poetic force put to communicative effect to achieve euphemism.

There are occasions, then, when some submission to the poetic force is functionally appropriate. There are other occasions, however, when the poetic force is allowed to exert itself for its own sake. *Euphemism* is a motivated use of the poetic force for the more effective communication of content. This is to be distinguished from *euphuism*, where content serves as the excuse for expression and where the poetic force is simply released from its confinement to content. The term derives from John Lyly's work *Euphues: The Anatomy of Wit* published in 1579. Here is a sample:

> The foule Toade hathe a fayre stoane in his head, the fine goulde is founde in the filthy earth, the sweete kernell lyeth in the hard shell. Uertue is harbored in the heart of him that most men esteeme misshapen. Contrarywise, if we respect more the outward shape, then the inwarde habit, good God into how many mischiefes doe we fall? Into what blyndenesse are we ledde? Doe we not commonly see that in paynted pottes is hidden the deadlyiest poyson? that in the greenest grasse is the greatest Serpent? in the cleerest water the uglyiest Toade? Doth not experience teach us that in the most curious Sepulchre are enclosed rotten bones? that the Cypresse tree beareth a fayre leafe but no fruit? that the Estridge carryeth fayre feathers but rancke flesh? How franticke are those louers which are carryed away from the gaye glistering of the fine face?

This is babu at its best. Or at its worst. The simple proposition that things are not what they seem by their outward appearance is used as an excuse for an elaborate display of expression, a kind of highly wrought verbal folly. The poetic force, once activated, is simply allowed to expend itself. Here is another instance. The speaker wishes to confide in his interlocutor and one can accept that he might indulge in a little verbal feet-shuffling before getting to the point, but the following is surely a little excessive:

> Well, well seeing the wound that bleedeth inwards is most dangerous, that the fire kepte close burneth most furious, that the Oouen dammed up baketh soonest, that sores hauing no vent fester inwardly, it is high time to unfolde my secret loue, to my secrete friende.

High time indeed, the reader might think.

Here is another example, which I cannot resist including. It comes from a book entitled *Impressive Interviews*, published in New Delhi, which is intended to serve as a candidate's guide to correct verbal comportment at interviews.

Impressive interview no. 26.

Chairman   Good morning, Miss Mohini. Take your seat.
Answer   Good morning, sir. Thank you.
Chairman   Why are you going for an administrative career?
Answer   That I am a woman should by no means militate against the chances of my carving out an administrative career for myself. Women have already figured conspicuously in the various depart-

ments of human life and activity. If they could prove accomplished scholars, renowned politicians, consummate administrators and, to crown all, orators of great repute, there seems no earthly reason why consideration of sex alone should constitute a bar to my building a career for myself. I hope that I shall not have any difficulty in adapting myself to surroundings and atmosphere, not otherwise happy or congenial.

Babu language, then, is marked by an elaboration of expression for its own sake, the result of the poetic force overwhelming the referential. It might be described as an elaborated code of a kind. This naturally brings up the question as to whether it can be related to Bernstein's elaborated code (see Samarin 1971: 130–132). Judging from Bernstein's own descriptions, the two are quite different. His elaborated code is represented as a more efficient instrument for conveying meanings: the elaboration of expression serves a referential need:

> An elaborated code, where prediction is much less possible at the syntactic level, is likely to arise in a social relationship which raises the tension in its members to select from their linguistic resources a *verbal* arrangement which closely fits specific referents. This situation will arise where the intent of the other person cannot be taken for granted, with the consequence that meanings will have to be expanded and raised to the level of verbal explicitness. The verbal planning here, unlike the case of a restricted code, promotes a higher level of syntactic organization and lexical selection. The preparation and delivery of relatively explicit meaning is the major function of this code.
> *Bernstein 1971: 128.*

Unfortunately, as has frequently been pointed out, Bernstein's description of his codes is somewhat speculative and is insufficiently supported by analysis of actual data. Other scholars, less inclined to trust intuition, do not find the qualities which Bernstein attributes to his elaborated code in the middle class speaking which Bernstein associates with it. What Labov, for example, finds is 'jargon and empty elaboration'. He asks:

> Is the 'elaborated code' of Bernstein really so 'flexible, detailed and subtle' as some psychologists believe? . . . Isn't it also turgid, redundant, and empty? Is it not simply an elaborated *style*, rather then a superior code or system?
> *Labov 1969b: 12.*

He then goes on to compare the performance of a speaker using what might reasonably be counted as restricted code in Bernstein's terms, with the performance of a speaker using what might reasonably be counted as elaborated code. Predictably enough, the former emerges from Labov's analysis as an altogether more effective user of language. We would be wise to be wary of this finding: Labov himself is not entirely free of prejudice. What is of relevance to the present discussion, however, is the way in which Labov describes the performance of the elaborated code speaker:

> . . . he makes every effort to qualify his opinions, and seems anxious to avoid any misstatements or over-statements. From these qualities emerge the primary characteristics of this passage—its *verbosity*. Words multiply, some modifying and qualifying, others repeating or padding the main argument.
> *Labov 1969b: 16.*

In this view, elaborated code does not achieve the balance between the opposing referential and poetic forces that Bernstein in effect claims. On the contrary, content is sacrificed to expression and the result is babu, the primary characteristic of which is, precisely, its verbosity.

Although one must be careful not to equate restricted and elaborated codes with non-standard and standard language (see Trudgill 1975), it would seem nevertheless to be the case that an increase in referential force will tend to result in a reduction of surface complexity. This tendency would account for the common characteristics of contact vernaculars like baby-talk, foreigner-talk, and pidgins (Ferguson 1971) and provide some explanation for the universal features of pidgin languages (Kay and Sankoff 1974). Referential force, we may say, moves language in the direction of deviation towards the simplicity of direct reference. Poetic force, on the other hand, moves language in the direction of deflection towards complexity of message form. The term 'deflection' is borrowed from Halliday: he uses it to refer to 'departures from some expected pattern of frequency', particularly as exemplified in literary discourse (Halliday 1973: Ch. 5). I am using the term in a somewhat wider sense to mean the exploitation of grammatical resources for widening the range of alternative message forms, for the elaboration of expression. Linguists concerned with different forms of speaking have in the past concentrated almost exclusively on deviation and have been much preoccupied with its formal characteristics and the social context of its occurrence. But deflection is, it seems to me, an equally important phenomenon. There does not seem to be any reason why one should concentrate on forms of speaking where the referential force is dominant while neglecting those where the poetic force is dominant. Both can be seen as illustrative of universal tendencies in natural language. These tendencies are realized to different degrees in different circumstances. It would seem, for example, that literacy provides conditions which favour the development of babu. Written language is of its nature independent of immediate context and something, therefore, that can be fashioned in detachment as an artefact. The association referred to earlier between the Indian clerk's mode of expression and his handwriting is not simply fortuitous.

Recent work on pidgin languages (Hymes 1971, De Camp and Hancock 1974) has considerably advanced our knowledge of the nature of deviation. To put this work into proper perspective we now need to turn our attention to deflection, to consider babu language, the other end of the post-creole continuum. But babu is not only a phenomenon of theoretical interest for sociolinguists: it is also one which has considerable significance for language teaching. We might consider, for example, the notion of error. This has almost always been associated with deviation, the extent to which the learner's 'interlanguage' does not match up with the standard code of the target language as a means of expression. Thus the learner is said to make errors if the message form of his utterance is non-standard, even though it might be referentially effective. But what if the learner's message forms are correct but convey no content worth expressing? Labov makes the comment:

> In high school and college middle-class children spontaneously complicate their syntax to the point that instructors despair of getting them to make their language simpler and clearer.
> *Labov 1969: 12.*

And in the L2 situation it is common to find learners producing linguistic patterns for their own sake without regard to their referential value. We do not normally consider these as errors, but why not? If we are to measure learner performance in terms of communicative effectiveness (and it is difficult to justify any other means of measurement) then it is surely just as reprehensible to err in the direction of over-elaboration as in the direction of over-simplification. In both cases communication is likely to be impaired. There seems no reason why we should deplore the pidgin and approve of the babu.

And yet I think that our approach to the teaching of foreign languages is indeed based on a belief in the overriding importance of expression. Our learners are taught submission to the poetic force from the very beginning. It does not matter what nonsense they produce so long as they produce it in correct sentences. The very design of most practice drills restricts the learner to the automatic repetition of linguistic expressions which become by repetition itself referentially vacuous. Of course, being speakers of natural language, learners will frequently feel the pull of the referential force. They then make errors, for which they are duly penalized. The language we find in most language teaching classrooms is a kind of classroom babu, a form of expression almost totally devoid of content representing the forced growth of syntactic elaboration for its own sake. The paradox of much of language teaching is that it emphasizes correctness by focusing on message form, and so insists on the operation of the poetic function, in circumstances which are socially impoverished and thus provide no justification for the emphasis. There is no motivation for elaboration. Correct forms, representing as they do an accretion of socially desirable redundancy, emerge as a consequence of communicative purpose and develop naturally only under pressure of increasingly subtle and complex social interaction. What would be more appropriate in the classroom would be an initial emphasis on the referential force, on getting learners to say something worth saying in language which approximates to pidgin rather than babu.

There seems to be no reason, in principle, why we should not try to develop a kind of classroom pidgin in the early stages of learning. The situation is, after all, precisely one which would favour the emergence of a contact vernacular. In this case we would expose the learner to standard language but aim at teaching a simplified form of expression for productive purposes to be used to conduct different sorts of classroom business and then gradually elaborate this into a kind of creole and then through the post-creole continuum towards the standard language. In this way we might hope to maintain a balance between the two opposing forces and get the learners to learn something which is more in accord with their own experience of language.

In Act II of *Hamlet*, Polonius, an inveterate babu speaker, addresses Claudius and Gertrude in these terms:

> My liege, and madam,—to expostulate
> What majesty should be, what duty is,
> Why day is day, night night, and time is time,
> Were nothing but to waste night, day, and time.
> Therefore, since brevity is the soul of wit,
> And tediousness the limbs and outward flourishes,
> I will be brief:—your noble son is mad:
> Mad call I it; for to define true madness,
> What is't but to be nothing else but mad?
> But let that go.

At which point, Gertrude comes in with the curt remark:

> More matter with less art.

This exchange illustrates the conflict of opposing forces which I have argued in this paper, is an intrinsic feature of natural language. Every utterance is an attempt to balance these forces in the interest of com-

municative effectiveness. When we fail to achieve the balance communication is impaired. The failure tends to be tolerated more readily
when it is caused by the poetic force overcoming the referential, rather
than the reverse. But Gertrude does not tolerate it. Neither, perhaps,
should we. In our language teaching it would perhaps be an advantage
to place our emphasis more on the referential force and less on the
poetic; more on those features of language use which characterize
pidgins and less on those which characterize babus. In Gertrude's
words (to put the point more referentially): what we perhaps need is
'more matter with less art'.

Notes

Paper presented at the fifth Neuchâtel Colloquium in Applied Linguistics, May 1976, and published in the proceedings: Corder and
Roulet 1977.

Descriptions and applications

The papers here investigate the relationship of the theoretical study to the practical teaching of language. They are concerned with establishing applied linguistics as an area of inquiry. They differ, however, in emphasis and attitude. The first paper (Paper 17) sees the main task of applied linguistics as the interpretation of findings from theoretical models of description. The second paper sees it as the initiation of models according to independent criteria of relevance.

Paper 17, then, focuses on the advantages that can be gained through the exploration of theory, showing how insights from micro and macro studies of language can, through the interpretative mediation of applied linguistics, be put to pedagogic service. It demonstrates, therefore, how one might proceed from one end of the applied linguistics spectrum to the other. In the course of this demonstration issues touched on in earlier papers are taken up for further discussion: in particular attention is given to how one might move beyond the sentence towards discourse through a consideration of propositions and illocutions.

There is an assumption in this first paper that micro-linguistic models of description as developed by grammarians must be relevant to language teaching even though this relevance may not be self-evident and so needs to be revealed by applied linguistic interpretation. The other paper in this section questions this assumption. The burden of the argument here is that the model of language devised by the analyst according to principles of objective inquiry may not be congruent with that of the language user. Furthermore it is suggested that the model most appropriate for learners is more likely to be one derived from that of the user rather than that of the analyst, and that the derivation of such a pedagogically appropriate model of description should be the main business of applied linguistics.

In the past, the basic source of reference, the authoritative model, for language teaching has been the different descriptive grammars of linguistic analysts. If, as I suggest here, these linguistic representations do not reflect the user's own experience of language use, then it would seem likely that at least some of the difficulties encountered by learners arise from the fact that the teacher has to train them in analytic attitudes. Such attitudes will often be difficult to adopt and may well be unfavourable to learning, involving as they must a dissociation from user experience. Hence many of the problems of the learner may, paradoxically, derive directly from the pedagogy designed to solve them.

17 Linguistic insights and language teaching principles

Linguistics is the systematic study of language through the observation of the characteristics of particular languages. It would seem to be self-evident that such a study would have an immediate bearing on the tasks of the language teacher, that it would provide a definition of the content of his subject. We might expect that the teacher would be able to draw what he has to teach from the findings of linguistic descriptions and so make his own procedures more systematic. But the relationship between theoretical linguistics and practical language teaching is not as simple and direct as it might appear to be. We need a mediating area of inquiry which will interpret the results of theoretical and descriptive studies in such a way as to reveal their relevance to the language teacher. This mediating inquiry is generally known as applied linguistics. The purpose of this paper is to demonstrate a number of ways in which this mediation can take place and by so doing to define the scope of applied linguistics in so far as it relates to the problems of language teaching.

Two assumptions have been made in this opening paragraph which are immediately open to objection and so they need to be examined in some detail. The first is that linguistics stands in need of interpretation. This assumption seems to run directly counter to one of the basic principles of contemporary linguistics that its statements should be absolutely explicit and exact. It is generally allowed that the rules of a linguistic description have their origin in the intuitive introspection of individual linguists, but once the rules have been formulated they are not open to the variable interpretation of intuitive judgements. How then can one speak of interpreting the findings of linguistics when these findings by definition leave no room for interpretation? Part of the answer to this puzzle is that where linguistic description is explicit it is so only at the expense of a severe restriction on its scope of inquiry, and where its scope of inquiry is extended it ceases to be explicit. In the standard version of the generative model of linguistic description, for example, language is reduced to a well-defined axiomatic system and there is no account taken of language variation or change, of the way in which language is put to communicative use. The rules are explicit but interpretation is required to relate them to the actual facts of language behaviour. In recent developments in generative linguistics, on the other hand, the scope is much wider: there are attempts to incorporate aspects of use into grammatical statements. But the statements have little of the explicitness and exactitude of the rules of the standard version of the theory. We have an abundance of insights into the nature of language but interpretation is required to organize them into some semblance of order. Linguistics has moved from the early period of classical precision to a current resurgence of romanticism. We need some detachment from these shifts of fashion in order to judge how far they provide a satisfactory account of those aspects of language as a whole with which we as language teachers are particularly concerned. We touch here on another reason why interpretation is necessary.

All systematic inquiry is based on an idealization of data, and all idealization is relative to the principal interest of the inquirer. As de Saussure pointed out, the whole phenomenon of language presents a picture of bewildering heterogeneity that must be reduced to order in some way if it is to be studied at all. His solution was to assume a static and well-defined system at the core of all the outward confusion. This solution, adopted also in its essentials by Chomsky and his associates, provides for a stable platform upon which linguistic models can be built. But it is a draconian one all the same. Its efficacy as a means of defining a discipline of linguistics rests on the fact that it excludes from consideration a wide range of phenomena which other people interested in language might well regard as absolutely central to its study. The point is that all systematic study is based on an idealization which adjusts 'reality' to make it conform to how the inquirer is inclined to conceive it. The methodological principles of linguistics which were first made explicit by de Saussure have yielded impressive results and enormously extended our knowledge of the nature of language in certain directions. But not in others. Different sets of methodological principles deriving from a different approach to idealization have to be set up to inquire into those aspects of language which linguistics, in the narrow sense we have been considering, cannot by definition account for. Thus, for example, the manner in which language is manifested in actual delivery, characterized by hesitation, self-editing and repetition, is disregarded by the linguist as grammarian but is clearly of immediate concern to the psychologist, who will frame his principles of inquiry in such a way as to bring these features into the focus of his attention. Again, the manner in which language is realized as actual communicative activity determined not only by knowledge of linguistic structure but also by a knowledge of what constitutes appropriate social behaviour in different settings is excluded by the linguist in his formulation of grammatical rules. But those who are interested in the study of language in its social context will obviously wish to frame their principles in such a way as to capture these aspects of language. And the language teacher too has his own principles of approach, a way of representing language which conforms to his own particular concerns; and the way language is dealt with in the theoretical and descriptive domains that have been mentioned has to be adjusted in the light of these principles. The findings of linguistics, psycholinguistics, and sociolinguistics have, in other words, to be interpreted so as to incorporate them into a language teaching pedagogy.

Linguistics, then, requires the mediation of an interpreter for its potential usefulness to language teaching to be realized. The interpretation involves two processes. The first is the selection of insights from the whole range of theoretical and descriptive studies of language, stripping them of their formal integuments where these are cumbersome, giving some reformulation to the insights where they are vague and haphazard. The second process is one of adaptation. Here the insights are recast in a form which will accord with the requirements of language teaching. It should be noted that neither of these processes is likely to find much favour with theoretical linguists since they run counter to their notions of consistency and rigour. But the language teacher has other conditions of adequacy to consider and it is these that the applied linguistic interpretation is intended to satisfy.

Mention of the language teacher's conditions of adequacy brings us to the second assumption that has been made which is open to objection. This is that language teachers have a need of insights deriving from theoretical studies. It might be argued, and indeed it has been argued, that the teacher can work out his own way to effective teaching without being troubled by the activities of linguists who seem intent only on complicating the issue. If these activities are such as to need a mediating interpretation, why should it be supposed that they have any bearing on the essentially practical business of teaching language?

Perhaps the first point to make in answer to this objection is that the teaching of language is in fact an essentially theoretical business. No matter how practical an attitude a teacher may assume, this attitude must ultimately be founded on beliefs about the nature of language and how it is learnt: in other words, it must be based on a theory of one sort or another. This theory may not be explicit, and it may indeed operate below the level of conscious formulation: the teacher may do his teaching according to intuitively held principles which he has never given formal expression to. Now if we could rely on all teachers acquiring sound pedagogic principles by simple experience, then there would be no need of training. Unfortunately we cannot. The very notion of training implies that there is something specific to impart through explicit instruction. Although the naturally gifted teacher may need no special guidance, the vast majority of teachers do, and this guidance must take the form of a set of basic pedagogic principles which they can bring to bear on particular teaching situations. It might be thought that it is enough to demonstrate a particular approach and require teachers to adopt it by imitation without troubling them with the principles which underlie it. But all kinds of factors come into play in actual teaching and no one approach can be imposed on all situations. Teachers need more than an approach which they can adopt; they need a set of underlying principles which will allow them to adapt particular approaches to meet the requirements of different circumstances. Without such a set of explicit principles the teacher will be imprisoned within a methodological orthodoxy.

It seems clear, then, that the language teacher needs an explicit conceptual framework within which he can devise particular teaching approaches. The relationship between the principles which make up this framework and a particular teaching approach is comparable to that between linguistic insights and a particular model of linguistic description. It has sometimes been assumed in the past that a teaching approach can be derived directly from a model of linguistic description. What I am arguing here is that the link between linguistics and language teaching lies in the relationship between insights and principles, and that it is this relationship that requires the interpretation of the applied linguist. Pedagogic principles can be developed through an interpretation of insights deriving from theoretical studies of language. Let us now consider examples.

I suggested earlier on that linguistics as conceived by de Saussure and Chomsky (among others) should not be equated with theoretical studies of language. We have to distinguish between a broad and a narrow definition of linguistics. A narrow definition restricts the scope of linguistics to a study of the abstract underlying system of a language assumed to represent the shared knowledge of all speakers. This is micro-linguistics or 'core' linguistics and its central concern is the writing of grammars. A broad definition includes the study of psychological and social factors which constrain the way that speakers of a language draw upon their knowledge of the language system, and how this system itself varies and changes over time under the influence of psychological and social factors. This is macro-linguistics. For the purposes of the present discussion I want to concentrate on that part of micro-linguistics which is concerned with syntax and that part of macro-linguistics which is concerned with the communicative function of language as a means of social interaction. I have selected these areas because I believe that they offer insights which can be exploited for the establishment of certain teaching principles.

Syntactic description, under the conditions of idealization which have already been mentioned, represents the rules which control the correct usage of a language. These rules yield a set of sentences. But they provide no indication about what acts of communication these sentences are used to perform when they are actually uttered in social contexts, nor how communicative import is carried along over stretches of language consisting of a number of sentence-like units connected together. They are rules of usage and not rules of use. To discover the latter we have to turn to a sociolinguistic description. In what follows I shall first consider what insights might be gained from certain ways of describing language usage and then go on to consider what insights might be gained from certain ways of describing language use.

We will begin by considering a set of sentences:

1 Macbeth killed Duncan.
2 Did Macbeth kill Duncan?
3 Duncan was killed by Macbeth.
4 It was Macbeth who killed Duncan.
5 It was Duncan who was killed by Macbeth.
6 What Macbeth did was to kill Duncan.
7 What happened to Duncan was that he was killed by Macbeth.

Here we have seven structurally different sentences and if we were making use of a structuralist model of linguistic description which analysed syntactic structures simply in terms of immediate constituents we would have to say that each of these sentences is structurally distinct and leave it at that. But it is intuitively obvious that sentences 1 and 3 are related in a way that sentences 1 and 2 are not. We might express this relationship in an informal fashion by saying that in some sense the first pair of sentences have the same meaning whereas the second pair of sentences do not. Now if we adopt a transformational-generative approach to linguistic description we can give a more formal account of this relationship by specifying that sentences 1 and 3 are surface variants deriving from the same deep structure source by different transformational routes. Once one accepts the notion of there being two levels in syntactic analysis, the deep level where basic meaning relations are established and the surface level at which these relations take on different formal appearances, then the way is open to the establishment of links between sentences which seem on the surface to be very different indeed. Consider, for example, sentences 4–7 in our collection. On the face of it, with reference only to surface appearance, these sentences have little resemblance to each other or to sentences 1–3. And yet they can all be said to express the same basic proposition and to this extent to be synonymous. Any of these sentences could be used, for example, to report an utterance of one of the others. Let us suppose that Macduff in the course of a conversation with Malcolm utters sentence 1. Malcolm can, without any misrepresentation, report what Macduff has said by using any of the other sentences except sentence 2. Alternatively, Macduff's utterance of, say, sentence 6 could be reported by the use of any of the other sentences except 2. We can illustrate this with the following invented extracts from an apocryphal version of *Macbeth*:

Scene 1

Macduff   Macbeth killed Duncan.
Malcolm   Are you sure?
Macduff   Yes.

Scene 2

Ross   What did Macduff say?
Malcolm   He said that it was Macbeth who killed Duncan.

Scene 1

Macduff   What Macbeth did was to kill Duncan.
Malcolm   Are you sure?
Macduff   Yes.

Scene 2

Ross   What did Macduff say?
Malcolm   He said that Duncan was killed by Macbeth.

The advantage of a transformational-generative model of usage is that it provides formal recognition of what we might call the propositional equivalence of structurally different surface forms. It would represent sentences 1 and 3–7 as relatable to the same deep structure, which is in effect a formulation of the basic proposition which they all express. Their differences are accounted for in terms of the transformational operations they undergo before they emerge on the surface. Exactly what form these operations take is a complex and controversial matter involving technical problems associated with the formal apparatus of a generative grammar. We need not be troubled with this. The essential insight for our purposes is that structurally different surface forms can be grouped together as expressing a common proposition. But having selected this insight from transformational-generative grammar and restated it in simple terms, how can we adapt it so that it can serve as a language teaching principle?

We can approach an answer to this by first recognizing that the main preoccupation of language teachers has generally been with correct sentence formation. Just as the grammarian has traditionally seen his main task as the construction of a device for generating correct sentences, so the language teacher has traditionally seen his

main task as the development of a set of techniques for teaching
correct sentences. But language does not occur as instances of isolated
sentences. The grammarian can afford to work within an idealized
framework of his own devising and concentrate his attention exclusively
on sentences, but the language teacher cannot. He has his pupils to
think about. Sooner or later he will want them to be able to handle
stretches of language consisting of a series of sentences combined
appropriately together to form *texts*. Sentences are the abstract units of
formal linguistic analysis but they have no special status in actual
language use. They can be taken over and pressed into service as
teaching units, as they very commonly are, but they can only provide a
basis for the knowledge necessary to cope with language as it is normally
used. There must at some stage be a transition from sentences in
isolation to sentences in combination, from sentence to what I have
called text. I think that the linguistic insight that we have been considering points to a principled way in which this transition might
be effected.

The transformational-generative model of linguistic description
enables us to recognize a deep structure equivalence underlying
different sentence forms. Let us say that it demonstrates how different
sentences can have the same signification in the sense that they express
the same basic proposition. But this does not mean that the differences
between these sentences can be ignored. Although they can be said to be
formally equivalent at a deep level of analysis, they are not functionally
equivalent as elements in a text. They are not simply free variants:
which surface form is selected on any particular occasion is determined
by textual conditions. To demonstrate this, we can invent some more
small scenes from *Macbeth*. Consider, for example, the following
exchanges:

1 **Ross**   What did Macbeth do?
  Malcolm   It was Duncan who was killed by Macbeth.

2 **Ross**   What happened?
  Malcolm   It was Macbeth who killed Duncan.

3 **Ross**   Wasn't it Macduff who was killed by Macbeth?
  Malcolm   What happened to Duncan was that he was killed by
                Macbeth.

There is clearly something wrong with Malcolm's replies in all of
these exchanges. The sentences he uses are all perfectly correct as
isolated instances of usage but they are inappropriate in form relative
to the form of Ross's questions. The two sentences in these exchanges

do not combine to create a cohesive text. In the following exchanges, on the other hand, the pairs of sentences do so combine:

1 **Ross**   What did Macbeth do?
  Malcolm He (Macbeth) killed Duncan.
              What he (Macbeth) did was to kill Duncan.

2 **Ross**   What happened?
  Malcolm Macbeth killed Duncan.
              Duncan was killed by Macbeth.
              What happened was that Duncan was killed by Macbeth.

3 **Ross**   Wasn't it Macduff who was killed by Macbeth?
  Malcolm No, it was Duncan who was killed by Macbeth.
              No, Macbeth killed Duncan.

We may say, then, that although the sentences we have been considering are equivalent in signification, they are not equivalent in value as elements in a text. We can now turn our attention to the relevance of these observations to language teaching.

I have said that language teachers have traditionally concentrated on the teaching of sentences. The tendency is to represent different sentences as different units of meaning and in consequence learners are inclined to associate differences of form with differences of proposition. In the early stages of a conventional structurally graded course sentence patterns are selected and arranged in sequence by reference to their distinctiveness of meaning. Later on, it is true, equivalent sentences are introduced, particularly in the teaching of such aspects of language as the passive and the formation of relative clauses, but this is not always done in any very principled way. Exercises which provide practice in transforming active sentences into the passive are given the same status as those which provide practice in converting verb phrases from one tense to another. But as the transformational-generative model of description makes clear, these are very different structural operations. If, however, we group structures which have a common signification together then we can show how active and passive sentences, together with the range of other surface forms we have been considering, express the same basic proposition. The advantage of this is that it counteracts the tendency for learners to equate different forms with distinct meanings and guides them to a recognition of underlying propositions through the distracting appearance of different surface forms. The ability to do this is of particular importance, of course, in comprehension.

One of the ways in which the notion of deep structure equivalence can benefit language teaching, then, is to provide the means of extending transformation exercises of the active/passive sort and of distinguishing them from grammatical exercises of a different kind in a systematic way. At the same time this distinction serves the purpose of getting the learner to discriminate between those structural differences which reflect essential changes of meaning and those which do not, to recognize that not all grammatical operations have the same status. I have suggested that the ability to recover basic propositions from different surface realizations is important for comprehension. The ability to select the surface form which has the appropriate textual value, on the other hand, is of particular importance for composition.

There is seldom any distinction made between grammar exercises which change the signification of sentences and those which do not. At the same time there is usually no indication given of the different textual values which alternative surface forms may assume. Learners are generally required to transform active sentences into the passive, but they do this simply as a straightforward formal exercise in usage: they are not usually led to consider the conditions under which they would make use of one form rather than another. Their attention remains focused on sentences and it is not directed towards text. Having established the common signification of different surface forms, the next step we need to take is to demonstrate their different value and so to move from sentence to text composition.

Here the language teacher must to a large extent explore for himself. Although a certain amount of work has been carried out on the textual function of different surface forms, notably by M. A. K. Halliday (e.g. Halliday 1970), there is as yet no definitive source of reference to which the teacher can turn for guidance. We need not be discouraged by this, however. Given the stimulus of the insight we have been discussing, the teacher can begin to work out his own principles of approach and formulate the facts in accordance with his particular teaching circumstances. The main principle that emerges from our discussion is that the transition from sentence to text involves a consideration of the way syntactic structure reflects the distribution of information in a proposition. In the case of the first of the exchanges cited above, for example, the use of the sentence *It was Duncan who was killed by Macbeth* is not appropriate because such a distribution of information brings into focus not what Macbeth did, which is what Ross is asking about, but who he did it to. This kind of explanation depends on an investigation into how the variable realization of the same proposition gives differential prominence to the information which the proposition contains. It requires a shift of emphasis from syntactic patterns to the propositions which they express.

We may say, then, that the linguistic insight which directs the transformational-generative grammarian to trace different sentence forms to a common deep structure proposition can provide the language teacher with a basic guiding principle. It is that when the learner makes the necessary transition from the comprehension and composition of sentences to the comprehension and composition of text he must be led to consider what propositions sentences express under the guise of different surface appearances, and think of these surface differences as having to do with the manner in which the information expressed in these propositions is organized.

So far we have been looking at how a particular model of language usage can point the way towards the transition from sentence to text by directing attention towards the relationship between sentences and propositions. From such a model we can develop the distinction between the signification of sentences and their textual value. We now turn our attention from micro-linguistics to macro-linguistics and in particular to attempts that have been made to study the communicative use of language as an instrument of social interaction. Whereas the description of usage we have been considering leads us to think of sentences in terms of propositions, the description of use which we will now consider leads us to think of sentences in terms of communicative acts.

We have seen that the transformational-generative model of grammar can be used to correct the assumption that difference in structure corresponds necessarily to difference in proposition. The same proposition can be expressed by different forms and (although we have not considered this matter) different propositions can be expressed by the same form, in which case we get instances of ambiguity. An example of the latter would be a sentence of the form:

The government is agreeable to returning hostages.

One interpretation of this sentence would yield the proposition alternatively expressed as *The government agrees to the return of hostages* and a second interpretation would yield the proposition alternatively expressed as *The government is pleasant to hostages who return.* Now when we consider the communicative acts which sentences count as in actual language use we find that a similar situation obtains: the same sentence form can be used to perform a number of different acts and the same act can be realized by a number of different sentence forms. Let us consider the following sentence, for example:

Macbeth will kill Duncan.

This sentence expresses a proposition which could be alternatively expressed as follows:

Duncan will be killed by Macbeth.
What will happen is that Macbeth will kill Duncan.

But in uttering such sentences the language user would also be performing an act of one sort or another. We do not simply express propositions in the uttering of sentences, we at the same time engage in communicative activity: we assert, confess, suggest, describe, explain, predict, promise, and so on. Let us suppose, for example, that Macduff actually utters the first of these sentences in the course of a conversation with Malcolm and that afterwards Ross asks Malcolm what went on in the conversation. If Malcolm wishes to report this particular utterance he can choose to do so in three different ways. First he can report Macduff's *sentence* by the use of direct speech:

Macduff said: 'Macbeth will kill Duncan.'

Secondly, he can report the *proposition* that Macduff expressed, drawing on the range of surface forms available:

Macduff said that Macbeth would kill Duncan.
Macduff said that Duncan would be killed by Macbeth.
Macduff said that what would happen would be that Macduff would kill Duncan.

Thirdly, Malcolm can report the communicative act that he understands Macduff to have performed in the uttering of the sentence:

Macduff predicted that Macbeth would kill Duncan.
Macduff predicted that Duncan would be killed by Macbeth.
Macduff warned me that Macbeth would kill Duncan.
Macduff warned me that Duncan would be killed by Macbeth.

It will be clear that whereas the character of a particular proposition is signalled grammatically so that it can be specified in the deep structure of sentences, the character of a particular act cannot be so signalled. Macduff's utterance could serve as a warning or a prediction, or, for that matter, if Macbeth were under his orders, a threat or a promise. Malcolm's interpretation of the remark as constituting one act as opposed to another will depend on certain conditions, like his knowledge of the situation in which the remark was made, and of the character of Macduff and his relationship with Macbeth. What the expression of a particular proposition counts as does not depend only on the nature of the proposition but also on the circumstances in which it is expressed.

The study of the conditions which determine what sentences count as in contexts of use has been undertaken by both philosophers of language and sociolinguists and we can now investigate what relevance their findings have for the language teacher, what insights they reveal that can be transferred into pedagogic principles.

Let us begin by considering the act of command, or the giving of an order. How is this act performed? One answer, favoured by some language teachers, is that it is performed by the uttering of an impera-tive sentence. This answer assumes an equation between form and function and a moment's reflection will reveal that it is inadequate. It is perfectly possible to give an order without using the imperative form. One can easily conceive of circumstances, for example, in which the uttering of the declarative sentence:

These windows are filthy.

would be intended by the speaker and construed by the hearer as an order to get to work to clean them. But which circumstances? We can draw on suggestions put forward by Labov (see Labov 1972a) and say that for an order to be effectively performed both speaker (S) and hearer (H) must agree that, at the moment of utterance, the following conditions hold:

A There is a certain state of affairs to be brought about, and S makes some reference to it.
B H has the ability to bring about the required state of affairs.
C H has the obligation to bring about the required state of affairs.
D S has the right to ask H to take the necessary action.

Now if the circumstances of S's utterance are such as to provide for three of these conditions, then his utterance need make reference to only one and it will thereby constitute an order. We can take the example that Labov gives of a teacher telling a pupil to do a piece of work again. He can perform such an act of command by focusing on the first of these conditions thus:

1 This has to be done again.

This declarative sentence functions as an order because the teacher assumes that the pupil will automatically acknowledge that the other conditions obtain and need not be verbally invoked. Alternatively, he could focus on any of the other conditions:

2 You can do better than this.
3 You'll have to do this again.
4 It's my job to get you to do better than this.

These declarative sentences, then, take on the communicative function of command because they are uttered in circumstances which provide for the satisfaction of the conditions to which they do not make refer-ence. But this is not the whole story. The teacher could also make use of interrogative sentences. In so doing he invites the pupil to overtly acknowledge the condition to which his sentence makes reference, again assuming that those conditions which are not referred to are recognized as existing in the situation. Thus, the teacher could issue commands of a more persuasive or mitigated kind:

1 Shouldn't this be done again?
2 Don't you think you can do neater work than this?
3 Don't you have to do neater work than this?
4 Can I ask you to do this again?

So far we have considered the utterance of sentences which make direct reference to one of the conditions attendant on a command. Thus a sentence like:

This has to be done again.

expresses the proposition that a certain state of affairs needs to be brought about. But what about the sentence which was cited earlier:

These windows are filthy.

Here the proposition has to do with a present state of affairs and does not refer to one which is to be brought about. The person at the receiving end of the utterance has to work out what implication lies concealed under what is overtly stated: he has to recover the covert proposition. If the circumstance under which this sentence is produced realizes the other conditions attendant on a command, then the hearer will be primed to discover ways in which the utterance can be interpreted as expressing the remaining condition. If the sentence we have been considering were uttered by a sergeant major, for example, the private soldier to which it were directed would have no difficulty in discovering the requisite underlying proposition:

These windows are filthy ⟶ These windows need to be cleaned.

There are, then, a variety of ways in which one can issue a command in English. We can reduce this variety to a number of simple formulae. First, the speaker may make use of a declarative sentence whose proposition refers, directly or indirectly, to one of the conditions to be met for the act of command to be accomplished, on the assumption that the hearer will recognize that the other necessary conditions obtain by virtue of the situation in which the utterance is made. We might express this by means of the following simple formula:

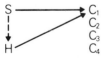   This work needs to be
done again.

If we wish to distinguish between a direct reference to a condition, where we have an overtly expressed proposition, and an indirect reference, where we have the proposition covertly implied, we may use a broken arrow between S and the conditions concerned. For example:

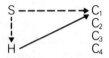　　　　This work is unsatisfactory.

The second way of issuing an order is to produce an interrogative sentence whose proposition makes reference to one of the requisite conditions. As I have suggested, the effect of this is to invite the hearer to acknowledge the condition concerned. We might express this as follows:

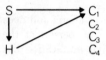　　　　Don't you think that this work
　　　　　　　　　　needs to be done again?

Again, the reference might be indirect so we need a modified version of the formula to account for this:

　　　　Do you think that this work is
　　　　　　　　　　satisfactory?

Finally, the speaker can make use of an imperative sentence. This might be thought of as the standard or explicit form of a command in which the nature of the act is signalled by the form the proposition takes. This does not mean that every time an imperative sentence is produced an order is given but it does mean that if the requisite conditions obtain in the situation it will be understood that the use of the imperative form invokes them all at once and there is no need for specification. We might express this in the following way:

　　　　Do this work again.

What relevance does all this have for language teaching? We saw earlier how the notion of deep structure equivalence could be used to indicate the distinction between sentence forms and the propositions which they are used to express and to point the way towards the necessary transition from sentence to text. This brief discussion of the communicative use of language indicates the distinction between sentence forms and the acts they are used to perform, and points the way towards the necessary transition from sentence to discourse. The way of describing usage which was considered earlier shows us how we can get our pupils to think in terms of propositions, and the way of describing use which we have just considered shows us how we can get pupils to think in terms of communicative acts. In both cases we are getting below the frequently distracting surface appearance of sentences to the manner in which they function in communication. What I want to do now is to first draw out certain implications from what has been said for the teaching of communicative acts as individual units of use and then to go on to talk about discourse.

So far in our discussion of use we have been concerned solely with the act of command, but it is not difficult to see that the same line of inquiry can be extended to deal with other acts of communication. We can begin by considering acts which are characteristically realized by the use of the imperative and which, to this extent, bear a family resemblance to commands. The following would be examples:

1 Instruction/direction: Turn left at the next street.
2 Advice: Invest in Premium Bonds.
3 Appeal: Give generously to Famine Relief.
4 Prayer: Forgive us our trespasses.
5 Warning: Beware of pickpockets.

What we have to do is to establish a set of conditions from which each of these acts selects a sub-set. That is to say, each act will be distinguished from the others by a unique selection of the conditions which together constitute the family resemblance. Of the conditions attendant on a command, for example, it is clear that the fourth, which has to do with the obligation of the hearer, does not figure in the sub-set of conditions which define an appeal and a prayer: a defining feature of such acts is precisely that the hearer is under no obligation to carry out what is proposed by the speaker. The same is true of the act of advising: the speaker, at the moment of utterance, assumes that he has the right to suggest a course of action, but the hearer is under no obligation to embark upon it. What, then, distinguishes between advice and appeal or prayer? Clearly we need to specify a condition other than those we considered in connection with the giving of orders. It has to do with whether what is proposed by the speaker is to the advantage or benefit of the speaker or to the hearer. In the case of advice, for example, what is proposed is of benefit to the hearer, but in the case of appeal, or prayer, what is proposed is of benefit to the speaker. But we now have to discover a condition which distinguishes between an appeal and a prayer. It would appear to relate to the third of the conditions which were specified for commands: in uttering a prayer, the speaker does not assume that he has the right to require the hearer to perform the action referred to. On the contrary, he tends to stress how unworthy he is even to address the personage, usually a supernatural figure, to whom he is speaking.

Instructions, or directions (I am assuming for the purposes of the present discussion that these are different names of the same act, although a case might be made out for distinguishing them), resemble pieces of advice in that they refer to a course of action which it is to the advantage of the hearer to follow. The difference would seem to lie in the fact that in the case of a direction the speaker provides information which is necessary for the course of action itself to be carried out in the undertaking of a larger task, like finding one's way to somewhere, or installing a piece of equipment, or carrying out some kind of operation. To distinguish advice from warning we need a different condition. Whereas advice is given by making reference to an action which will be to the advantage of the hearer, warnings are given by making reference to an action which the hearer needs to take to avoid something happening which is to his disadvantage, or by making reference to a state of affairs which is to the disadvantage of the hearer, with the implication that he will take action to avoid it. With warnings, therefore, it is assumed that unfortunate consequences will follow if the hearer does not take evasive action, but there is no such assumption with pieces of advice.

What we have just been doing is working our way in somewhat informal and discursive fashion towards the specification of a set of conditions whose sub-sets serve to define the different acts we have been considering. What we would eventually hope to arrive at would be a distinctive characterization of acts in terms of a simple index. For example, having fixed upon a group of acts which by virtue of their apparent formal resemblance seem to constitute a family, we would then draw up our set of conditions and specify each act within the family by reference to it. In the case of those acts we have been exploring, for example, it would appear that in addition to the conditions attendant on a command, we need to postulate others, and that these might be informally expressed as follows:

E S makes reference to an action which needs to be carried out to achieve a particular goal.

F S makes reference to an action which needs to be carried out if H is to avoid undesirable consequences.

G S makes reference to an action which benefits H.
H S makes reference to an action which benefits S.
I S has knowledge which H does not have.
J The action referred to by S cannot be carried out by S.

We can then provide a distinctive characterization of the acts we have been discussing by giving each an indexical specification drawn from the above set of conditions in the following manner:

> command: A B C D
> instruction: B D E I
> advice: B D G I
> appeal: B D H J
> prayer: B H J
> warning: B F I

As our inquiry proceeds, of course, these conditions would be given more precise expression and would need to be adjusted to accommodate other acts which we might wish to include within the same family. All I wish to do at the moment is to point out a possible procedure developing from a sociolinguistic insight. And it is a procedure which the language teacher can himself follow, framing the expression of relevant conditions in a manner which is suited to his own situation, and getting his pupils to participate in their discovery. This second point is an important one and has to do with the use of translation.

In our discussion we have been trying to isolate conditions which have to be met for certain acts of communication to be effectively performed. These acts are referred to in English by the terms *command*, *instruction*, *advice*, and so on but although the terms are specific to English, the acts themselves are not specific to English-speaking societies. It is likely that similar (though not necessarily identical) acts form part of the communicative repertoire of all cultures. The conditions which determine whether a certain utterance counts as a *Befehl* or *Warnung* are likely to be the same as those which determine whether a certain utterance counts as a *command* or a *warning*. This being so, German learners of English, for example, can be asked to work out the conditions attendant upon those acts to which the German terms refer as a preliminary to considering how such acts are realized in English. Any lack of correspondence between conditions will naturally emerge as a result of the comparison. What I am suggesting, then, is that the teacher can proceed to elicit sets of conditions which relate to acts with which their pupils are already familiar and which they know by their German names and then demonstrate how the same, or similar conditions, operate to give English sentences their communicative value. We can represent this process in simple form as follows (where the capital letters indicate an act common to both cultures):

COMMAND

Befehl   Command
C_1
C_2
C_3
C_4

A consideration of the different ways in which these conditions can be realized in German sentences will then prepare the way for the pupils to recognize the different ways in which the same, or similar acts can be realized in English. Thus we draw upon the learner's own knowledge and experience of the communicative functioning of language to develop a knowledge of English use.

Enough has been said perhaps to indicate how the insight we have been exploiting can point the way towards a transition from a concentration on sentences to a concentration on the acts they can be used to perform. We must now turn to the transition from acts to discourse. Just as propositions do not generally occur in isolation but combine to form cohesive text, so acts do not generally occur in isolation but combine to form coherent discourse. For an example, let us return to the classroom situation we were discussing earlier and consider the following exchange between the teacher and the pupil:

T This work needs to be done again.
P My pen is broken.

Now there is no formal link between these two utterances as sentences and no link either between the propositions which they express: in other words, they do not constitute a cohesive text. We can, however, make sense of this exchange by relating each utterance to the conditions on a command. The teacher performs this act by focusing on the first condition but the pupil, drawing on his knowledge of English rules for use, performs what we might call a counteract, a refusal to obey, by drawing attention to the second condition and suggesting that, contrary to what the teacher assumes, this condition does not hold: he is not able to carry out the action referred to by the teacher. At this point the teacher could produce his own counteract by restoring the condition which the pupil has removed. In this case he might come up with a remark like:

T You can do your work in pencil.

Again, there is no cohesive link between this utterance and the ones which have preceded, but the three form a coherent discourse because they are all relateable to the same set of underlying conditions.

The examples we have just taken are of spoken discourse, but the same sort of observation can be made of written discourse as well. Consider the following sequence of sentences from a newspaper article:

> The unions refused to accept the government's proposal. Unemployment has been rising steadily over the past few months.

At the level of form, we have two separate sentences here, and at the level of content we have two separate propositions. But the reader makes sense of the two by inferring a coherent link between them: he understands that the second sentence expresses a proposition which counts as an explanation of the state of affairs described in the first sentence. It is because he interprets what is said here as something like *report + explanation* that he can recognize it as an instance of coherent discourse, and his ability to impose this kind of interpretation on instances of language use of this sort depends on his recognizing how the propositions expressed in the sentences satisfy conditions which define different communicative acts.

The language learner has ultimately to deal with actual language use and to concern himself with the way in which the language he is learning conveys propositional content and functions as communicative activity. What I have tried to do in this paper is to indicate how certain insights in the description of use can help us to formulate principles for effecting the transition from sentence to act to discourse. The insights I have discussed have still to be developed and realized as detailed descriptions, and when they are, the teacher will have a source of reference upon which to draw. Meanwhile, he can develop and realize these insights in his own manner and for his own purposes, using them to establish principles which he can then use as a basis for the design of teaching approaches relevant to his own circumstances.

Notes

First published in *Forum Linguisticum* 3.

18 The partiality and relevance of linguistic descriptions

It is a common assumption among language teachers that their subject should somehow be defined by reference to models of linguistic description devised by linguistics. This does not mean that they try to transfer such models directly into the pedagogic domain (although such attempts are not unknown): there is usually a recognition that they have to be modified in one way or another to suit a teaching purpose. But the basic theoretical orientation is retained. The same assumption dominates applied linguistics. The very name is a proclamation of dependence. Now I have nothing against linguistics. Some of my best friends, etc. But I think one must be wary of its influence. In this paper I want to question the common assumption, axiomatic in its force, that a linguistic model of language must of necessity serve as the underlying frame of reference for language teaching. And I want to suggest that it is the business of applied linguistics as the theoretical branch of language teaching pedagogy to look for a model that will serve this purpose. I think that applied linguistics can only claim to be an autonomous area of inquiry to the extent that it can free itself from the hegemony of linguistics and deny the connotations of its name.

So much for the clarion call. Now the argument. We may begin with a quotation which makes quite explicit the assumption of dependence that I want to question:

> This is the main contribution that the linguistic sciences can make to the teaching of languages: to provide good descriptions. Any description of a language implies linguistics: it implies, that is, a definite attitude to language, a definite stand on how language works and how it is to be accounted for. As soon as the teacher uses the word 'sentence' or 'verb' in relation to the language he is teaching, he is applying linguistics, just as when he says 'open your mouth wider' he is applying phonetics. It is a pity then not to apply the linguistics best suited to the purpose. The best suited linguistics is the body of accurate descriptive methods based on recent research into the form and substance of language. There is no conflict between application and theory; the methods most useful in application are to

be found among those that are most valid and powerful in theory.
Halliday, McIntosh, and Strevens 1964: 167.

But how can these authors be so sure that the 'best suited' description
for language learning is one which derives from theoretical linguistics?
I know of no evidence myself that would support such an assertion, and
one looks in vain for any in the book from which this quotation is taken.
I think one should interpret these remarks as a kind of propaganda or as
a declaration of faith. It seems to me that actually there is reason to
suspect that a description deriving from linguistic theory is *not* the best
suited one for language teaching. I want now to try to give some
substance to this suspicion.

Let us first consider how language is represented by these 'accurate
descriptive methods' that Halliday *et al* talk about. One of the
favourite pursuits of modern linguists is to poke fun at traditional
definitions of parts of speech. No introduction to linguistics, it seems,
is complete without it. Thus Palmer sets out to demonstrate the
absurdity of Nesfield's definition of a noun as 'a word used for naming
anything', that is to say, a person, place, quality, action, feeling,
collection, etc. He comments:

> In fact the definition is completely vacuous as we can see if we ask
> how on the basis of this definition can we find the nouns in *He
> suffered terribly* and *His suffering was terrible*? Is there any sense in
> which the last sentence has reference to things in a way in which the
> first does not? For these sentences are identical in meaning.
> *Palmer 1971: 39.*

Are they identical in meaning? Who says so? Again I know of no
evidence obtained from elicitation tests on informants that would
support this assertion. What Palmer means, I suppose, is that it is
convenient for the purposes of formal linguistic analysis to consider
these two sentences to be identical in meaning. This is presumably why
the argument he uses for rejecting Nesfield's definition is not a language
user's argument but a language analyst's. It is the analyst, not the user
who needs to *find* nouns. All the language user needs to do is *use* them.
And if he is called upon to describe what they are he is likely to do so
notionally in terms of their use rather than in terms of their formal and
distributional properties. It is probable, it seems to me, that this would
incline him to say that these two sentences are *different* in meaning.

The linguist tends to be intolerant of such 'folk' ideas, believing
himself to be in a position to observe from outside and to distinguish
what is true from what is not. In effect he simply exchanges one kind of
ethnocentricity for another. And he clings to his beliefs in spite of
contrary evidence with just as much tenacity as does the common man.

Furthermore, it would appear that, with his frequent appeals to what seems to be 'intuitively correct', he cannot quite free himself from the influence of folk ideas. Thus Chomsky is reluctant to part with the notion of the kernel sentence:

> The notion 'kernel sentence' has, I think, an important intuitive significance, but since kernel sentences play no distinctive role in generation or interpretation of sentences, I shall say nothing more about them here.
> *Chomsky 1965: 18.*

But if such sentences have important intuitive significance, then why, one is prompted to ask, do they have no role to play in the description of language? I suppose that what we must conclude from this really rather remarkable statement is that it is convenient from the analyst's point of view to deny the intuitive reality of the language user's sense of language. One might also suggest (while we are on the subject) that Chomsky's refusal to accept the generative semanticist position might derive in part from his intuitive (common) sense of the psychological reality of the word as a linguistic unit.

There is no reason to suppose, then, that linguists have any privileged access to reality. Yet they constantly talk as if they did. Here are Halliday *et al* again:

> Conceptually defined categories can be held precisely because they are incapable of exact application; some of the definitions have survived to this day, protected by a cosy unreality. But it is doubtful if any English schoolboy, having to find out whether a certain word is a noun or not, asks: 'Is this the name of a person, living being or thing?' More probably he will test whether it has a plural in -*s*, or whether he can put the definite article in front of it. Since he is probably required to decide that 'departure' is a noun whereas 'somebody' is not, he is more likely to reach the right conclusion by this method.
> *Halliday et al 1964: 145.*

Once more it is assumed that only the analyst's model can be a valid one. Clearly the schoolboy learning *about* language will be required to adopt an analytical point of view. But even so there seems no reason why he should be persuaded that this is the only correct way of seeing things, 'the right conclusion'. It is important to distinguish between education and indoctrination, but they are dangerously close in these comments. What, for instance, is all this about a 'cosy unreality'? The fact that these deplorable definitions have survived so long surely suggests that they correspond in some way to a deep-seated intuitive reality in the minds of language users. There is nothing 'cosy' or unreal about that. One could argue, I suppose, that this is only because such notions have been passed down through the generations by misguided educators. But this is only to say that these notions have something of the character of folklore and persist because they are congruent with some kind of cultural reality.

It is interesting to note that Hudson makes a similar appeal to tradition in support of his recent proposals for a 'daughter dependency' grammar:

> This similarity to traditional grammar lends not only academic respectability but also psychological support, since schoolchildren and their teachers, and other theoretically naive people, must have found this way of viewing sentence structure reasonably convincing for two thousand years. For all its claims to represent the views of the rationalist philosophers of the Enlightenment, transformational grammar can scarcely trace the notion of the phrase-marker back much further than the neo-Bloomfieldians, the inventors of 'immediate constituent analysis'.
> *Hudson 1976: 19.*

How far such a similarity does in fact lend academic respectability and psychological support to a *formal* model of linguistic description is, I would have thought, open to debate. But my concern is with the relevance of the tradition that Hudson mentions to the validation of a user's model of language.

What I am suggesting, then, is that the language user's intuitive sense of the nature of language as expressed through these much maligned definitions has its own legitimacy and we would do well, I think, to respect it. Linguists may find it methodologically convenient to set themselves apart and to analyse the user's knowledge in disassociation from his experience of language, and in terms of categories that can be precisely formulated. But it does not follow that the only ideas that are 'real' or 'true' or 'correct' are those which can be given precise formulation. Consider again the definition of the noun. The case against it is that it cannot be reduced to the formal terms that define the concept of reality that the linguist happens to find convenient. The distinction, one might conclude, is not between conceptually defined categories which are invalid and formally defined categories which are not, but between categories conceptually defined in different ways.

This distinction has to do with the familiar anthropological question of the relationship between 'structural' and 'psychological' reality in ethnographic descriptions based on formal analysis. Chapter 4 of Tyler (1969) entitled 'Relevance: psychological reality', bears upon this issue. It presents a number of papers concerned with the basic question:

> . . . how do arrangements constructed by the anthropologists
> correspond to arrangements used by the people being studied?
> *Tyler 1969: 343.*

The definition of a kin category like 'uncle' by means of componential
analysis, for example, may fail to capture the underlying sense of
'uncleness' in the minds of the members of the society concerned. This
sense may be realized through the extension of the term in reference to
non-kin, or in the creation of metaphorical expressions and so on. In
much the same way the formally defined category 'noun' may fail to
capture the language user's sense of 'nounness'.

With this in mind, we can return to Palmer and his strictures on
traditional definitions. When he asks if there is any sense in which
His suffering was terrible has reference to a thing whereas *He suffered
terribly* does not, the answer is: Yes, there is. The language user senses
that they are different in meaning, that yes, in some sense not easy to
identify and define, the first sentence does refer to suffering as something, some thing, some entity having some notional correspondence
with tables, books and bags, shoes and ships, and sealing wax. The
language user senses that grammatical categories have an underlying
semantic significance, that they represent a potential in the language
for making subtle distinctions in meaning. This potential is sometimes
actually realized and in a way that lends support to the user's intuition.
I am thinking in particular of poetry. Consider, for example, Hopkins'
line in *The Windhover*:

> My heart in hiding.
> Stirred for a bird,—the achieve of, the mastery of the thing!

Here, we might say, Hopkins has created a noun which realizes the
semantic quality associated with 'verbness' and so gives direct expression
to the language user's sense of meaning potential inherent in the category
'verb'. *The achieve of* just does not mean the same as *the achievement of*:
we recognize the difference by reference to the same underlying sense
of conceptual distinctions as lead us to distinguish between *He suffered
terribly* and *His suffering was terrible*. It may be extremely difficult to
describe these differences, and so one falls prey to the linguist and the
sharp edge of his precision, but this does not mean that the differences
are any the less real. Much of poetry, and other forms of creative
expression, crucially depend for their effect on such a vague awareness
of the implicit and not normally exploited semantic resources of the
language. The persistence of the notion of a noun being the name of a
person, place or thing and the capacity to appreciate poetry have a
common origin in the language user's intuitive sense of the communicative possibilities in his language.

If, then, one takes these pronouncements about the noun as deriving from the 'accurate descriptive methods' that Halliday *et al* refer to, it would seem that the concept or model of language that is developed by analysts does not correspond with that acquired by users. There are signs, however, that with an increasing concern with the communicative properties of language the two models are beginning to converge. It is hard to see how it could be otherwise. If one is to talk about communication one has to be involved in the attitudes and beliefs of users: one can no longer separate out an underlying knowledge to be treated as an idealized abstraction in isolation from its natural context of experience. A communicative orientation to description must take into account the orientation of communicators. One interesting consequence of this converging of models is that the 'conceptually defined' categories that Halliday *et al* and Palmer (among many others) are so scornful of take on a more respectable character. The criteria for a 'good' description now change in their favour. Whereas previously it was assumed that formal distributional criteria could be invoked to define parts of speech as discrete and invariant categories, it now appears that they cannot be dealt with so neatly. Thus Ross (1973), for example, points out that the four items, *Harpo*, *headway*, *there*, and *tabs*, exhibit degrees of 'nounphrasiness' which can be specified in terms of their tolerance of certain transformational operations. He is thus able to range them along an implicational scale which in effect is a variable definition of the notion noun phrase. Instead of a well-defined category, we have a 'squish'. The most 'nounphrasey' of the items that Ross considers is *Harpo*—he describes it in his characteristically whimsical way as a 'copperclad, brass-bottomed' NP. What needs to be noticed here is that such copperclad and brass-bottomed NPs turn out to be names of persons, places, and things, so that the old-fashioned conceptual definition does not seem to be quite so vacuous after all, even with reference to formal criteria. We can now account for the user's definition by saying that he simply associates the whole range of the squish with the semantic features which characterize the full blown nominals at the end of the scale. Thus his conceptual definition has just the same degree of exactitude as the formal distributional one: the difference is that he generalizes from the semantic characteristics of the copperclad nominals, whereas Palmer, Halliday, and others generalize from their syntactic characteristics. It is not a matter of precision but of point of view.

I think we should recognize that there is no model of language which has the monopoly on the truth, that captures reality. All descriptions, no matter how apparently objective they might appear, are really only projections of personal or social attitudes. Skinner is disposed to see language in terms of operant behaviour and tends in consequence to equate human beings with pigeons. Chomsky is disposed to see language in terms of mathematical systems and so tends to equate human beings with automata. Which is to be preferred depends on such factors as usefulness, prejudice, and correspondence to the prevailing intellectual and cultural climate. Theorists are just as subject to the forces of fashion as anybody else: they really have no vantage point from where they can observe in privileged detachment. All this is obvious. And yet, in our search for security, we constantly fall into the same error of supposing that an absolute truth is attainable and we look for revelation. It might be instructive to consider another case. In Hockett (1968) a powerful argument is presented against the adequacy of Chomskyan grammar. The central point of the argument is expressed as follows:

> Since languages are ill-defined, mathematical linguistics in the form of algebraic grammar is mistaken.
> *Hockett 1968: 61.*

Hockett acknowledges that, although mistaken, such a grammar may achieve a 'practically useful approximation'. But he has his reservations:

> This may be so if one's concern is, say, the programming of computers for the helpful manipulation of language data. But an approximation is always made possible by leaving some things out of account, and I believe the things left out of account in order to achieve an approximation of this particular sort *are just the most important properties of human language*, in that they are the source of its openness.
> *Hockett 1968: 62.*

What Hockett's complaint amounts to is that Chomskyan grammar leaves unaccounted for certain aspects of natural language which he is inclined to value highly. He is not content that it should be useful (which he admits it is): he also wants it to be comprehensive. He wants it to reveal the truth. This is the absolutist expectation: doomed to be disappointed at the outset. Interestingly enough, Chomsky himself uses the same argument for rejecting a model of language which does not suit *his* predilections. Hockett objects to a well-defined model on the grounds that natural language is not well-defined, and in the same way Chomsky objects to a finite-state model on the grounds that English at any rate is not a finite-state language. Chomsky, too, acknowledges that the model he rejects might be useful. Here is the relevant passage:

> In view of the generality of this conception of language, and its utility in such related disciplines as communication theory, it is important to inquire into the consequences of adopting this point of view in the syntactic study of some languages such as English or a formalized system of mathematics. Any attempt to construct a finite state

grammar for English runs into serious difficulties and complications at the very outset, as the reader can easily convince himself. However, it is unnecessary to attempt to show this by example, in view of the following more general remark about English:
English is not a finite-state language.
Chomsky 1957: 20–21.

But, of course, as Hockett points out, English is not a 'formalized system of mathematics' either, although it is clear that Chomsky is disposed to think of it in these terms, and there are aspects of the language that can be explored most effectively by assuming that it is. The observation that English is not a finite-state language is itself no argument for rejecting finite-state models of linguistic description. The justification of such an assumption, like the equally false assumption that English is a well-defined language, must lie in the kind of insights it allows into certain aspects of language and in the relevance of such insights for the different groups of people who need linguistic descriptions.

It does not seem to make very much sense, then, to talk about a 'good' description as if there were some universal criteria for assessment. It is interesting to note that Halliday is inconsistent on this point. In the passage already cited and discussed, he seems to be expressing the view that there are such criteria. A few pages earlier, however, he seems to be expressing the opposite view:

Linguistics has various aims, and different types of statement are appropriate to different purposes: a grammar for the teaching of language does not look like a grammar written for linguists while a grammar written for speech pathologists would differ from either.
Halliday et al 1964: 150.

This attitude (further elaborated in Halliday (1964)) is not, however, allowed to prevail and ten pages on we find it contradicted. We are invited to play the familiar game of exposing the absurdities of language teachers. Thus we are given a quotation from Thomson and Martinet's *A Practical English Grammar for Foreign Students.*

It is used to replace an infinitive phrase at the beginning of a sentence; e.g. instead of: '*To be early* is necessary' we usually say: 'It is necessary to be early.'

This, say Halliday *et al*, is a 'fiction' and they add:

It is not clear what is gained by 'explaining' one pattern by reference to another which it is held in replace.
Halliday et al 1964: 162.

I suppose that one answer to this is that what is gained is a transformational-generative grammar of English. Thomson and Martinet are stating here, in appropriately informal and pedagogically orientated terms, syntactic relations which the transformational-generative grammarians formalize in terms of precise rules. And this, surely, is one way in which 'a grammar for language teachers does not look like a grammar written for linguists'. What Thomson and Martinet are doing here is making a statement about syntactic relations which will be consistent, with a less formal model of language which has to meet conditions of pedagogic adequacy. Talk of one structure 'replacing' another may not meet the approval of linguists; they will prefer to talk about extraposition transformational operations. But then they are developing a different model for different purposes, and they have other conditions of adequacy to consider.

What, then, we might ask, are the conditions of adequacy attaching to a pedagogic model of linguistic description? One of them, I would venture to suggest, is that it should be in some way congruent with the language user's concept of the nature of language rather than the analyst's. Once again, Halliday has insightful things to say that touch on this matter. In a paper entitled, significantly enough in the present context, 'The relevant models of language', he distinguishes between a number of different concepts or models of language which the child develops in the acquisition process. One of these is what Halliday calls the 'representational model'. He defines it as a 'means of communicating about something, of expressing propositions', and he comments:

> This is the only model of language that many adults have; and a very inadequate model it is, from the point of view of the child.
> *Halliday 1973: 16.*

But this is precisely the model that Palmer appeals to when he declares that the two sentences we considered earlier (*He suffered terribly* and *His suffering was terrible*) are identical in meaning. It is the model which is generally given preference by the linguistic analyst. Halliday goes on:

> . . . this presents what is, for the child, a quite unrealistic picture of language, since it accounts for only a small fragment of his total awareness of what language is about.
> *Halliday 1973: 16.*

One might make the same sort of observation about the language user in general to the extent that the analyst only captures a small fragment of *his* total awareness of what language is about. It would appear from this that it is the linguist's model rather than the language user's that is 'protected by a cosy unreality'.

In the remarks that I have been making in this paper I have been circling around two points. The first is that models of description are developed from models of language in a conceptual sense which derive from predispositions to see language in a certain way. They are, therefore, inevitably partial, in both senses of the word. It is, of course, a common human failing to assume that personal predisposition and universal truth are the same. The first point, then, is ontological.

The second is heuristic. It is, simply enough, that the model of description to be preferred should be that which is likely to be relevant to a particular purpose. Our particular purpose in what we call applied linguistics is the teaching of language. The question then is: what model can be developed which realizes the necessary coincidence of partiality and relevance? As I said at the beginning, the common assumption has been that it must be some version of the most recent model emanating from theoretical linguistics. And so we have been led off dancing in the footsteps of one pied piper after another.

It seems to me that the purpose of applied linguistics is not to take random pot shots at pedagogic problems using the occasional insights from linguistics as ammunition, but to devise in a serious and single-minded way a coherent model of linguistic description which will be relevant to language teaching. I have no very definite idea about what such a model might look like in detail but I would expect it to embody the user's concept of language rather than the 'detached' view of the analyst, to be participant rather than observer orientated. This does not mean that we would not continue to exploit whatever insights are offered by studies which are methodologically precise in their partiality, but I suggest that these insights would need to have their relevance assessed against the independently motivated applied linguistic model. Eclecticism should not serve as an excuse for irresponsible ad-hocery as it sometimes has in the past. Whatever piper we choose to pay, we should make quite sure that we call the tune.

For we must, I think, accept the possibility at least that the analyst's model is not only inadequate but actually incongruent in certain crucial respects with that of the user. For example, whereas linguistic analysis based on scientific principles must of its nature be exact, communication of *its* nature, cannot be. This is not a matter for regret. If meaning could be conveyed by exact specification, if it were signalled entirely by linguistic signs, then there would be no need of the kind of negotiation that lies at the very heart of communicative behaviour, whereby what is meant is worked out by interactive endeavour. There would be no room for the exercise of practical reasoning, for the ongoing accomplishment of making sense that is the central concern of ethnomethodology (see Turner 1974, Cicourel 1973, Gumperz and Hymes 1972).

A number of recent studies in language acquisition and use have a bearing on the development of the kind of user model I have in mind. The exploration of a communicative orientation to description and the consequent consideration of social context and variation are, as I suggested earlier, favourable to its emergence. And such a model is perhaps beginning to assume some shape through recent work on natural semantax (see Traugott 1973, 1977), natural sequences of acquisition (see Ervin-Tripp 1974, Dulay and Burt 1974, Bailey, Madden, and Krashen 1974, Krashen 1977) and other work on performance analysis (see Corder 1975 for a brief review). Also of relevance, of course, is the work of Labov and others on the varying prominence given to different functions of language by different social and ethnic groups within a speech community (see, for example, Bernstein 1971, Labov 1972). Related to such ideas of functional difference are the suggestions that have been made about broad distinctions in cognitive style and mode of conceptualization between serialists and holists (see Pask and Scott 1972), between convergers and divergers (see Hudson 1966) or for that matter between hedgehogs and foxes (see Berlin 1957). All of these are sources of insight for applied linguistics in its quest for an appropriate way of representing language to the learner as a phenomenon congruent with his own experience as a language user.

The description of language in terms of *process*, of natural cognitive and communicative strategies for the exploitation of linguistic resources, is likely to be very different from one which treats language as a *product*, as an acquired and complete body of knowledge which can be reduced to component parts and rules for their operation. The former is likely, too, to conform more closely to the user's own concept of language, since presumably such a concept has its intuitive roots in experience.

It is this kind of description, participant rather than observer oriented, deriving from the beliefs and behaviour of learners as users and not as analysts of language, that I believe applied linguistics needs to develop as relevant to its concerns. And it is one that we need to develop actively and strategically, on our own initiative, and not simply as a tactic in expedient response to recent linguistic research. Such a description will be necessarily partial, and it will probably not meet the approval of others with different axes to grind. This should not be allowed to trouble us. We have our own conditions of relevance to meet and our own independent way to make in the world.

Notes

Paper presented at the sixth Neuchâtel Colloquium in Applied Linguistics, May 1977, and published in the proceedings: *Studies in Second Language Acquisition*. University of Indiana Linguistics Club, Volume I No 2.

Reprise

The theme introduced in the first section and developed in subsequent ones is here restated as we return to the question of what constitutes a communicative approach to the teaching of language.

I argue here, as I have before, that such an approach does not simply consist in representing language as notions or functions but involves extending the learner's ability to realize discourse from his mother tongue to the language he is learning. What is needed therefore is an investigation into the nature of this discourse realizing ability as a preliminary to the task of devising a pedagogy which will engage the learner's participation as a language user.

It seems to me, indeed, that the principal and perhaps the only reason for adopting a communicative approach is that it is likely to lead to a representation of the language to be learned which is in accord with the learner's own linguistic experience. Other reasons have been suggested, but I do not find them very convincing. One of them, more often presupposed perhaps than openly stated, is that theoretical studies have now demonstrated the essential communicative character of language and so the teacher needs to redefine his subject accordingly. Actually, I do not think that theoretical studies have demonstrated anything of the kind, but (as I argue in the preceding section) even if they had, we would need further demonstration to establish its relevance to pedagogy. And this brings us back again to learner experience.

Another reason which is current at the moment relates to the purpose in learning. The argument here is that since learning objectives can most satisfactorily be specified in communicative terms, an approach which concentrates on teaching communication is needed to achieve them. I do not find this reason very convincing either. It does not seem to me to follow that what is learnt needs to be explicitly taught. It is perfectly possible to teach one thing in order to facilitate the learning of something else. One might argue, indeed, that if this does not happen no real learning takes place and teaching is ineffective. The 'structural' approach would appear to embody this belief, which seems to me to be quite sound from a pedagogic point of view. The basic flaw in the structural approach is not that it fails to teach communication directly, but that it represents language in a way which dissociates the learner from his own experience of language, prevents real participation, and so makes the acquisition of communicative abilities particularly (and needlessly) difficult. One does not avoid this fault simply by basing one's pedagogy on a specification of learning objectives.

Both papers in this final section, then, are reconsiderations of what is involved in adopting a communicative orientation to language teaching pedagogy. The first of them is a somewhat curt critical assessment of the principles that appear to underline proposals for notional syllabuses. The issues it raises are then treated in less summary fashion in the final paper, which attempts, more positively, to demonstrate how one might approach the presentation of discourse so as to develop communicative competence in the learner.

19 Notional syllabuses

Notional syllabuses are represented by their proponents as an alternative to, and an improvement on, structural syllabuses. How do they differ? And what are the grounds for believing them to be better?

The two types of syllabus differ most obviously in the manner in which the language content is defined. In the structural syllabus it is defined in *formal* terms, as lexical items and grammatical patterns *manifesting* the system of English. In the notional syllabus, language content is defined in *functional* terms, as notions which are *realized* by formal items. In both cases the essential design is an inventory of language units in isolation and in abstraction. In the structural syllabus the inventory is ordered by reference to grading criteria. In the notional syllabus it is not.

The question then arises: what are the grounds for favouring a functional rather than a formal definition of language content? We can, I think, discern two arguments in the supporting literature. One refers to linguistic description. The other to learner needs.

The first argument rests on the assumption that descriptions provided by linguists capture the 'real' nature of language so that units for teaching should correspond with units of linguistic description.

The structural syllabus was developed at a time when linguists conceived of language in terms of the distributional properties of surface forms. So the subject matter for teaching language was similarly defined. The notional syllabus is being developed at a time when linguistic interest has shifted to the communicative properties of language, when meaning has moved to the centre of the stage with speech acts, presuppositions, case categories, conversational implicatures, and what have you all dancing attendance. It looks as if linguists have now decided that language is 'really' communication. As before the syllabus designer follows the fashion.

If you do not believe that we progress towards the truth of things by recurrent revelations, or if you do not believe that there should be a necessary correspondence between units of linguistic analysis and units for language teaching, then you will not be impressed by the fact that the notional syllabus can drum up current linguistic support. So we will turn to the second argument: the one relating to learner needs. The question to consider here is this: what kind of knowledge or behaviour does a learner need to have acquired at the end of a course of instruction?

Proponents of the structural syllabus will argue that the learner needs a basic knowledge of the language system, of lexical and grammatical forms constituting a core linguistic competence, and that this will provide the essential basis for communicative behaviour when the learner finds himself in a situation which requires him to use the language to communicate. The belief here is that what has to be *taught* is a knowledge of the language system: its exploitation for communicative purposes can be left to the learner.

Proponents of the notional syllabus will argue that the learner needs to learn appropriate behaviour *during* his course since one cannot count on him learning it later simply by reference to his linguistic knowledge. The belief here is that communicative competence needs to be expressly taught: the learner cannot be left to his own devices in developing an ability to communicate.

Both types of syllabus recognize that the learner's goal should be the ability to communicate. They differ in the assumption of what needs to be actually taught for this ability to be acquired. In both cases there is a gap between what is taught and what is learnt, both leave something for the learner to find out for himself. They differ again in their awareness of this fact.

The structural syllabus quite openly—brazenly, you might say—leaves the learner to realize his linguistic competence as communicative behaviour when the occasion arises. A tall order.

The notional syllabus, it is claimed, develops the ability to do this by accounting for communicative competence within the actual design of the syllabus itself. This is a delusion because the notional syllabus presents language as an inventory of units, of items for accumulation and storage. They are notional rather than structural isolates, but they are isolates all the same. What such a syllabus does not do—or has not done to date (an important proviso)—is to represent language as discourse, and since it does not it cannot possibly in its present form account for communicative competence—because communicative competence is not a compilation of items in memory, but a set of strategies or creative procedures for realizing the value of linguistic elements in contexts of use, an ability to *make* sense as a participant in discourse, whether spoken or written, by the skilful deployment of shared knowledge of code resources and rules of language use. The notional syllabus leaves the learner to develop these creative strategies on his own: it deals with the *components* of discourse, not with discourse itself. As such it derives from an analyst's and not a participant's view of language, as does the structural syllabus. Neither is centred on the language user.

The focus of attention in the notional syllabus, then, is on items, not strategies, on components of discourse, not the process of its creation, and in this respect it does not differ essentially from the structural syllabus, which also deals in items and components. In both cases what is missing is an appeal to cognition, to the language processing ability of the learner. For example, in a notional syllabus functions of different kinds are correlated with various linguistic forms. But the relationship between function and form is not just fortuitous: the form itself has what Halliday refers to as 'meaning potential' and it is this which is realized on particular communicative occasions. This realization of meaning potential depends on a knowledge of the conventional code meanings of linguistic items *and* of the ways in which these meanings can be conditioned by context. A notional syllabus presents certain common formal realizations of a range of communicative functions but does so *statically* without any indication of the dynamic process of interpretation that is involved. There is no demonstration of the *relationship* between form and function, of the meaning potential in the language forms which are presented. And so there is no attempt to develop an awareness of how this potential is realized by interpretative procedures which provide linguistic items with appropriate communicative value. But what is important for the learner is not to know what correlations are common between certain forms and functions, but *how* such correlations and innumerable others can be established and interpreted in the actual business of communicative interaction.

It seems to me, then, that the focus of the notional syllabus is still on the accumulation of language items rather than on the development of strategies for dealing with language in use. And in practice once you start writing materials or applying teaching procedures it may turn out not to make much difference whether you define these items as forms or functions.

I have spent most of my time pointing out what I see as the deficiencies of the notional syllabus, as it has been developed to date. I want to end on a more positive note. What the work on notional syllabuses has done, I think, is to sharpen our perception of what is required of a syllabus if it is to develop communicative competence in learners. It is an attempt to look afresh at the principles of syllabus design and it thus directs us to a reappraisal of these principles. I have said, for example, that the notional syllabus, in its present form, does not develop an awareness of meaning potential. But then how does one go about developing such an awareness? This question might then take us back to the structural syllabus to find out if there are not ways of reforming it, so that there is an emphasis on the meaning potential of forms and the varied ways in which this is realized in contexts of use.

We can now return to the two questions I posed at the beginning.

How does the notional syllabus differ? Its proponents represent it as an alternative to the structural syllabus, so forcing us into taking sides. This is unfortunate. The work on notional syllabuses can best be seen, I think, as a means of developing the structural syllabus rather than replacing it, and if it were seen in this light, the extent of difference between the two would become clear and we would be less likely to be deluded by false visions, which we are all rather prone to be. How far are notional syllabuses an improvement? In the attempt rather than the deed, I think. They are the first serious consideration of what is involved in incorporating communicative properties in a syllabus. We must give full credit for that. Work on the notional syllabus, properly interpreted, opens up the horizons and does not confine us to a creed. It indicates a direction to follow and ground to explore. But it is a starting point, not a destination.

Notes

Paper presented at the Tesol Convention, Mexico City, April 1978, and published in *ON TESOL 78*.

It seems self-evident that if we are to claim to be teaching English for specific purposes, then the first task must be to specify what these purposes are. Such a specification will enable us to define what needs to be learnt. It does not, however, necessarily tell us what needs to be taught. Nor does it tell us how the teaching is to be done. Having established the desired terminal behaviour of learners, we then have to work out the best way of getting there. The best way may not be what appears to be the most direct route, although one is generally inclined to think that it is. Consider, for example, the case of a group of technical college students who need English for the quite specific purpose of reading textbooks in metallurgy. One's immediate inclination might be to design a course whose exclusive concern is with reading and whose content derives directly from the textbooks which the students will eventually have to deal with. This is the direct route. But it may be that the students could be more effectively prepared by a course which developed more general communicative strategies over a wider range of language use, which concentrated not so much on direct teaching as on setting up the kind of conditions which created a favourable set towards later learning. I am not saying, please note, that the direct route is necessarily the wrong one, but only that it is not necessarily the right one. We need to examine the pedagogic terrain.

My point is that a specification of learner needs, though a crucial matter, does not relieve us of the responsibility for devising a methodology. I think that this is a point that needs to be stressed because there is a tendency in some quarters to allow terminal needs to *determine* teaching procedures. This is the case, for example, with those who insist, as a matter of pedagogic principle, on the presentation of what they call 'authentic' language on the grounds that since the learner will have to deal with such language eventually he should be exposed to it right from the beginning. I have discussed the notion of authenticity and its pedagogic validity in some detail elsewhere (see Paper 12 in this volume) and I shall refer to it again later on. Here I simply want to suggest, in passing, that it comes from an uncritical belief in the direct route, an undue compliance with need specification. The learner will have to be able to cope authentically with genuine language use at the end of his course. It does not follow at all that the only way of achieving this is to expose him to genuine language use at the beginning. It may be one way and in some circumstances it may indeed be the best way. But this is not axiomatic: it has to be established by reference to pedagogic criteria.

The specification of learner needs should not, then (or so it seems to me), determine methodology. At the same time it obviously will have to be taken into account as a crucial factor, since it defines what methodology will ultimately have to achieve and in so doing indicates a theoretical orientation to the teaching task. To maintain my metaphor, it does not provide us with a route but it points us in the right direction. It suggests an approach. Thus if in our specification we establish that a group of learners needs English for the purposes of communication of some kind, then this suggests that we should adopt an approach which represents what is to be learnt not simply in terms of formal linguistic units but also in terms of the communicative functions they fulfil. In ESP a communicative approach seems to be the obvious one to adopt because even the most elementary assessment of needs reveals that learners will have to put the language they learn to actual use outside the language teaching context. Where need specification and examination requirements are not distinct, where language activity is thus confined within the language teaching context, the relevance of a communicative approach is not so obvious.

Nor is it obvious how such an approach can be realized as a workable methodology, whether this is designed for ESP or not. The communicative approach is being rapidly adopted, adopted indeed with almost indecent haste, as the new orthodoxy in language teaching: adopted, almost inevitably, without critical examination. It is always easier to join the ranks of the faithful than to question the creed, and as usual the more recent converts are the most zealous and the most embarrassing to the cause. But how exactly is a (or the) communicative approach to be characterized? What are its principles and how can a methodology be devised which will effectively apply them?

These are the questions that I want to explore in this paper. They are very difficult questions and involve issues of a complex kind. I shall not come up with any definitive answers. All I can hope to do is to make a suggestion or two about the kind of answer we might most profitably be looking for.

One view of what constitutes a communicative approach, and probably the most influential, finds expression in the work emanating from the Council of Europe, and in particular in Wilkins (1972, 1974, 1976) and Van Ek (1975). It is based on need specification and arises from the recognition that in the actual use of language people do not just produce sentences, but express concepts and fulfil communicative functions in so doing. On this basis, it is proposed that the content of language teaching courses should be defined in terms not of the formal elements of syntax and lexis, as is customary in structural syllabuses, but of the concepts and functions these elements are used to realize. Wilkins groups these concepts and functions under the general heading of 'notions' and outlines a preliminary inventory (Wilkins 1976). Van Ek (1975) provides a more detailed specification of notions together with a selection of English exponents. The rationale behind this approach is very simple. Wilkins puts it in this way:

> The whole basis of a notional approach to language teaching derives from the conviction that what people want to do through language is more important than mastery of the language as an unapplied system. *Wilkins 1976: 42.*

We would all, I think, share this conviction. The question is whether the notional approach as proposed by Wilkins and Van Ek (and others) really does account for what people want to do through language. Earlier in his book, Wilkins gives grounds for preferring notional to grammatical and situational syllabuses in the following terms:

> The advantage of the notional syllabus is that it takes the communicative facts of language into account from the beginning without losing sight of grammatical and situational factors. It is potentially superior to the grammatical syllabus because it will produce a communicative competence and because its evident concern with the use of language will sustain the motivation of the learners. *Wilkins: 1976: 19.*

But to what extent does an inventory of notions of the kind proposed take the communicative facts of language into account? There is one rather crucial fact that such an inventory does not, and cannot of its nature, take into account, which is that communication does not take place through the linguistic exponence of concepts and functions as self-contained units of meaning. It takes place as discourse, whereby meanings are negotiated through interaction. What the notional inventory presents us with is a collection of idealized elements of which discourse is compounded: idealized because, listed as they are in isolation from context, they are exemplified in such a way as to make their conceptual and functional meanings linguistically explicit. In discourse such meanings are not signalled with such convenient clarity: it would often be damaging to communicative effectiveness if they were since contextual dependence is a necessary condition for discourse development. In discourse one has to work out what concepts, or propositions, are being expressed and what functions, or illocutions, they count as.

What we are offered in Wilkins (1976) is really only a very partial and imprecise description of certain semantic and pragmatic rules which are used for reference when people interact. They tell us nothing whatever about the procedures people employ in the application of these rules when they are actually engaged in communicative activity. These are 'communicative facts' which are ignored. So it is hard to see how a notional syllabus of the sort proposed can, of itself, *produce* communicative competence since it does not deal at all with one of its most fundamental aspects. It is also hard to see why, this being so, such a syllabus should provide so much more motivation for learners than the structural syllabus. The learners are presented with language items called notions rather than with language items called sentences. The items are organized and labelled differently, but unless learners are persuaded of the relevance of this to a development of an ability to deal with discourse, an ability which they associate with a natural use of their own language, they are likely to regard it as yet another pedagogic confidence trick. There will be no motivation then.

I have discussed the notional approach in some detail, and perhaps a little harshly, because many people assume that this is *the* communicative approach, the only form a communicative approach can take. It is important, therefore, to recognize its limitations. These can be summarized by saying that it does not deal with language use in context but only with concepts and functions in idealized isolation, informally described and exemplified by citation forms whose very explicitness signals their ideal character. The move from sentence to notion is, I believe, an advance. But it still leaves us with a long way to go. We still have to face the complexity of real communication, the way in which notions are realized in discourse.

If we are to adopt a communicative approach to teaching which takes as its primary purpose the development of the ability to do things with language, then it is discourse which must be at the centre of our attention. What kind of 'communicative facts' would such an approach have to take into account? The most fundamental of them might, perhaps, be expressed as follows:

When a sentence is used, or its use is apprehended, in a normal communicative context, it activates a range of different relationships; or, to put it in an alternative (and Hallidayan) way, its meaning potential is realized in a number of different ways. The concept, or ideational content, is realized as a particular proposition which links up with and develops from the propositions previously expressed. This is the relationship of *cohesion* (see Halliday and Hasan 1976). As an example, consider the following:

One of the important mechanisms by which the individual takes on the values of others is *identification*. The term is loosely used to sum up a number of different ways in which one person puts himself in the place of another.

Here the second sentence is used to express a proposition which combines with the first by virtue of the anaphoric link between 'the term' and 'identification'. This is not, however, the only relationship that can be recognized between the two sentences as they occur together in this context. We may note that the second proposition is to a very considerable degree a paraphrase of the first: the expressions *the individual takes on the values of the others* and *one person puts himself in the place of another* are conceptually alike. So we recognize that the second proposition functions in a certain way in relation to the first, that it acts as a clarifying restatement or gloss. This relationship is of *coherence*, the manner in which the illocutionary functions which propositions count as combine into larger units of discourse. Here coherence is realized in the recognition that the second proposition functions as some sort of elucidation of the statement expressed through the first.

So far I have been talking about cohesion and coherence as relationships which obtain between propositions and illocutions. In fact, I think it is preferable to conceive of these relationships not as existing in the text but as established by the interactive endeavour of participants engaged in a discourse. In this view, they are dependent on a third kind of relationship which the sentence in context realizes: the relationship of interaction. The sentence can be said to represent a set of clues provided by the writer, or speaker, by reference to which the reader, or listener, can create propositional and illocutionary meanings (see Paper 13 in this volume). One kind of clue is the manner in which propositional content is organized so that what is assumed to be recoverable from shared knowledge, what is given, appears first, and what is assumed to be informative, known only to the addresser and new to the addressee, appears last. Consider, for example, the first of our two sentences. Here 'identification' is presented as new and this indicates to the reader that what is to follow will provide more information about it. The italics serve to point out the clue more clearly. The same proposition could be expressed by the use of a different sentence, one in which given and new are reversed:

Identification is one of the important mechanisms by which the individual takes on the values of others.

The indication here is that 'identification' is assumed to be given, so that the reader will not expect any further elaboration. Hence if this sentence were to be followed by our second sentence, he would find it unpredictable and puzzling. The two propositions could still be recognized as having a cohesive relationship, but there would be a breakdown in interaction in that the writer would be misleading the reader and denying him the opportunity to participate. What the reader would expect to follow from this second version of the first proposition would be some elaboration of the ideas expressed in the predicate noun phrase. Thus he might expect some substantiation of the assertion that identification is important, in which case he will be primed to anticipate something like:

Its importance can be assessed by considering the behaviour of children.

Alternatively, the reader might fix on the clue provided by the expression *one of* and expect a concessive statement to follow, like:

It is not, however, the only one.

The reader, then, predicts, on the basis of the clues provided, what the possible functions of the succeeding proposition are likely to be. The success of his predictions is a measure of the effectiveness of the interaction relationship which the sentence in question mediates between the participants.

Of course, as he proceeds, the reader may find that he has favoured the wrong clue and followed the wrong lead. Thus in the case we have just been considering, he may fix on the expression *important* as the clue and predict that a substantiation is to follow. If instead a concession follows, then he has to adjust his interpretation so that he recognizes the preceding sentence as having the function of a summary of an earlier discussion. He may not pick up a necessary clue at all and in this case he has to retrace his steps and have a closer look. If he still makes no sense of the text, the interaction breaks down and there is no discourse.

When a sentence is used in context, then, the reader or listener has work to do to make sense of it. This work is directed by what Grice (1975) calls the 'co-operative principle', which provides the basis for interaction. The addressee uses the clues provided by the addresser to create cohesive links between the proposition expressed in the sentence and those expressed through other sentences, and coherent links between the illocutionary functions which these propositions count as. The sentence, then, can be said to activate an interaction relationship which in turn enables the addressee to create the relationships of cohesion and coherence.

An approach to teaching which concentrates on the business of communication must, it seems to me, concern itself with discourse. I have given here only a sketchy and imprecise idea of what this might involve. The whole field of discourse analysis is busy with exploration at the moment (for a review see Coulthard 1975 and Paper 9 in this volume) and it is not easy to find oneself around it, let alone establish significant common principles of investigation. Ethnomethodologists, sociolinguists, philosophers, semanticists are all digging away at their own particular claims. For our present purposes I want to suggest that there are two basic characteristics of (or 'communicative facts' about) discourse which we need to account for in a communicative approach to teaching. The first is that it is essentially interactive, and involves negotiation of meanings. This aspect of discourse is particularly stressed by the ethnomethodologists (see Turner 1974) and is demonstrated (in different ways) in Labov (1970), Grice (1975), Harder and Kock (1976). In this view, what is presented on a page as written text has to be converted by the reader into discourse whereby meanings are negotiated. The second characteristic is that this interaction creates hierarchical structures whereby the combination of propositions and illocutions builds up to larger units of communication. This aspect of discourse is given prominence in Sinclair and Coulthard (1975). Their concern is with spoken language. Recent work in the University of Washington examines the structure of written discourse in terms of the rhetorical development of the paragraph in technical writing (see Selinker, Trimble and Vroman (1974) and the papers cited there).

Let us then assume that a specification of needs indicates that the appropriate teaching approach is one which concentrates on the development of communicative competence, and that this is defined as the ability to cope with the interactive structuring of discourse. Let us further assume that it is written discourse of an academic kind that is to be dealt with. What methodology can we devise which will incorporate this approach and meet these needs? I want to propose that the structural characteristic of discourse should inform the manner in which language items are sequentially graded in a syllabus and that its interactive characteristic should inform the manner in which these items are presented. I am proposing, then, that the two basic characteristics of discourse that I have identified should be converted into basic methodological principles. Let us now consider, in a very tentative way, how these principles might work.

In designing the syllabus, our aim is to order the language items to be learned in such a way that they build up into larger communicative units. We might conveniently take paragraph units as defining the scope of each section of the syllabus. Within each section there are stages which introduce new coherence relationships and these can be labelled by the overt clues which are used to mark them: *for example* marking exemplification, *that is to say* marking restatement, *however* marking concession, *on the other hand* marking contrast, and so on.

Thus we devise a syllabus which is not a collection of structures or situations or notions but a sequence of relationships which build up into a structured paragraph, and subsequently into a series of paragraphs which approximate to the kind of reading material which the learner will ultimately have to handle.

Let us suppose that after due consideration of the question of teaching and learning objectives that I raised at the beginning of this paper, we have decided that our starting point in preparing such a syllabus is the point the learners will arrive at on the completion of the course: instances of genuine reading matter derived from their textbooks. Our task is to analyse it into teaching materials, to contrive a pedagogic presentation which will develop in the learners a capacity for ultimate authentic response. Let us suppose that we want to design a reading course for students of sociology, and let us suppose that we wish to begin with the simple relationship of exemplification. We search through our corpus of genuine passages for instances of this. One such passage, we will suppose, is the one on *identification* which appears as an appendix to this paper and from this we can extract the following:

> The child takes the same attitude towards himself that others take towards him.

> Children take the same attitudes towards their environment that adults take towards them.

The learner is then presented with a set of sentences and asked to select from them those which could be used to provide an example. Among these would be:

> If the average child does not steal, it is because he takes the same disapproving attitude towards such behaviour that others take towards it.

> The little girl who is spanked by her mother may in turn spank her dolls.

Appropriate combinations will yield the sequences:

> The child takes the same attitude towards himself that others take towards him. If the average child does not steal, for example, it is because he takes the same disapproving attitude towards such behaviour that others take towards it.

> Children take the same attitude towards their environment that adults take towards them. The little girl who is spanked by her mother, for example, may in turn spank her dolls.

At the next stage we might move on to consider how these embryonic instances of discourse might be extended by other supporting acts. The learners can be asked to consider the combinations they have produced and to select a sentence which can be used to restate the idea in the example, which can be linked with it by means of the markers *that is to say* or *in other words*. The set of sentences provided would include the following (again extracted from our original text source):

She acts towards her dolls as her mother acts towards her.

By combining this with what has been produced before, the second of our instances of discourse is extended as follows:

Children take the same attitude towards their environment that adults take towards them. The little girl who is spanked by her mother, for example, may in turn spank her dolls. That is to say she acts towards her dolls as her mother acts towards her.

We might then at a further stage go on to ask the question: what do you conclude from this? Among the sentences which the learner has to choose from are the following:

She identifies with her mother according to her experience of what a mother does and feels.

He identifies with the adult point of view, and the thought of stealing prompts feelings of guilt.

The discourse can now be extended further by use of the marker *thus*:

The child takes the same attitude towards himself that others take towards him. If the average child does not steal, for example, it is because he takes the same disapproving attitude towards such behaviour that others take towards it. Thus he identifies with the adult point of view, and the thought of stealing prompts feelings of guilt.

Children take the same attitude towards their environment that adults take towards them. The little girl who is spanked by her mother, for example, may in turn spank her dolls. That is to say she acts towards her dolls as her mother acts towards her. Thus she identifies with her mother according to her experience of what a mother does and feels.

What we are aiming to do here is to get the learner to participate in developing a paragraph which has roughly the following structure:

Main statement   support

                            exemplification (*for example*)
                            clarification (*that is to say*)
                            conclusion (*thus*)

The paragraph can be said to consist of two parts: main statement and support. The support in turn consists of three acts, which I have labelled (for the nonce) exemplification, clarification and conclusion, which exhibit increasing degrees of generalization, the last coming close to the level of generalization of the main statement.

The display given above represents a simple plan of one section of the syllabus. At each stage of the course a number of different paragraphs are being simultaneously developed along similar lines, so that this display, and others representing different paragraph structures in other sections of the syllabus, can be regarded as a device for generating different textual tokens of essentially the same discourse type.

Obviously I do not have the time here and now to work out in detail the kind of syllabus I am proposing. Such a task would need careful and collaborative effort in the context of actual teaching circumstances. All I have outlined, by way of example, is how one unit might be organized around the relationships marked by *for example*, *that is to say*, and *thus*. Other units would deal with other patterns, with other types of discourse development concentrating on relationships marked by *therefore*, *however*, *on the other hand*, and so on. Later units would then go on to combinations of paragraphs.

The raw material used in this operation is extracted from genuine texts. In these examples I have been giving this extraction has not involved very great changes. If one wanted to begin at a linguistically less complex level one could decompose the original texts into simple propositions and begin the paragraph build-up from a more elementary base. The methodological principle informing the design of the course would remain the same. As the course proceeds, then the learners create paragraphs of different patterns and then combine these paragraphs into sequences which constitute reading passages, which are simplified versions of the passages from which they originally derived. At these points they can be presented with these genuine passages and others like them, having been prepared to respond to them authentically as discourse by what has preceded. The learners will be practised in recognizing underlying rhetorical patterns through stylistic variation. They will have acquired interpretative strategies for textual use. That, at least, is the theory of the thing.

The kind of methodology that I have in mind, then, organizes the syllabus in such a way as to develop in the learners the interactive capacity to create structured discourse with each stage focusing on a coherence relationship, and each unit focusing on a paragraph type, with later units bringing different paragraphs into an appropriate sequence to form passages which represent in simple form the underlying structure of the genuine texts from which they derive and to which the learners can now be exposed.

I have already suggested how such a syllabus might be presented, how learners might be involved interactively in the discovery of discourse structure. As the course proceeds, the learner's scope for participation would quite naturally widen. Thus, he might at some point be presented with the beginnings of paragraphs and be invited to predict possible developments, guided by the provision of alternatives. An exercise of this kind could be designed as a branching programme. Another, and similar, activity is suggested by the kind of 'logical trees' described by Sheila Jones (Jones 1968) which transpose passages of written language into visual graphs, and list structures representing question and answer sequences. There would also be a place, I think, for the procedures of information transfer and gradual approximation (see SECTION TWO in this volume), both of which are designed to engage the learner's active participation in the writing, and therefore in the interpreting, of discourse.

All of the procedures I have just mentioned are thought of as directly realizing the syllabus. At the same time, one has, I think, to allow for supplementary activities of various kinds. One may need, for example, exercises on the different forms which are customarily used to perform the communicative functions we are concerned with. Such exercises would be concerned with the ideal linguistic realizations of Wilkins' concepts and functions. Again we might need exercises which familiarized the learner with common cohesive devices such as are described in Halliday and Hasan (1976). Other exercises might deal with the different ways in which propositional content can be organized in sentences and with the presuppositions which are thereby created. This last would offer plenty of scope for interaction and for the representing of speaking and reading as alternative realizations of the same underlying ability. I think of all of these activities as loops: they extend from and return to the main teaching point which they serve and which gives them their *raison d'être*. I conceive of them as optional practice elements in the course, to be exploited or by-passed as required, and to provide the flexibility which is necessary in classes of uneven attainment or varying rate of progress.

All of this is, I am aware, very sketchy and very imprecise: more of a gleam in the eye than a reasoned set of proposals for immediate application. What I am certain about is that any approach to the description and teaching of language that claims to account for communicative competence (a very large claim indeed) must deal with discourse. What I am uncertain about is the way in which our as yet imperfect understanding of discourse can be applied to the design of an effective methodology. What I have done in this paper is to suggest one or two possibilities that I think might be worth exploring. A lot more exploration needs to be done. This is a painful and frustrating business, especially when you find only that you have been following a false trail. But I think we must persist. Above all we must deny ourselves the comfort of dogma which deals in the delusion of simple answers.

Notes

Paper presented at a conference on the Teaching of English for Specific Purposes, Paipa, Colombia, April 1977, and published in the *Indian Journal of Applied Linguistics*, Volume III No 1, September 1978.

Appendix

Identification

One of the important mechanisms by which the individual takes on the values of others is *identification*. The term is loosely used to sum up a number of different ways in which one person puts himself in the place of another. People are said to identify with others when they are able to feel sympathy for another's plight, to understand and perhaps even experience the emotions someone else is experiencing, and to treat others as they themselves would like to be treated.

The normal tendency of the child to take the same attitudes towards himself that others take towards him is also a form of identification. If the average child does not steal, it is not because he has reached the rational conclusion that it is unwise or inexpedient to do so. Rather he takes the same morally disapproving attitude towards such behaviour that others take towards it. He identifies with the adult point of view, and the thought of stealing prompts feelings of guilt.

It is also normal for the child to take the same attitudes towards his environment that his 'significant others' take towards him. The little girl who is spanked by her mother may in turn spank her dolls, acting towards her dolls as her mother acts towards her. She identifies with her mother according to her limited experience of what a mother does and feels.

There is a stronger and more specific sense in which children identify with others. Some adults in the child's experience appear to him as ideal figures; the child wants to be like them and *models* himself upon them. In early childhood, he identifies with one or both of his parents. Later, he may develop 'crushes' on teachers and peers and take them as ideal images to be emulated. Identification of this sort is often temporary, but it can permanently shape character and personality[1].

Notes

1 Extract from L. Broom and P. Felsnick (1955). *Sociology*. Harper and Row.

Bibliography

Alexander, P. (1963). *A Preface to the Logic of Science.* London: Sheed and Ward.

Allen, J. P. B. and **S. P. Corder** (eds) (1974). *The Edinburgh Course in Applied Linguistics.* Vol. 3: *Techniques in Applied Linguistics.* London: Oxford University Press.

Allen, J. P. B. and **P. Van Buren** (1971). *Chomsky: selected readings.* London: Oxford University Press.

Allen, J. P. B. and **H. G. Widdowson** (1974a). *English in Physical Science.* English in Focus Series. London: Oxford University Press.

Allen, J. P. B. and **H. G. Widdowson** (1974b). 'Teaching the communicative use of English.' *IRAL* Vol. XII No. 1 (reprinted in MacKay and Mountford 1978).

Austin, J. L. (1962). *How to do things with words.* London: Oxford University Press.

Bach, E. and **R. T. Harms** (eds) (1968). *Universals in Linguistic Theory.* London: Holt, Rinehart and Winston.

Bailey, C.-J. N. and **R. W. Shuy** (eds) (1973). *New Ways of Analysing Variation in English.* Washington D.C.: Georgetown University Press.

Bailey, N., C. Madden and **S. D. Krashen** (1974). 'Is there a "natural sequence" in adult second language learning?' *Language Learning* Vol. 24 No. 2.

Bar-Hillel, Y. (1971). 'Out of the pragmatic wastebasket.' *Linguistic Inquiry* II/3.

Bauman, R. and **J. Sherzer** (eds) (1974). *Explorations in the Ethnography of Speaking.* Cambridge: Cambridge University Press.

Berlin, I. (1957). *The Hedgehog and the Fox.* New York: Mentor Books.

Bernstein, B. B. (1971). *Class, Codes and Control* Vol. 1. London: Routledge and Kegan Paul.

Bolinger, D. L. (1971). 'Semantic overloading: a restudy of the verb "Remind".' *Language* 47 No. 3.

Bronowski, J. (1960). *The Common Sense of Science*. Harmondsworth: Penguin Books.

Burt, M. K., H. C. Dulay and **M. Finnochiaro** (1977). *Viewpoints on English as a Second Language*. New York: Regents Publishing Company.

Campbell, R. and **R. Wales** (1970). 'The study of language acquisition' in Lyons 1970.

Candlin, C. N. (1972). 'Acquiring communicative competence.' Paper presented at 32nd Conference of Philologists, Utrecht, mimeo.

Candlin, C. N. (1973). 'The status of pedagogical grammars' in Corder and Roulet 1973.

Catford, J. C. (1965). *A Linguistic Theory of Translation*. London: Oxford University Press.

Chomsky, N. (1957). *Syntactic Structures*. The Hague: Mouton.

Chomsky, N. (1965). *Aspects of the theory of syntax*. Cambridge, Mass.: M.I.T. Press.

Chomsky, N. (1968). 'Deep structure, surface structure, and semantic interpretation.' Mimeo reprinted in Chomsky 1972.

Chomsky, N. (1972). *Studies on Semantics in Generative Grammar*. The Hague: Mouton.

Cicourel, A. (1973). *Cognitive Sociology*. Harmondsworth: Penguin Books.

Cole, P. and **J. L. Morgan** (eds) (1975). *Syntax and Semantics Vol. 3: Speech Acts*. New York: Academic Press.

Corder, S. P. (1967). 'The significance of learners' errors.' *International Review of Applied Linguistics* Vol. V No. 4. Reprinted in Richards 1974.

Corder, S. P. (1973). *Introducing Applied Linguistics*. Harmondsworth: Penguin Books.

Corder, S. P. (1975). 'Error analysis, interlanguage and second language acquisition.' *Language Learning and Linguistics: Abstracts* Vol. 8 No. 4 and in Kinsella 1978.

Corder, S. P. and **E. Roulet** (eds) (1973). *Theoretical Linguistic Models in Applied Linguistics*. Brussels: Aimav and Paris: Didier.

Corder, S. P. and **E. Roulet** (eds) (1974). *Linguistic Insights in Applied Linguistics*. Brussels: Aimav and Paris: Didier.

Corder, S. P. and **E. Roulet** (eds) (1975). *Some Implications of Linguistic Theory for Applied Linguistics*. Brussels: Aimav and Paris: Didier.

Corder, S. P. and **E. Roulet** (eds) (1977). *The Notions of Simplification Interlanguages and Pidgins and their Relation to Second Language Pedagogy*. Faculty of Letters, University of Neuchâtel and Librairie Droz, Geneva.

Coulthard, R. M. (1975). 'Discourse Analysis in English: a short review of the literature' in *Language Teaching and Linguistics: Abstracts* Vol. 8 No. 4 and in Kinsella 1978.

Crystal, D. and **D. Davy** (1969). *Investigating English Style*. London: Longman.

Dakin, J., B. Tiffen and **H. G. Widdowson** (1968). *Language in Education*. London: Oxford University Press.

De Camp, D. (1971). 'The study of pidgin and creole languages' in Hymes 1971.

De Camp, D. and **I. F. Hancock** (eds) (1974). *Pidgins and Creoles: Current Trends and Prospects*. Washington D.C.: Georgetown University Press.

de Saussure, F. (1955). *Cours de Linguistique Générale*. Paris: Payot, 5th edition. (First edition 1916.) English translation by Wade Baskin, *Course in General Linguistics*. New York: Philosophical Library 1959.

Dressler, W. (1970). 'Towards a semantic deep structure of discourse grammars.' Papers of the 6th Regional Meeting of the Chicago Linguistic Society.

Ducrot, O. (1972). *Dire et ne pas dire*. Paris: Hermann.

Dulay, H. C. and **M. K. Burt** (1974). 'Natural sequences in child second language acquisition.' *Language Learning* Vol. 24 No. 1.

Dundes, A., J. W. Leach and **B. Özkök** (1972). 'The strategy of Turkish boys' verbal dueling rhymes' in Gumperz and Hymes 1972.

Ervin-Tripp, S. M. (1974). 'Is second language learning like the first?' *TESOL Quarterly* Vol. 8 No. 2.

Fanselow, J. F. and **R. H. Crymes** (eds). *ON TESOL 76*. Washington D.C.: TESOL.

Fasold, R. W. and **R. W. Shuy** (1975). *Analyzing Variation in Language*. Washington D.C.: Georgetown University Press.

Ferguson, C. A. (1971). 'Absence of copula and the notion of simplicity: a study of normal talk, baby talk, foreigner talk and pidgins' in Hymes 1971.

Fillmore, C. J. (1968). 'The case for case' in Bach and Harms 1968.

Fillmore, C. J. (1971). 'Verbs of judging: an exercise in semantic description' in Fillmore and Langendoen 1971.

Fillmore, C. J. and **T. D. Langendoen** (eds) (1971). *Studies in Linguistic Semantics*. New York: Holt, Rinehart and Winston.

Firth, J. R. (1957). *Papers in Linguistics* (1934–51). London: Oxford University Press.

Fodor, J. A. and **J. J. Katz** (eds) (1964). *The Structure of Language*. Englewood Cliffs: Prentice Hall.

Fowler, R. (1969). 'On the interpretation of nonsense strings.' *Journal of Linguistics* Vol. 5 No. 1.

Frake, C. O. (1964). 'How to ask for a drink in Subanum.' *American Anthropologist* Vol. 66 No. 6 Pt 2.

Freedle, R. O. and **J. B. Carroll** (eds) (1972). *Language Comprehension and the Acquisition of Knowledge.* Washington D.C.: V. H. Winston and Sons.

Garfinkel, H. (1967). *Studies in Ethnomethodology.* Englewood Cliffs: Prentice Hall.

Garfinkel, H. (1972). 'Remarks on ethnomethodology' in Gumperz and Hymes 1972.

Glendinning, E. (1975). *English in Mechanical Engineering.* English in Focus Series. London: Oxford University Press.

Goodman, K. S. (1967). 'Reading: a psycholinguistic guessing game' in *Journal of the Reading Specialist* No. 6.

Greene, J. (1972). *Psycholinguistics: Chomsky and Psychology.* Harmondsworth: Penguin Books.

Grice, H. P. (1975). 'Logic and Conversation' in Cole and Morgan 1975.

Gumperz, J. J. and **D. Hymes** (eds) (1972). *Directions in Sociolinguistics: the Ethnography of Communication.* New York: Holt, Rinehart and Winston.

Gutknecht, C. (ed) (1977). *Grundbegriffe und Hauptströmungen der Linguistik.* Hamburg: Hoffmann und Campe Verlag.

Halle, M. (ed) (1962). *Preprints of Papers for the 9th International Congress of Linguists.* Cambridge, Mass.

Halliday, M. A. K. (1964). 'Syntax and the consumer' in Stuart 1964.

Halliday, M. A. K. (1967/68). 'Notes on transitivity and theme in English.' *Journal of Linguistics* Vols. 3 Nos. 1, 2, and 4 No. 2.

Halliday, M. A. K. (1969). 'The relevant models of grammar.' *Educational Review* Vol. 22 No. 1, reprinted in Halliday 1973.

Halliday, M. A. K. (1970a). 'Language structure and language function' in Lyons 1970.

Halliday, M. A. K. (1970b). 'Functional diversity in language as seen from a consideration of modality and mood in English.' *Foundations of language* Vol. 6 No. 3 (see Ch. 13 Kress 1976).

Halliday, M. A. K. (1973). *Explorations in the Functions of Language.* London: Edward Arnold.

Halliday, M. A. K. and **R. Hasan** (1976). *Cohesion in English.* London: Longman.

Halliday, M. A. K., Angus McIntosh and **Peter Strevens** (1964), *The Linguistic Sciences and Language Teaching.* London: Longman.

Hancock, I. F. (1971). 'A map and list of pidgin and creole languages' in Hymes 1971.

Harder, P. and **C. Kock** (1976). *The Theory of Presupposition Failure.* Travaux du Cercle Linguistique de Copenhague XVII, Copenhagen.

Harris, Z. (1952). 'Discourse analysis.' *Language* 28, reprinted in Fodor and Katz 1964.

Hasan, R. (1968). *Grammatical Cohesion in Spoken and Written English.* London: Longman (see Halliday and Hasan 1976).

Hinde, R. A. (ed) (1972). *Non-verbal communication.* Cambridge: Cambridge University Press.

Hockett, C. (1968). *The State of the Art.* The Hague: Mouton.

Householder, F. W. (1970). Review of Hockett (1968). *Journal of Linguistics* Vol. 6 No. 1.

Huddleston, R. D., R. A. Hudson, R. A. Winter and **E. O. Henrici** (1968). *Sentence and Clause in Scientific English.* Communication Research Centre, University College London.

Hudson, L. (1966), *Contrary Imaginations.* Harmondsworth: Penguin Books.

Hudson, R. A. (1976). *Arguments for a Non-transformational Grammar.* Chicago: Chicago University Press.

Hymes, D. (1970). 'On Communicative Competence' in Gumperz and Hymes 1970.

Hymes, D. (ed) (1971). *Pidginization and Creolization of Languages.* Cambridge: Cambridge University Press.

Jacobs, R. A. and **P. S. Rosenbaum** (eds) (1970). *Readings in English Transformational Grammar.* Waltham, Mass.: Blaisdell.

Jakobson, R. (1960). 'Concluding Statement: linguistics and poetics' in Sebeok 1960.

Jakobson, R. and **M. Halle** (1956). *Fundamentals of Language.* The Hague: Mouton.

Jones, S. (1968). *Design of Instruction.* London: HMSO.

Kac, M. B. (1969). 'Should the passive transformation be obligatory?' *Journal of Linguistics* Vol. 5 No. 1.

Karttunen, L. (1970). 'On the semantics of complement sentences.' Papers of the 6th Regional Meeting of the Chicago Linguistic Society.

Karttunen, L. (1971). 'Implicative verbs.' *Language* 47.

Katz, J. J. (1964). 'Semi-sentences' in Fodor and Katz 1964.

Katz, J. J. and **P. M. Postal** (1964). *An Integrated Theory of Linguistic Descriptions.* Cambridge, Mass.: M.I.T. Press.

Kay, P. and **G. Sankoff** (1974). 'A language universals approach to pidgins and creoles' in De Camp and Hancock 1974.

Kinsella, V. (ed) (1978). *Language Teaching and Linguistics: Surveys.* Cambridge: Cambridge University Press.

Kiparsky, P. and **C. Kiparsky** (1971). 'Fact' in Steinberg and Jakobovits 1971.

Krashen, S. D. (1977). 'The Monitor Model for Adult Second Language Performance' in Burt, Dulay and Finnochiaro 1977.

Kress, G. R. (ed) (1976). *Halliday: System and Function in Language.* London: Oxford University Press.

Krzeszowski, R. P. (1975). 'Is it possible and necessary to write text grammars?' in Corder and Roulet 1975.

Labov, W. (1966). *The Social Stratification of English in New York City.* Washington D.C.: Center for Applied Linguistics.

Labov, W. (1969a). *The study of non-standard English.* National Council of Teachers of English (U.S.A.).

Labov, W. (1969b). 'The logic of non-standard English' in Georgetown Monographs 22. Washington D.C.: Georgetown University Press.

Labov, W. (1970). 'The study of language in its social context.' Studium Generale Vol. 23, reprinted in Labov 1972a.

Labov W. (1972a). *Sociolinguistic Patterns.* Philadelphia: University of Pennsylvania Press.

Labov, W. (1972b). 'Rules for ritual insults' in Sudnow 1972.

Lackstrom, J. E., L. Selinker and **L. Trimble** (1970). 'Grammar and technical English' in Lugton 1970.

Lackstrom, J. E., L. Selinker and **L. Trimble** (1972). 'Technical rhetorical principles and grammatical choice.' Papers of the 3rd A.I.L.A. Congress (see Verdoodt 1974).

Lakoff, R. (1970). 'Tense and its relation to participants.' *Language* 46.

Laver, J. and **S. Hutcheson** (eds) (1972). *Communication in Face to Face Interaction.* Harmondsworth: Penguin Books.

Levin, S. R. (1962). 'Poetry and grammaticalness' in Halle 1962.

Levi-Strauss, C. (1958). *Anthropologie Structurale.* Paris: Plon.

Lugton, R. C. (ed) (1970). *English as a Second Language: Current Issues.* Philadelphia: Center for Curriculum Development.

Lyons, J. (1968). *Introduction to Theoretical Linguistics.* Cambridge: Cambridge University Press.

Lyons, J. (ed) (1970). *New Horizons in Linguistics.* Harmondsworth: Penguin Books.

Lyons, J. (1972). 'Human language' in Hinde 1972.

Lyons, J. (1977). *Chomsky* (2nd edition). London: Fontana/Collins.

Maranda, P. (ed) (1972). *Mythology.* Harmondsworth: Penguin Books.

MacKay, R. and **A. Mountford** (eds) (1978). *English for Specific Purposes.* London: Longman.

Nemser, W. (1971). 'Approximative systems of foreign language learners.' *IRAL* Vol. IX No. 2 (reprinted in Richards 1974).

Nyyssonen, H. K. (1977). *Towards a pedagogically relevant model of discourse analysis.* Acta Universitatis Oulensis. Series B. Humaniora No. 5. University of Oulu.

Olson, D. R. (1972). 'Language use for communicating, instructing and thinking' in Freedle and Carroll 1972.

Palmer, F. R. (1971). *Grammar*. Harmondsworth: Penguin Books.

Pask, G. and **B. C. E. Scott** (1972). 'Learning strategies and individual competence.' *International Journal of Man-Machine Studies* 4 No. 3, pp. 217–253.

Perren, G. (ed) (1971). *Science and Technology in a Second Language*. Reports and Papers 7. London: Centre for Information on Language Teaching and Research.

Postal, P. M. (1970). 'On the surface verb "Remind".' *Linguistic Inquiry* 1.

Powlison, P. S. (1965). 'A paragraph analysis of a Yagua folk tale.' *International Journal of American Linguistics* 31 No. 2.

Propp, V. (1972). 'Transformations in fairy tales' in Maranda 1972.

Richards, J. C. (1972). 'Social factors, interlanguage, and language learning' in *Language Learning* Vol. 22 No. 2 (reprinted in Richards 1974).

Richards, J. C. (ed) (1974). *Error Analysis: Perspectives on Second Language Acquisition*. London: Longman.

Richards, J. C. and **G. P. Sampson** (1974). 'The study of learner English' in Richards 1974.

Ross, J. R. (1970). 'On declarative sentences' in Jacobs and Rosenbaum 1970.

Ross, J. R. (1973). 'A fake NP squish' in Bailey and Shuy 1973.

Sacks, H. (1972). 'On the analyzability of stories by children' in Gumperz and Hymes 1972.

Samarin, W. J. (1971). 'Salient and substantive pidginization' in Hymes 1971.

Searle, J. R. (1969). *Speech Acts*. Cambridge: Cambridge University Press.

Searle, J. R. (1975). 'Indirect speech acts' in Cole and Morgan 1975.

Sebeok, T. A. (ed) (1960). *Style in Language*. Cambridge, Mass.: M.I.T. Press.

Selinker, L. (1972). 'Interlanguage' in *International Review of Applied Linguistics* Vol, X No. 3 (reprinted in Richards 1974).

Selinker, L., L. Trimble and **R. Vroman** (1974). *Working papers in English for Science and Technology*. College of Engineering. Seattle: University of Washington.

Sinclair, J. McH., and **R. M. Coulthard** (1975). *Towards an Analysis of Discourse: The English used by Teachers and Pupils*. London: Oxford University Press.

Spencer, J. (1966). 'The Anglo-Indians and their speech' in *Lingua* 16.

Steinberg, D. D. and **L. A. Jakobovits** (eds) (1971). *Semantics*. Cambridge: Cambridge University Press.

Strawson, P. F. (1950). 'On referring.' *Mind* LIX, reprinted in Strawson 1971.

Strawson, P. F. (1971). *Logico-linguistic Papers*. London: Methuen.

Stuart, C. I. J. M. (ed) (1964). *Report of the 15th Annual Round Table Meeting on Linguistics and Language Study*. Georgetown Monographs 17. Washington D.C.: Georgetown University Press.

Sudnow, D. (ed) (1972). *Studies in Social Interaction*. New York: Free Press.

Sutherland, J. (1948). *Preface to Eighteenth Century Poetry*. Oxford: The Clarendon Press.

Swales, J. (1974). 'Notes on the function of attributive *–en* particles in scientific discourse.' *Papers in English for Special Purposes* No. 1, University of Khartoum.

Thomson, A. S. and **A. V. Martinet** (1960). *A Practical Grammar for Foreign Students*. London: Oxford University Press.

Thorne, J. P. (1965). 'Stylistics and generative grammars.' *Journal of Linguistics* Vol. 1 No. 1.

Todd, L. (1974). *Pidgins and Creoles*. London: Routledge and Kegan Paul.

Traugott, E. G. (1973). 'Some thoughts on natural syntactic processes' in Bailey and Shuy 1973.

Traugott, E. G. (1977). 'Natural semantax: its role in the study of contact languages' in Corder and Roulet 1977.

Trudgill, P. (1975), *Accent, Dialect and the School*. London: Edward Arnold.

Turner, R. (ed) (1974). *Ethnomethodology*. Harmondsworth: Penguin Books.

Tyler, S. A. (ed) (1969). *Cognitive Anthropology*. New York: Holt, Rinehart and Winston.

Van Buren, P. (1974). 'Contrastive analysis' in Allen and Corder 1974.

Van Dijk, T. A. (1972). *Some Aspects of Text Grammar*. The Hague: Mouton.

Van Ek, J. A. (1975). *The Threshold Level*. Strasbourg: Council of Europe.

Verdoodt, A. (ed) (1974). *Proceedings of the 3rd International Congress of Applied Linguistics*. Heidelberg: Julius Gross Verlag.

Widdowson, H. G. (1968). 'The teaching of English through science' in Dakin, Tiffen and Widdowson 1968.

Widdowson, H. G. (1972). 'The teaching of English as communication.' *English Language Teaching Journal* Vol. XXVII No. 1.

Widdowson, H. G. (1973). *An Applied Linguistic Approach to Discourse Analysis*. Ph.D. Dissertation, University of Edinburgh.

Widdowson, H. G. (1974). 'Stylistics' in Allen and Corder 1974.

Widdowson, H. G. (1975). *Stylistics and the Teaching of Literature.* London: Longman.

Widdowson, H. G. (1978). *Teaching Language as Communication.* Oxford: Oxford University Press.

Wilkins, D. A. (1972). 'An investigation into the linguistic and situational common core in a unit of the credit system.' Strasbourg: Council of Europe.

Wilkins, D. A. (1974). 'Grammatical, situational and notional syllabuses.' Papers of the 3rd A.I.L.A. Congress (see Verdoodt 1974).

Wilkins, D. A. (1976). *Notional Syllabuses.* London: Oxford University Press.

Winburne, J. N. (1962). 'Sentence sequence in discourse' in Halle 1962.